LETTERS OF JOHN MASEFIELD TO FLORENCE LAMONT

LETTERS OF JOHN MASEFIELD TO FLORENCE LAMONT

edited by
Corliss Lamont
and
Lansing Lamont

Columbia University Press
New York   1979

Library of Congress Cataloging in Publication Data

Masefield, John, 1878–1967.
    Letters of John Masefield to Florence Lamont.
    1.   Masefield, John, 1878–1967—Correspondence.
    2.   Lamont, Florence Haskell Corliss, 1873–1952.
    3.   Poets, English—20th century—Correspondence.
    I.   Lamont, Florence Haskell Corliss, 1873–1952.
    II.   Lamont, Corliss, 1902–   III.   Lamont, Lansing, 1930–
    IV.   Title.

PR6025.A77Z546 1979   828'.9'1209   [B]   78–27134
ISBN 0–231–04706–1

To the Masefields and the Lamonts

Contents

Acknowledgements

The letters from John Masefield quoted in this book are printed by the kind permission of the Society of Authors, London, England, on behalf of the Masefield Estate. For permission to publish the Masefield letters, and to reproduce the sketches, we also wish to thank the Houghton Library, which owns the original autograph letters, and its director William H. Bond. Special thanks, too, for their help in research and consultation and for extra editing and the typing of the manuscript should go to Marcia Bradley, Constance Hirsch, Helen Mac Lachlan, Rya Rosenzweig and Sir Peter Masefield, cousin of the poet.

We are especially grateful to Dr Glen Cavaliero, who carried out a great deal of research in the later stages of preparing the book. Even so, there inevitably still remain a few instances where we have not been able to track down John Masefield's references to people or places.

PLATE 1 *John Masefield with the family cat, Mickey, about 1949*

PLATE 2   *Florence Lamont in her summer flower garden at North Haven, Maine, about 1928*

PLATE 3   *Oil portrait of John Masefield by Sir John Lavery, 1937*

President:
Miss PENELOPE WHEELER.

General Director:
JOHN MASEFIELD.

Costume Director:
Mrs. HARRISSON.

Properties Director:
Miss J. MASEFIELD.

THE HILL PLAYERS.

Vice-Presidents:
THOMAS LAMONT.
JOHN GALSWORTHY.
JOHN DRINKWATER.
Miss LILLAH McCARTHY.

Musical Director:
Mrs. PEARCE.

Hon. Treasurer & Secretary:
Mrs. MASEFIELD.

Publicity Managers:
R. A. W. HUGHES.
Miss ADDIS.

Subscription 10/- per annum

PLATE 4   *Flier used by the Hill Players, producers of plays staged by Masefield at Boar's Hill*

Introduction

This House of Books set open here,
May it bring light, may it bring cheer.
May it bring Man a thing most dear,
A mind alive,
A quiet of wisdom fenced from fear.

Thirty years after he first began sharing his quiet of wisdom with Florence Lamont, John Masefield wrote those lines for the opening in London of the National Book League. The League had been one of Masefield's special devotions and in gratitude for his long friendship with the Lamonts, Florence and Thomas W., he had invited them to join it as honorary trustees. The Second World War had ended, Europe was digging itself out from the rubble, Masefield was celebrating his sixteenth year as England's Poet Laureate – and the spirited correspondence between him and Florence had survived it all, undiminished.

It had flowed through wars, censors and family misfortunes as indomitably as Masefield's Thames, as inexorably as the Hudson they both so loved. It would remain flowing brightly for another six years until Florence's death.

Out of the pages of that correspondence, which spanned nearly four decades, emerged not only an uninhibited commentary on their turbulent era but a portrait of two sensitive people concerned for the world about them while deeply attracted to each other's ideas and feelings. Theirs was a friendship that thrived on communicating the exuberance of their respective lives, on sharing a mutual curiosity about changing fashions in thought and literature. It was a friendship that never lagged in shared respect and affection.

What brought the struggling poet and banker's wife together?

I

The beginnings for such a lasting friendship seemed improbable enough.

He was all sea-feverish, salt and worldly; she was manor-bred and sheltered. Long before they met, they were figures from vastly different worlds: she, the Smith-educated bride of a Morgan partner rising to great influence in international finance; he, a wander-lusting mariner with no riches save the gift of verse and loving family. She spent her early years earning a Master's Degree in Philosophy from Columbia, living the comfortable life of a suburban housewife across the Hudson from New York. He came to America first in 1895 as a youth looking for adventure, earning his keep as a worker in a Yonkers, N.Y., carpet factory.

By the time they met, however, both Florence and John had matured in age and reputation. The strands of intellect and patriotism connected their otherwise disparate lives. At 44, Florence Lamont had blossomed into the beauteous, literate, well-traveled wife of one of Wall Street's pillars; she and her husband cultivated and entertained the great and the creative. Masefield, at 38, was becoming a one-man cottage industry of verse and plays in England; his reputation had bloomed with the publication of *Salt-Water Ballads*, his first book containing the famous 'Sea-Fever', and he was in demand as a lecturer and public icon. When the First World War began, the Lamonts were in the forefront of notable Americans supporting the Allied cause; Masefield had been assigned by the British government to an international lecture tour designed to quicken public sympathy in the West for England and the Allies. In February 1916, while lecturing in New York, Masefield met Florence Lamont.

One can surmise from Masefield's earliest letters to her that each of the protagonists saw in the other luminous qualities that would enhance their own lives: in Masefield, Florence had found a warm and informing link to the fascinating inner world of English letters; in Florence, Masefield had discovered a generous and understanding spirit who might help his and his country's fortunes through her influence in America. Both conversed in the graceful language of inquiring minds; both were blessed with a gentle teasing humor.

Florence was plainly intrigued with Masefield's erudition in so many fields, his willingness to share it with so eager if untutored a pupil. Masefield was captivated by the New-World vigor and artlessness that Florence personified. (He was an admirer of Jack

Dempsey the boxer, but she once proclaimed to have never even heard of Babe Ruth.)

It is an obvious disappointment that few of the letters from Florence to Masefield survive, and none that would fit in this sampling of Masefield's letters chosen for publication. They would have rounded the dialogue nicely. Yet in a way their absence lends a poignancy, a mystique almost, to this collection. The reader is left to imagine what sparkling, thoughtful or playful inquiries from Florence prompted Masefield to such philosophical or satirical flights. Her letters, one suspects, were by design mostly foils to draw him out on a multitude of subjects. She was beguilingly adept in her design.

What letters!

From the more than 2000 of them housed in Harvard University's Houghton Library, we have selected the following three hundred or so that seemed best to display the remarkable catholicity of Masefield's interests. Whether he was touring the war fronts in Europe, traveling through western America or composing new works in his beloved Oxfordshire, Masefield could always turn a poetic or journalistic eye on the world around him. When he focused that eye in his letters to Florence, fresh observations about the most worn topic leapt off the page, biting opinions about the fashions and major figures of his day crackled in the lines.

Freed from the stern constraints of poetry writing, Masefield the lettrist poured out his wit and humanity in an informal, stream-of-consciousness style that touched on every facet of his experience from Freud to the joys of English fruit. His letters bring out a subtlety and complexity in Masefield's character, a contradiction in moods, that were not apparent in his published works of poetry and prose. With equal parts of relish and wisdom he dissected the fraudulent and the redeeming.

From his protean knowledge of writers and writing, Masefield provided Florence with a running critique of figures like Shakespeare, Stendhal, Dostoievsky, Hardy, H. G. Wells, A. E. Housman and dozens of other literary giants. Many, like Housman or the novelist John Galsworthy, were his friends. His letters are studded with parodies of Chaucerian verse (which he obviously enjoyed), plus a delightful dollop of his own rhymes, some of them composed to fit a particular thought or a paean to Florence, some of them almost subconsciously buried in the singing prose of his letters. Always, however, Masefield reminded his American friend how tortuous was, and is, the task of composing seriou verse for a critical readership.

One of the passions in which Masefield, an ascetic man indulged himself was the regular staging of plays and verse drama near his home at Oxford, an activity he reported in energetic detail to Florence. The material acted out by Masefield, his wife Constance and a small group of literary intimates, sometimes consisted of Shakespearean classics; much of it was Masefield's own work. (One of the editors, Corliss, recalls that as an Oxford student in the 1920s he used to attend such stagings as a friend of the Masefields and one evening, while taking tickets at the door, ushered in the George Bernard Shaws.) In his letters to Florence, Masefield was scornful of the commercial productions of finer English drama and verse, preferring his own small amateur efforts as a purer reflection of the art. At any rate, the Oxford experiments by Masefield were said to have led the way for T. S. Eliot in similar stagings of *his* work, most notably at Canterbury.

Another of Masefield's passions, the sea, he conveyed to Florence in a series of vignettes about long-departed ships of grandeur and in mini-essays about the vagaries of Moby Dick and other beasts of the briny. His letters contain a wondrous succession of salty quatrains and ichthyological sign-offs such as,

> "Lobsters and whales,
> John."

He wrote of the harbor of Athens that it had the last great 'forest of masts' in the world and mourned the passing of the legendary *Cutty Sark*. As a token of his affection for Florence, Masefield laboriously constructed miniature ship models and posted them to her in New York. Many of his letters were illustrated with charming doodles of schooners and sloops, the sketchiest hints of the really fine marine water-colors he was capable of. (Masefield once drew for another of the editors, Lansing, a full-sail multi-colored brigantine carving the waters of the Atlantic – all on the back of an envelope.)

But it is Masefield's sharply stroked impressions of events normally outside his and Florence's ken that brings much of the yeast to these letters.

He wielded a trenchant pen on such diverse subjects as Parisian women, Russia, Teddy Roosevelt, Jesus Christ, Mexican bullights, the obstreperous Irish and the blighted hell of an industrial city in England's 'Black Country'. He could dream magnificently. A near victim of strafing by a German plane in World War I, Masefield dismissed the incident in a sentence and went on to expound his vision of an airborne cavalry of bombers and fighters that would determine the outcome of future wars the way the infantry and tanks had in this one. Though not a name-dropper, he could raise to an art form the gossip about his contemporaries in the literary and political worlds; he was unforgiving toward politicians as a genre.

Something, too, of the lyrical narrative flow that epitomized Masefield's best work imbues this correspondence: he moves in tidal rhythms from sweeping condemnation of war through deep thoughts about death and hope to bright pools of chat about English flowers and the sounds of water he loves most.

No epic stirred Masefield so deeply as the First World War. It was in its third cruel year when he met Florence and many of his earliest letters to her depicted the numbing carnage of the battlefield. After touring the bone-littered valley of the Somme, where he'd been sent by His Majesty's Government to do a report on the great battle there, Masefield must have found it almost therapeutic to spend an hour or so penning his thoughts to Florence, so many thousands of miles from the horror, on the virtues of Macaulay or the latest styles in Paris. If his only salvation from the horror was to sound occasionally lighthearted, Masefield could not for long disguise his shock at the inferno of trench warfare and his hatred for the Germans. It poured out in those first letters – and then again twenty-five years later.

The other event which transfixed England and Masefield was the royal abdication. Masefield, a staunch royalist who owed his Poet Laureateship to George V, wrote first in almost awestruck tones of the scandal that had divided his country, then in hot rage about the way so many of his countrymen had treated the young King and his American love. Mrs Simpson, Masefield had convinced himself, would have developed into an admirable Queen; the Church and much of the aristocracy had behaved abominably. Masefield's views of the episode revealed much about his romantic, basically populist leanings and his innate distrust of those elite institutions, the Crown excepted, which ruled England at the time.

Throughout the 1920s and '30s, the Lamonts and Masefields

frequently saw each other, usually in England, which Florence visited whenever she could manage a respite from her busy life in Manhattan. Her husband after the First War shuttled back and forth between Europe and America as a participant in the Versailles peace talks, and Florence often accompanied him. Masefield's letters vibrate with his anticipation of these visits, his suggestions for special excursions through the English countryside or a theatre outing in Oxford. It was an idyllic two decades and the attachment between the two families, between Florence and Masefield, grew even as the bonds between their countries tightened under the shadow of another world war.

When it came, Florence and Masefield were in their sixties and the letters from him spoke of old wounds reopened, old hatreds rekindled. Masefield raged at the Germans, their atrocities, but for him the new war was the extra reel in an epic film he'd already lived. There was no more vivid reportage in his letters, only the frustrations of a peaceful man of talents, disturbed in his labor by the alarums of yet another battle. For Florence, relatively untouched by the First War, the Second brought lengthy anxiety and sadness: her oldest grandson died in the Pacific while serving as a submariner; her oldest son, an Air Force colonel, spent two years amidst the bombs and V-2s of wartorn London. Masefield's letters were often snatches of consolation ending with his hopes for brighter days ahead.

The postwar years were the last relatively brief epoch in the Lamont–Masefield alliance. His letters became more philosophical, reflecting the mellowing of age, ever solicitous of Florence's fragile health, ever uncomplaining about his own infirmities.

Thomas W. Lamont had made a magnificent bequest to Canterbury Cathedral for its restoration from the ravages of bombs, and Masefield gratefully authored an inscription for a plaque honoring the couple, which rests today in a courtyard of the church. A few years later in 1948, T.W.L. died in Florida after a prolonged illness. Masefield sent words of comfort to Florence, reminding her ever again of how much her friendship had meant through the years. Amidst the shadows of death the correspondence between the two shone steadfast like a beacon, recalling the lines from Masefield's little known poem about the Palisades:

> Friendship is sunlight scattering man's cloud,
> Making a life a sunbeam's spangled dust.

Florence Lamont died four years after her husband. Masefield's letters to her were turned over for safe-keeping, and eventual use by scholars, to the Houghton Library at Harvard which already housed a considerable collection of Masefield works. In late 1959, after a correspondence between the Lamont family and Masefield in which he agreed to the release of the letters twenty-five years after Florence's death, Masefield asked that if any of the letters were published, they be accompanied by the following statement:

> These letters have not been seen by their writer since they were posted to their recipient long years ago. Like other writers he cannot but regret that these things come to the readers unread, uncorrected, unexcised by him. He would much prefer that all his letters were not even the memory of ashes in long forgotten grates.
>
> (signed) John Masefield.

It would perhaps be small consolation for Masefield to know that two editors who grew up admiring his works and who once partook of his hospitality tried in their small way to read and edit this correspondence without diminishing its spirit. The letters were written often casually or in haste, and Masefield's imaginative spelling and punctuation (or lack thereof) remain for the most part in their original state. Where material was dropped, it was done so in the interests of clarity and continuity.

John Masefield died in the spring of 1967. He had developed gangrene in one leg, but refused to have an amputation that might have saved him. At the memorial service in Westminster Abbey, his ashes were placed in an urn in the Poet's Corner.

Corliss Lamont, Florence's second son, represented the family and the Academy of American Poets at the service. His older brother, Tommy, who had died exactly a month before Masefield, had had an exchange of letters with the poet a few years before. In one of them, Tommy had written to Masefield:

> I detect in your letter a note of pessimism as to the world's future. I remain an optimist. I think that twenty-five years from now – and a hundred years from now – the world is going to be inhabited and that its people will still be able and willing to read. Indeed, I believe that some thousands of them will find delight in your letters.

We think that a prescient remark.

Not only because these letters were written to a woman he deeply admired by a man of great human understanding and liberal outlook, but because, as Masefield himself had once said,

> Though the soul shrink, though the heart ache,
> From Man's debasement and mistake,
> Nothing can null, or quench, or shake
> A mind alive.
> A quiet of wisdom will remake.

C.L.
L.L.

The Letters

On 28 February 1916, while on a wartime visit to America on behalf of His Majesty's Government, Masefield gave an afternoon talk at the Aeolian Hall in New York City. His lecture, on the subject of 'The Tragic Drama', was enthusiastically received by the audience, some of whom crowded around him afterwards. It was at this point that Masefield was introduced to a smiling and eager woman, Florence Corliss Lamont, then aged 44 and the wife of a well-known figure in American banking circles, Thomas W. Lamont.

New York.
18 March. [1916]

Dear Florence,

This to bring my goodbye greetings to you & say that I have loved getting to know you & that you must look on our friendship as only beginning now. All greetings & blessings & good wishes be about you from me.

Your friend
John

En route back to England, an enthused Masefield wrote of his entente cordiale with his new-found friend from New York. It was the beginning of a nearly four-decade-long Anglo-American alliance.

U.S.M.S. "St. Paul".
21 March. [1916]
(at sea)

Dear Florence,

We are three days out now, & I've written all my 55 letters (the ones which I ought to have written) and now I am free to write to my friends.

You would be pleased to see how I miss you. It breaks my heart across to think of all your goodness & kindness & frank merry-heartedness, & all your gentle thought for my pleasure. I never had such a friend, & ever since the elevator took you down & away I've felt as heartbroken as you could wish. You were good to me, & I can't begin to thank you; and oh I am homesick for America which was so kind to me, & which holds you.

We had some good times, our reading, & our going to New Haven, & our walks together. I can never forget them all.

By the way, Julia[1] did turn up at the pier, with Consuelo,[2] but I gave you no occasion for jealousy.

I want to see you & to hear from you & to hear your voice. We must set to work, we two, to make England & America tremendous friends, & then come from our respective countries to each other's as ambassadors continually. That would be one way.

You are getting ready for another of your famous dinner parties as I write this. I, too, shall have to dress in a few minutes, but no Florence to sit beside & look at; nothing but 5 commercial travellers & a one armed soldier; & we shall not talk about élan vital, but about whether the soup is fit to eat & how the oysters are, & no "historic Claremont"[3] to look at, only the monotonous Atlantic.

Your lovely gifts of fruit have kept me from being seasick. So far I have not felt a single qualm, though it will not do to boast. This last paragraph reads like a quotation from the Sorrows of Werther;[4] but it is really from the Sorrows of John.

Dear Florence, you have taught me so much & given me so much that I seem unable to begin to write to you. I must put this off till another day. Good night to you. All greetings to your husband[5] & Corliss[6] & Eleanor.[7]

Your friend
John.

1. Mrs Simeon Ford of Rye, N.Y., 1859–1950. Writer and friend of both Masefield and Florence C. Lamont. Author of *Consequences* and co-author with Thomas W. Lamont of *George Frederick Watts*.
2. Mrs Ellsworth Ford, daughter-in-law of Mrs Simeon Ford.
3. The Claremont Inn, a well-known New York restaurant on Riverside Drive just north of Grant's Tomb. It is no longer in existence.
4. *The Sorrows of Werther:* a romantic novel by the German poet and philosopher, Johann Wolfgang von Goethe, 1749–1832, published in 1774.
5. Thomas W. Lamont, 1870–1948, banker, philanthropist and author. Partner in J. P. Morgan & Co., becoming Chairman of the Board in 1943.
6. Corliss Lamont, born in 1902, second son of Thomas W. and Florence C. Lamont. Author and educator.
7. Eleanor Allen Lamont, 1910–61, only daughter of Thomas W. and Florence C. Lamont. Married Charles C. Cunningham in 1932.

U.S.M.S. "St. Paul"
24 March. 1916.
(at sea.)

Dear Florence,

I've been reading a little philosophy book which you might like to know, Gilbert Murray's[1] brief summary, or lecture, on Stoic Philosophy. If it be still in print in England I must send it to you, as it will interest you. It has been the only thing I have managed to read here.

A week ago we were cruising in a taxi, as of old, & now we are all these miles apart. Tell me, when you write, how Corliss's party went off, & how you have managed your week of feasting? What new pretty dresses have you had, & what effect have you noticed in Mr. Housman[2] & Mr. Bynner?[3] Be kind to Mr. Bangs if you see him, for our eloping a fortnight back robbed him of a looked-for talk, & he is a nice young man. It is only two weeks since that happy day of ours & it seems like years & years, with this dreary ship in between.

There used to be a song the sailors sang at the pumps:

> Only one more day for Johnny,
> One more day,
> O, rock & roll me over,
> Only one more day.

and one gets a kind of comfort from repeating it in the boredom of being at sea. I wouldn't be bored if Florence were here, not I, for we would walk up and down & quarrel about philosophy, & sit next each other at meals, & have a grand time, & I should watch the captain & the purser & the stewards & the male passengers one by one succumbing to you, just as our policemen & waiters & taxi drivers did. None could hold out long against Florence.

All greetings to you & your husband & Eleanor & the boys.

Your friend
John.

1. Gilbert Murray,1866–1957, Professor of Greek at Oxford University and translator of Greek dramatists. An author, active in the cause of international peace.
2. Laurence Housman, 1865–1959, English dramatist and brother of A. E. Housman. Author of *Victoria Regina* (1937).
3. Witter Bynner, 1881–1968, American author and poet. President, Poetry Society of America, 1920–2.

Lollingdon, Cholsey,
Berks.
May 20. 1916.

Dear Florence,

Once again I find it difficult to write to you, with such a press of work on hand, but I must send you a note, if only to thank you for the jolly letter from North Carolina. I'm glad you've had a good holiday. I wish I'd been there to have watched your delight, but it was pleasant anyway to hear of it, for your letters, as you know very well, can never be too long to me, nor too frequent.

Your spellings of Shakespeare differ from mine. I spell him thus [finger pointing to above spelling] I have nothing to do with people (so called men and women) who call him Shakspere, in their superior thin-lipped way, nor with those well-meaning (perhaps) people who call him Shakespere or Shakspear. These latter may be doing their best, but I say they straddle the rail & equivocate & try to be on both sides at once. Away with such, I say: is this a time to be straddling the rail? Of course it isn't. Its a time to be speaking out, as Lincoln says, though his precise words I find I forget.

Then as to why so much good poetry is sad. Probably because the world presses rather hard on sensitive people, & perhaps because men only take to poetry when something has unfitted them for action. But I don't really know. Perhaps no really deep feeling is really joyous.

I hope that you will meet Murray[1] when he comes: he is a fine fellow, & has a truly beautiful mind, & he will answer you all these things like one o'clock.

My going to France is again postponed. This task of mine is very difficult & takes time.

Blessings on you, good lady, & on all your household. What fun when there is peace & we can meet again. You will have to come down to the Pier to meet me (not with Philip, though). Goodbye.

Yours
John

1. Gilbert Murray.

Lollingdon, Cholsey,
Berks, 25. VI. 1916.

Dear Florence,

Thank you ever so much for your wonderful letter. It has been a great help to us to hear what the Boche are up to, & saying & doing, in America, & your letter was a revelation. If you will tell me always things of that kind you will help us, for although we will not answer their lies (their own foul acts expose them) we follow what they say with great care, as it shews us what Germany is wanting & thinking; & their present attitude is very very interesting. A wet harvest in Central Europe would pretty nearly finish the war.

You asked me. Does the Censor read your letters? The Censor is a British Officer & reads all letters, certainly all of yours, for by this time he must look out for them, & say to his man, "By the way, the St. Paul is in, is there any letter from Florence?" "Yes, sir," says the man "I put it on top, sir". "Thank you", says the

Censor, "I will begin with that. By Jove, that woman has a mind".

Long after the war he will say "Ah, when I was Censor, I used to see some wonderful letters from a woman named Florence to a man called John. I often think of Florence, she must have been a very beautiful soul, but I'm afraid she was thrown away on John. John's letters were just like eating glue. He was certainly a poor stick beside her".

Would you like these photographs of my wife,[1] Judith,[2] Lewis[3] & the little governess, standing outside Lollingdon?

All greetings to you & your husband & Eleanor & Corliss. I hope the yacht is the queen of Dark Harbour.[4] Is she a cutter or a schooner?

from
John

[Drawing of a ship]

1. Constance Crommelin Masefield, 1867–1960.
2. Judith Masefield, born in 1904, only daughter of Constance and John Masefield. Author and illustrator.
3. Lewis Crommelin Masefield, 1910–42, only son of Constance and John Masefield, killed in action in Africa in the Second World War.
4. A vacation resort on the island of Islesboro, Penobscot Bay, Maine, where the Lamonts spent the summer of 1916.

Lollingdon, Cholsey,
Berks. 30, July. [1916]

Dear Florence,

Thank you for your thought & for sending the cheque, which was altogether wrong of you, for who would not gladly pay duty to get a letter from you? Besides you've spent any amount too much, in your royal way, or republican way as you would call it, so I'm going to buy a lot of puzzles & cigarettes for French wounded with the surplus; & they will be playing with the one & smoking the other before you receive this letter.

I have applied for a wonderful job, & if I get it it will be the most amazing thing. I start off anyway on a job in a few days. You know how difficult it is to write anything but the barest scraps in war time, so when I'm in France you mustn't mind bald letters or no letters.

The Bergson article is eagerly expected. I expect it will quite alter the shape of my head; thus.

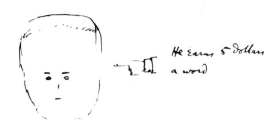

Before reading Bergson.

After reading Bergson.

I hope you're having a jolly time with your yacht. All greetings to your husband & Eleanor & Corliss & you.

from
John

Lollingdon, Cholsey,
Berks,
2nd Augt. 1916.

Dear Florence,

Thank you very much for the Bergson[1] article, which I've rec'd with pleasure & interest, though I don't agree with more than about half of it as you know. I still feel, that the thing life is made better by living, that we are given 5 copper senses, & make a sixth, of silver, if we have the wit, in our good moments, & that the notion that we are swimming in a stream of life, buoyed up & swung along by a current of life, is a wrong one. Still, the task is to get to heaven, & any way there is good.

I wish that I were standing on a rock 8 or 10 feet above an expanse of sea not less than "12 feet deep & as clear as gin", for if I were I would jump off the rock into the sea, & be the better for it; and by doing so I wd illustrate the superiority of my view of life to

Bergson's; for he would say, you are already a part of the sea, so do not jump, but go on rejoicing.

Well, I am off for France, & I won't begin a philosophical discussion, for truth is a personal thing, & no other person's truth opens the door.

The Search for Truth.

Greetings to you & your husband & Eleanor & Corliss.
from
John

1. Henri Bergson, 1859–1941, noted French philosopher. Author of *Time and Free Will* (1888) and *Creative Evolution* (1907).

Lollingdon, Cholsey,
Berks, Augt 25. 1916.

My dear Florence,

I was glad to have your letter about the Murrays:[1] what a time you must have had. I looked at myself in the glass as I read & saw that I had gone quite green. I told you he was a superior being. Lady M I've never met, but saw her once in a theatre: G.M. I've met & corresponded with a good deal for some years past. His mind is not very powerful, but it is acute & delicate & wise & has that beauty without which there is never any fineness in men or things. He is one of the best minds now in England.

As to Flecker,[2] I've never much cared for his work, though it is accomplished & very well done. All that school, from Swinburne down, seems to me to be a school of glass-cutters. What they do is frightfully difficult, & very expensive & looks well on the dinner table, & glitters & flashes & takes the eye, but it gives no meat & drink to the mind. Flecker came under the French (Heredia &

that set) & was an Orientalist & a strange clever man who died young. I must try to remember to send you something by him. He made a deep impression at Oxford, where, before the war, a new school of that kind was beginning, but probably the war will turn the young writers of that school more towards mysticism. I always think that that is what Flecker was aiming at, but got caught, as it were, in the painted glass over the altar. "John", you will say, "You are jealous of Flecker.

> 'O the artist's jealousy
> Is the poison in the honey bee'."

"Tush", as they say in the Bible, "go to". I am nothing of the kind.

You will say, "why aren't you abroad, serving your country, instead of writing rubbish?" Well, I've been laid up with a poisoned arm & haven't been able to go, but I start on Tuesday, the 29th inst, & shall have no fixed address, except this, for some time to come. I do not know how long I shall be away; it is a special job; not the artillery yet; that will come later.

What do you think? How far possible is it for America ever to be cordial friends with England? We fought France for 150 years & look at us now. We have wrangled with America ever since our German Court & King decided that America should be taxed. Well, it is time all that should end, & the very possibility of quarrel between us removed by an act of will. That is the thing I want to work at for the next few years, (see what comes of taking one out to dine at Claremont) and I want you, if you will, when you have time, to let me know what you think stands in the way.

All blessings & good wishes to you

from

John

1. Gilbert Murray and his wife, Lady Mary Murray.
2. James Elroy Flecker, 1884–1915, English poet and playwright. Author of *The Golden Journey to Samarkand* (1913) and the verse play *Hassan* (1922).

After a brief sojourn in England, Masefield reported for further service to his country. Over the next year or more he divided his time between home and the Continent where he performed special services on behalf of the Allied war effort.

Paris.
7 Sept, 1916.

My dear Florence,

So many thanks for your charming letter of Aug 18th. Alas, my nice kind friend, we are 20 days apart now, but never mind, the heart's all, & often you seem very near indeed.

Now I am not officially in the army at all. I was medically rejected, then accepted for the reserve of officers, & then, being supposed to be a writer & known to be in sympathy with America (this is where you came in) I was switched on to my present task, which is to make a report on all that America has done for the Allies since the war began, in France & England. So I am here at present, bothering your country people at Neuilly till they are ready to drop. I don't know whether I am glad or sorry; a little sad & ashamed that I can't be used instead of these young fellows who have never known the heart of life, & in a way relieved, for the Gallipoli business has made me feel very old, & I don't seem to get back my jump. I used to be just like this [drawing of a man jumping] and now I am just like this [drawing of a man with cane].

In 2 or 3 days I go to Verdun to see your Field Service at work. I shall be there a fortnight probably, & then come back here, & after that shall be here on & off, if you care to write, as of course I want you to.

I won't let you send any money anywhere till I find a really crying need. I have my eye on an armless man at Neuilly. I will find out about him.

My head didn't swell so much as we expected over the Bergson article; but over my new French accent, my good lady, it is beginning. I get the workmen to tell me the names of things & then I go to other workmen & fire them off, & they think, "c'est lui, c'est Jean, c'est épatant; il a du panache". So I go on, getting more panache each day.

Panache.

There is something that draws me towards Frenchmen & repels me in French women. Sisters of Charity are the only French women I can make friends with.

Good Florence, I often think of you.

All blessings & good wishes to you

from

John.

Paris.

20. IX. 1916.

My dear Florence,

I am back here again for a few days, & then go away, either to the Eastern front or to the south.

I've been principally in & near Verdun, a forlorn, unconquerable city, like some of the dead men who were lying round her, full of pathos, & all broken, & yet in a way not touched; I can't explain it.

War is like life, my dear Florence; there is no élan vital, but a kind of effort, full of patience & endurance & suffering, with other great things, too, love & friendship & agony of the soul, which all together do not bring the world far, but hold it from slipping & make good a new line, here & there, perhaps; I don't know.

I've seen so many die & so many suffer in this war that I would to God I could be taken by the gods & burnt piecemeal, as an atonement or as a scapegoat for the rest.

In one place there was a little country churchyard where the dead of ten centuries had been buried, & where rank on rank of French soldiers lay, often so mangled that the buriers could only say "Un Francais. Inconnu".

Then the enemy shelled the little churchyard with heavy shells, till it was dug with holes seven feet by seven feet, and all the dead, new & old, were flung up broadcast, so that one walked on bones & rags of flesh & broken crosses.

Then in another place was an old wayside cross, beside the cemetery of a hospital, where 2000 dead soldiers had been buried since March, and going by the cemetery I read the words on the cross:

C'est ainsi que Dieu a aimé le monde.

Well, dear Florence, all greetings to you.
from
John.

You will want to know about the Paris fashions. They are rather like this at present

Very jupes courtes, & huge heels on the boots, & the boots away up to the knee like the soldier's combined boot-gaiter. You stick to your own fashions, no French woman can dress as well as an American.

Then for the sort of finish of the fashion, the person puts a little rice powder on her face & a little red on her lips & touches up her eyes with something & out she goes with her little dog, & finishes off those who have survived the war. All along the Avenues you see the brave of France succumbing, Generals & Croix de Guerres & Colonels with the Legion of Honour. Faint sighs of Je me rends, come from their collapsing frames.

Dear Florence, I hope you & yours are all very well & happy. The best of greetings to you & your husband & Eleanor & Corliss.
from John.

Paris.
Sept 29. 1916.

Dear Florence,

I don't know what sort of world is to come out of this cauldron here; but some things strike profoundly, & rather bear out your Bergson. In all the scenes of war & desolation one repeats the text "the heart of men is upright always continually but they have sought out many inventions". I have found the hearts of men simple & profound & noble & true, & the brains full of the devil of hell, the ingenious devil, who is so stupid. Sometimes I feel that the intellect is hell, & then that we have to pass through a purgatory of imperfect intellect, in order to reach a state of intelligence, & then that men use their intellects because they are too proud or too restless to use their imaginations, & that life really offers nothing but a little hour in which, in the imagination, one can live all an eternity. "Golly", I think I hear you saying, "John did ought to have been in the church".

But as Balzac used to say "Now let us talk of real things. Let us talk of Modeste Mignon". Did you ever read Don Quixote? A lot of it you would hate, but if you would read it steadily through, & get into the sweep & the heart of it, & all the wisdom & the heroism, & the grand style, which makes one feel like a worm in the presence of the greatest gentlemen who ever lived, & would then tell me what you think of it, it would be a topic for all through the winter, & it would make you write me jolly long letters. It is the greatest book of modern times, and I don't know what it is really driving at, but it is a profound & beautiful thing. Unamuno,[1] the best critic now in Spain, thinks that it is a sort of dramatization of the soul of Spain, "fighting for the Middle Ages against the Renaissance, so as to keep the treasure of its childhood". The phrase is arresting, but it (the book) must be more human than that, & deals with the spirit & the sense of man, at war with this half baked ingenious thing that is so stupid, the human intellect.

I shall be at the front again about the time you get this, but only for a few weeks, so write here; it is nicer to suppose that one will survive. One nice thing about this front is that they aren't forever potting at one with rifles. They keep to good big shells, & plump little bombs.

All greetings & good wishes to you
from
John.

---

1. Miguel de Unamuno, 1864–1936, Spanish philosopher, poet and novelist. Author of *The Tragic Sense of Life in Men and Nations* (1913).

Aix-les-Bains
Oct. 6. [1916]
(waiting for a train.)

Dear Florence,

I've gone & lost your letter, silly owl that you always said I was, so I can't answer your remarks exactly, but you rejoiced (I think) that you had a restless mind, & that somebody else with a restless mind had said that restless minds were the thing, & that in a way I was in the wrong about something, & that you were happy that that was so.

Alas, alas, I want minds to follow the laws of their own beings, for that is the only way of life & happiness & the making of an eternal kingdom here. Let the restless be restless & the quiet calm, each to the fullest of its power, for only so is God served & the mind developed & the world made happy. God forbid that after this war one should say anything but thanksgiving, that any one ever should possess his own soul in peace, & delight his own mind as seems good to him.

I travel all night tonight & hope to reach Paris tomorrow morning, & there perhaps there will be a letter from you; not that I expect one; one expects nothing good in war time; but if there is one I shall call you many friendly names. Supposing you were there in person. Golly, wouldn't that be great?

I've been all day in this whited sepulchre, waiting, so to speak, for the stone to be rolled away, that is, for the Paris train to come. If you were never here, let me urge you never to come. It is a white town, full of people with diseased livers. There is a sort of common mountain, or calm mountain, not very good, at the back, & a sort of unusual mountain, or restless mountain, not very remarkable in the front. You have to pay a fearful lot for a view of either.

But in happy peace you can see it at its best, in the pitch dark night, as you go through to Rome. That's the way to see it, to wake up from a snug sleep & hear someone bawling something & see a light & a blackness & then turn over comfortably with a yawn & go to sleep, & not wake again till you're in Italy.

Did you ever read Stendhal's Chartreuse de Parme?[1] It is a good book for a long railway journey; and then what do you think of Les Dieux ont Soif, & Thais, & the Reine Pedauque?[2]

Golly what a talk we would have if you were here. I've not had a real talk about anything with anybody for 40 days & 40 nights;

though God knows I've had my mind restless enough. There is a gloomy hymn which begins

> 40 days & 40 nights
> I was starving in the wild.[3]

Now I must stop right here, for I mustn't begin another sheet of paper because the waiter's looking & he – O Lord I shan't have time, I mean space, to say all my farewells to you. All greetings & good wishes to you. from John.

---

1. *La Chartreuse de Parme* (1839) by Stendhal (Henri Beyle), 1783–1842.
2. *Les Dieux Ont Soif* (1912), *Thaïs* (1890), and *La Rôtisserie de la Reine Pédauque* (1893) are novels by Anatole France (Jacques Anatole Thibaut), 1844–1924, novelist, journalist and political satirist. He supported Emile Zola in his exposure of the Dreyfus affair.
3. Hymn by G. H. Smyttan and F. Pott. It opens with the words;
> Forty days and forty nights
> Thou wast fasting in the wild.

J.M.'s misquotations will be left uncorrected in the letters.

Paris.
Oct 15. 1916.

Dear Florence,
   I am going to the front again on Tuesday for a while; perhaps not for very long; & shall be there on & off at intervals, perhaps, for the rest of the war; but for all I know I may go home soon to join the artillery, the future is very uncertain. I shall be in bangy places this time. This is still the only address I can give you. In my next letter I may be able to send you a permanent address, but anyhow the people here will forward to me.
   I've been seeing some marvellous things in hospitals. Did you ever hear of a stuff called Ambrene? It is transparent (more or less) like glue, & it feels & looks like chocolate, & it is made of wax and paraffin & amber & things & it is amazing for burns. You go out to the war & have all your skin burnt off you with a bomb or a flame projector; but you just grit your teeth, & the people say "Golly, voilà un héros; il ne crie pas, le pauvre. Vite, Donnez-lui la Croix d'Honneur avec la cravate". But you just grit your teeth & say "C'est rien de tout. Je vais me panser avec un peu

d'Ambrene, et alors Guillaume me payera, sacré nom d'un nom",
etc. So then you go to hospital, & the nurses & people say "Golly,
what a wound. C'est effroyable". Then they rinse you over with
oxygenated water & dry you with an electric séchoir, then they
melt up a chunk of Ambrene over a chafing dish, & paint your
burn with it, & in seconds your pain stops & in about 2 weeks you
have a new skin, & go around the wards chaffing the Sisters. I
never saw such a stuff, but they say that it is less good for deep
burns.

Then there is another stuff for wounds, which seems amazing,
but this seems to me to depend more upon personal application,
though even so the results are extraordinary.

I've not had any time for reading or thinking during this last
week, but perhaps in time one will have these things again. Just
think of being able to settle down to some course of reading, all the
novels of Voltaire, say, or a lusty big boxfull of French memoirs, or
some Spanish stories of the conquest, or folios of English poetry
with the romantic bits like the glows in old wood. Golly, isn't
reading a fine thing?

> If I don't go tomorrow
> I shall go the day after
> Hooray hooray hooray
> This town is my abhorrence
> And now I'm going to be gay
> And share my joy with Florence
>
> I shall go on board the boat
> Whose screws will lash the foam
> Whether I'm seasick or noat
> I shall be going home.

Dear Florence, I don't know how long I shall be at home,
probably only a few days, but still, I'm going. Send letters either
to the Maurice or to Cholsey. Cholsey perhaps would be best, for
I'm hardly likely to be much in Paris, though a good deal in
France, after this. All greetings & good wishes to you & your
husband & all your household.

                              from
                              John.

Cholsey,
Nov 10. 1916.

Dear Florence,

I hope the epidemic is dying down with the year so that you can bring the children home without risk. I want you to tell me what "home" is going to be with you. You said something about a new house, but not where the new house was to be. I suppose you hesitate between two sites, one on the Avenue, overlooking silly old Sherman[1] with the peroxide angel, & the other overlooking our famous Reservoir, where we walked in the thaw & afterwards in the snow. I suppose by a "house" you mean a palace, with an Italian Wing, and perhaps a private observatory from which you could signal across the Park to Julia.[2] As I told you, I did not see Julia, but I should have liked to have seen her, because she was the cause of our meeting, & was a great preventative of our quarrelling on that drive out to the Bronx.

I don't know how much longer I shall be here, but probably only a day or two more, & then abroad again. You shall have my address.

You don't know what an effect war has upon people. You go out, & the beastly shells scare the life out of you, & then you think, not at all that you've been wicked, but that you haven't half loved people enough, & that they have been jolly good friends, & worth a lot more than you thought, so then you come home, & see them, & the good in them, a lot more clearly, & prize them a great deal more, & love them & their letters, & write to them much more lovingly, & shew your affection for them. So be very sure that when I go out again I shall long for letters from you as often as you can manage, for this war has taught me the worth of friendship.

I am not telling you about the war, because it is better not to write about it; probably the letter would be censored anyway; so I will only say that it is a noisier war than the last, & as dull, as dirty, & as dangerous as all other wars put together.

Bless you my dear friend Florence, & all my greetings to your household.

from
John.

---

1. Equestrian statue of Civil War General William Tecumseh Sherman, 1820–91, in the plaza at Fifth Avenue and 59th Street, New York City.
2. Mrs Julia Ford.

Cholsey,
Nov 29. [1916]

Dear Florence,

(Notice how my hand is coming to resemble yours. This is partly affection & partly because I'm writing in a train) It was such a joy to have your letter this morning (your 3rd of November letter, forwarded from France) Hooray I said, dear good Florence is well & her children are well, & she isn't angry with me, but still thinks me a valued friend. O my dear Florence if you knew how I've worried at not hearing from you, & how deeply I care for my real friends, you would not wonder whether I like you, nor why I write.

All the same, I'm going to roast you, now, for still misunderstanding me about Anatole & his inquietude. My point is that Inquietude has its merits & quiet has its merits, & that action & reaction are equal & opposite, but that what I like in people is not one thing nor the other, but their essential quality, the thing which they defend & carry the banner of, the quality which defines them from the rest of the world, & if that is quiet, I love it & thank God for it, & if its inquiet I love it & wonder at it & thank God for it, too; & if you were not you, but, say, Nefrekepta,[1] or Ella Wheeler Wilcox,[2] or Mrs. H. B. Stowe,[3] I shouldn't get quite the note you strike in me, but some other note, no doubt valuable, but not yours.

I know you think you rattled me & got on my nerves. My good Florence, if you'd got on my nerves I'd have bitten a piece right out of you, like this [drawing] & that I did not. I was as gentle as a lamb all the time.

Alas, no least chance of coming to the U.S., I'm afraid till after the war. I am in doubt still as to what will be done with me. A very very interesting job is talked of for me, but I'm waiting still to hear if it is to be. Failing that, & I must soon hear if I'm to have it, I shall be in the guns, as I told you.

O that some divine wisdom would touch the mind of a certain man & make him say, "John is the man we want in the U.S. He is the goods. Let John go. He'll smooth the thorny road". But there is no chance of that, there is nothing they can use me for there, so I shall be on this side, probably in France. But the thought that perhaps you will be coming here is wonderful; not that I expect it, though; one expects nothing in war time; and then, too, it might not be possible to meet. I might be at the front, or the Lord knows where, unable to get leave.

As to Gibson:[4] I have met him twice, but do not really know him. He is a gentle, quiet man. Rupert[5] was very fond of him. He lives away from London, near my old home in the country, which is a part I never go to now, & with the best will in the world I cannot get great joy out of his work. It is very sweet & good, but I suppose it wants inquietude or something. He would be very grateful for a kindly boost & it would be splendid of you if you could perhaps see him. Perhaps his wife will be with him. I met her once.

You ask, why one, with the realities of war under his eyes, should think of anything else. But one must think of something else, one thinks of the real realities, lying at the foundations of one's life, & these are the deep imaginings & the deep affections, for stronger & deeper things than a pash of dead bodies in the mud, & the tumult & terror going & coming outside and inside.

Whenever one isn't in a blind funk one is continually thinking of all the things & people one loves. I never realized how much I loved people till this war; nor how much I would like to survive it in order to write certain things which I now imagine.

I'm in the train for London, going to see Harley,[6] & then I shall lunch with Hamilton,[7] my admired chief, & then I shall see one or 2 people & catch a train home. John & Ada[8] have gone to do massage in a French hospital, dear souls.

O Golly I wish I could be definitely appointed consul in New York, or some quiet post of that kind; but since this is impossible we must just write oftener to each other. My future address will be my London house

> 13, Well Walk,
> Hampstead,
> London, N.W.

All greetings to you & yours

> from
> John.

---

1. Nefrekepta. Refers to *The Story of Nefrekepta*, from a demotic papyrus, put into verse by Gilbert Murray (Oxford 1911).
2. Ella Wheeler Wilcox, 1850–1919, popular author of sentimental verse.
3. Harriet Beecher Stowe, 1811–96, author of *Uncle Tom's Cabin* (1852).
4. Wilfrid Wilson Gibson, 1878–1962, English poet. Contributed to the anthologies of *Georgian Poetry* (1912–22).
5. Rupert Brooke, 1887–1915, English poet whose great promise was cut short by his premature death while on his way to take part in the Dardanelles expedition against Turkey in the First World War.

6. Harley Granville-Barker, 1877–1946, English actor, dramatist, producer and Shakespearean critic.

7. Sir Ian Standish Monteith Hamilton, 1853–1947, a distinguished British general who in the First World War was in command of the second stage of the abortive Gallipoli campaign against Turkey to force open the Dardanelles. When in 1915 Masefield was serving with the British Red Cross at the Dardanelles, he became a friend of Hamilton.

8. John Galsworthy, 1867–1933, English novelist and dramatist, author of *The Forsyte Saga* (1916–22). He married his wife Ada in 1905.

London.
9 Dec. [1916]

Dear Florence,

I'm still here, working, but expecting orders for France again. They may come at any moment. I've been expecting them for 5 weeks. When I go, I shall be at the front, & not able to write to you at all fully, but only just to say that I am well, & that the weather is good or bad. I want you to imagine all the friendship & pleasant philosophy which I shall not be able to write, & to think that anyhow I am going on being your friend & that I hope you will write to me. You shall have an address as soon as my orders come. There'll be danger of course, but there is no sense in crossing rivers till you reach the water: I have come back so far & may come back again.

But in peace time, in 1918, or whenever it is, there will be a tumult along 5th, past old gold Sherman, & historic Claremont will have to outdo itself.

All greetings & blessings to you for now & Christmas & the New Year

from
John.

You'd never seen me a year ago & probably never heard of me!

London.
18. xii. 1916.

Dear Florence,

Look here, did you ever get Gallipoli¹ from me? I have sent you three, one from France, months ago, one from here & one from New York, & I'm afraid all have gone astray, & I am worried, because I would like you to feel that my books come to you before they come to the public, & if they have not come to you, you may think that I have not been thoughtful of you, which is not true.

No, we won't *talk* of time, when we next go to Claremont. We will *have* a Time, or, as the book of Revelations puts it, "a Time and Times". What are the new ideas? It is odd that ideas should give you such pleasure, but you make friends with thoughts just as you do with people, & I suppose the thoughts, like the people, flush with pleasure & show up brighter than usual. Will you not send me your criticism of Mr. Rashdall's[2] book? I would love to see it, & you know that I love your mind however much we may wrangle.

The Greeks didn't really get much time for talk; they had wars most of the time; but the wars cleared away all the rubbish of what does not really matter to the mind or to life, & when they did have a little leisure they were profound on the right things. We are as wise as they, & our brains are as powerful, but our minds are not cleared, as theirs were, of knowledge & the past & the means of touching other minds. Imagine the gain to a thinker to have to use his mind directly upon his antagonist instead of through some book or pamphlet. The old Greek sat in the sun & his critic sat opposite & a gang of idlers sat about to listen, & ragged them both when they seemed off the point. Now he need never see his antagonist, nor read what the idlers say, & the quarrel of ideas is less alive & less passionate & no longer involves the whole man.

I don't think: I never could: it belongs to a different kind of brain from mine: I just see, or fail to see. So if I'd been an ancient Greek, like you, I should have sat outside the circle, & listened, & gone away silent, & then told you that both men were perfectly right, & that truth is a very beautiful thing, like something that passes, & no man knows what she is like, nor ever will know. I suppose she is only the good in things.

I'm still waiting for orders, & when they come I shall go back to the Somme, & shall be on that great field somewhere, I do not yet know where, nor could I tell you if I did. The Somme is a regular chalk river, at the foot of some rolling chalk billows of land, & all the way up to the battlefield it is exactly like the land near my home at Lollingdon, most strangely like; but beyond the Somme, & in the great & bloody patch between the Somme & Ancre, it is different; & at present it is different from anything man ever yet looked upon.

Please do not worry about danger & the rest of it. Life is an ordered business, conducted with mystery & art, & one is very subtly arranged for, as fits the scheme. I've had a beautiful time & hope we may have some more, & if we hope hard enough we shall.

Bless you & all kind & gentle thoughts to you
from
John.

1. J.M.'s book *Gallipoli* was published in September 1916, and gives an account of the unsuccessful British attempt to outflank Turkey and capture Constantinople in the First World War by breaking through at the Straits of the Dardanelles.
2. Hastings Rashdall, 1858–1924, English philosopher, theologian and historian.

London.
Jan. 19. 1917

Dear Florence,

I am grieved over your Christmas trouble, but I do not see that you are to blame in any slightest way. Life isn't a simple matter but a highly complex one, & extraordinarily inter-involved and interdependent, & the intellects of men are forever snatching at various half seen threads of the tangle, so that they may make for themselves some kind of a pattern. This is where the forger came in. Well, he snatched at the half-seen threads, & found, when he got them, that they were utterly different from anything he had imagined, & that instead of making him a pattern they blew his life & all the lives near his into misery. It is a cruel thing for the poor old father, & I am grieved for you, who think it partly your own fault; but it was not in any way your fault; only your Fate, that it should happen & make you thoughtful & sad. I will think of it at the front, to see if I can hit on anything that will be a comfort to you.

Dear Florence, you ask why I go to the front? I have been appointed, to write the history of the battle of the Somme, as a sort of pendant to Gallipoli, & that is why I am going. It has been in my mind for many months, that this is the biggest thing England has ever been engaged in, & that it must be a possession of the English mind forever, faults & splendor & all, & that we now living have a chance of beginning its tradition. I hope to make something of the battle. I cannot write what I feel about it, but I went over the field in the autumn, just after the most bloody & terrible fighting, when the ground was not ground at all, but the flesh and bones of men, all mixed with wreck and little half burnt scraps of their letters, & the photographs of their mothers & wives, & bits of the weapons they were carrying, & it gave me a feeling for this race deeper than any I have had. And then to come home & read the newspapers.

And do not blame my fellows. Old J.G. is 55 & a Sybarite, but he has learned massage & is massaging in a hospital. Gibson[1] is a crock, with no heart & no lungs & not much liver, & I daresay the rest of him is diseased, so that he could not serve anyway. Harley[2] is in the Army, but has been granted leave on very urgent grounds. De la Mare[3] is over military age. He is too old to be of much use at the front, & may not be physically fit anyway.

As to the danger. I shall be on the battlefield every day, & shells fall at random all over it, & if it be my Fate, I shall be hit by one of them. But not many people are hit by these random shells, and it will be rather bad luck if one of them gets me. As far as I can see, it will take me 6 weeks to learn the whole battlefield by heart, & after that, I suppose that most of the Records are now in England, as they were for Gallipoli. So it is a very feeble kind of service for one's country, though all I can do, for I am not up to much now.

Did you ever read the Iliad? It is the only book really like war. It is a profound study of the causes & the nature of war, & it leaves one with this sense of Fate, the big thing which is the Cat to our mouse, & decides the big issues, whatever we do.

All greetings, dear Florence,

from
John.

1. Wilfrid Wilson Gibson.
2. Harley Granville-Barker.
3. Walter de la Mare, 1873–1956, English poet, anthologist, novelist and short story writer.

13, Well Walk, N.W.
21 Jan. 1917.

Dear Florence,

I wrote to you a few days ago, to thank you for your letters, but I thank you again in this, lest the other should not reach you. As far as I can see, I shall be starting for France tomorrow. Of course, I will write to you from France, pretty often, but shall not be able to tell you where I am nor where I go, nor with whom I am, nor anything at all. Philosophy & affection must be my sole topics, as they were in America. I shall say, "I am extremely fond of you. What do you think of Berkeley's theory of matter?" and you will have to figure out the rest for yourself.

One thing puzzles me. It is that probably America is growing up with an aesthetic sense quite unlike the European aesthetic sense. Will you please tell me what is the admired type of American beauty? Is it the Mrs. Edward Reed type? I know the type I admire; but you aren't going to catch me making compliments. The English beauty seems to have changed very little in 700 years. The type I admire so here I find in medieval paintings & carved on country churches & in countless portraits of later times, & I see it daily in the London Tube railways. It is a type which is intellectual, that is, of the nature of the person, & owes nothing to flesh & colour & tint, but changes, on the whole, very very little throughout life, & gets from old age quite as much as it loses.

You ask me, do I think there will be another time for us? Why yes, certainly I do, if I do not get knocked out, & this war will come to an end, as perhaps it may this year. If I keep well & the war ends, I shall hope to be in America, actually talking to you, on this day twelve month. And if the war would only end soon, why, you might dash over in the summer, perhaps. Though I see little chance of such luck as that.

Mr Britling[1] is pretty good, I think, but it seems so old fashioned. It must have been finished about May or June, & centuries have passed since then; we are living in a different era; it is like the stone age to me. My dear Florence, an Italian city, in the Ghibelline time, is dull to this place & time. Life was never so interesting, or so passionate & so full of colour to me. If only I could be writing real things, instead of at the war.

All greetings & blessings to you
from
John.

---

1. Refers to First World War novel, *Mr. Britling Sees It Through*, by H. G. Wells, 1866–1946.

Back in France, Masefield journeyed to the Western Front to survey the battlefield carnage and gather first-hand material for his report on the Battle of the Somme.

France.
14 March, 1917.

My dear Florence,

Nearly a year since I saw you, & a fearful time since I had a letter from you; what are you doing, & what (as they say in plays) is "the name of my supplanter?"

Golly, golly; it is a year tomorrow since we held that feast in the Astor,[1] & I sat next to old Talthybins & cast sheep's eyes at you from the dais. O my dear Florence, life is running from us & we aren't meeting or talking or anything. It is the very devil, o dear, o dear.

This may never reach you, my dear Florence, & if I tell you anything about the war it certainly never will.

The war is still going on. I was strafed today, & I haven't had a bath for 17 days, but expect to have one soon. I love my fellow man, & I'm very well, & eat like an alderman.

All greetings to you

from
John

1. On 15 March, 1916, the Poetry Society of America held a big dinner in honour of John Masefield at the Hotel Astor. Several hundred persons were present, including a number of America's most distinguished poets.

Amiens, France.
18. III. 1917.

Dear Florence,

Your letter of the 10th Feb came today. Thank you so much. It was jolly nice to have it. The above address is more likely to find me than the other, though Lord knows; at the present speed of the mails, it may be June before I get an answer. Besides, the war is moving, the ice has broken up, & so much may happen. Pray good & hard for us. The old Iliad idea of war is the right one; it is a matter of the gods, & the nations make their gods, & the gods serve them.

I was saddened by your letter, for I felt that you were weary, & I don't think you know how to rest. You know a whole lot of other things, jolly well; but that one is beyond you; so that when you see an old Spanish mañana kind of a slacker, like me, you think him the real goods:—

Portrait symbolique.

I pass my days wandering on the battlefield, & have seen the last look of the enemy from the Bapaume ridge. He has gone, & his desecration passes elsewhere, & there'll be less iron flying about during our walks, which is something to the good. Pray good & hard for us, for prayer, which is intense thought mixed with feeling, is the only power. That was what Christ meant when he said that faith removes mountains; faith is imagination, it is of the nature of energy, of the sun, of God himself.

It is no good wishing oneself another person. The heart knoweth its own bitterness but never the bitterness of another heart; so cheer up & don't think of being anyone but yourself, the nice valiant attractive lady with whom taxi-cab drivers fall in love at sight, & poets try to put into sonnets, but can't, so go & hang themselves.

You would be interested in seeing this place, now, just after the fighting, & before the grass has grown. It cannot be described, it cannot be imagined, it must be seen. Imagine an infinite land-scape of the moon, made of mud instead of light, & burnt instead of illumined, & know that in all that vast expanse of death, destruction & corruption, there is no life, nor sign of home, nor trace of man's joy or man's quiet, no complete tree, almost no living blade of grass, but an awful tossing of mud & dirty water, littered with the wreck of men & things, & whining & crashing with the passing & the coming of death. Golly it is a sight; & if the Boches sinned, they paid part of the price in blood for it on the Somme battlefield. Golly, Golly, Golly. It is the limit. It was one of the battles of the world.

I must stop, for it is dinner time, which stirs my drowsy blood a

ood deal. After dinner time it will be bed time, & then, very soon,
he jovial time of breakfast.

All greetings to you & blessings on you.

from

John.

Amiens.

April 8. 1917.

Dear Florence,

Hurray; a letter from you, only 22 days in transit (your letter of
the 17th March) & what is more it brings reassuring news about
my rival. This is splendid of the Fates & of my kind friend. But
please do not go on in this New York way of yours. I am anxious
every time I open a letter of yours. It generally begins, "I have had
a fearful month of anxiety & have had no sleep for 3 weeks
together, but tonight I am going to take coffee & strychnine, so
that I may sit up all night reading philosophy, because tomorrow
I am motoring to Pittsburg, Pa. to talk with the Sage of Osh Kosh,
& I expect to talk all night; then early next morning I am riding in
a speed trial at the Harvard stadium, & then go to lunch with the
wise men of Gotham, so I am having my cook make me some more
coffee for them, because they are so subtle on the idea of Time,
that I have to have my brain quite clear," & so you proceed.

I wish I could think of you not "awfully done up" as you say.

Only think, you may get this letter this month.

So now you are an Ally as well as a great friend, & I suppose I
may talk about the war a little.

I believe the Boche are spreading their usual cloud of lies
around their movements, & set great store by their phrase
"strategic retirement". I saw much of the fighting for the
Bapaume Ridge & have been over most of the ground (nearly all
of it) & it is quite plain that he was beaten & booted out of every
position on the ridge. He had a stronghold which he might have
held as the French held Verdun, & we shelled & stormed him out
of it, & he got out of it in a hurry, & tried to stand in two or three
places, & traced new lines & began to dig, & ran up some more
barbed wire, but our guns found him out & killed him, & there he
lies, buried, & partly buried & unburied, with his bombs & his
spades & poor little kit bags, while the rest of him fell back further
& further, leaving a lot of stuff behind, shells by the hundred,

bombs by the thousand, rifles, helmets barbed wire, spades, iron
(to prop the wire) & boxes of cartridges & fuses.

Sometimes, as he fell back, he had time to destroy the towns &
villages, utterly & completely, after he had pillaged them, but
sometimes he had not time to do more than smash & defile
Peronne was a fair little city, a little well-built jewel of a city, with
a little toy cathedral like that church on the *west* side of 5th Ave
about 53rd Street,¹ where you met me once (do you remember?)
& fine old Vauban fortifications & a moat of clear water. These
people blew up the cathedral with a mine, they sacked & stole &
took away every bit of gear worth taking in the town, & then
brought down the rest & smashed it in the street. They fouled
books, they hacked pictures & furniture, they hung the statue of
the heroine of Peronne with indecencies, & then they pulled out
the fronts of half the houses by means of hooks & gun teams. They
hacked through & killed every fruit tree & bush & shrub in & near
the town; & every bed, & floor they smeared with filth, & then
they went away. This I saw, with my own eyes. Just after they had
gone, for I was in Peronne.

I can imagine mental degenerates doing these things, but not
grown men.

All Blessings to you

from
John

1. St Thomas Episcopal Church at Fifth Avenue and 53rd Street, New York City.

[Amiens]
April 16. [1917]

My dear Florence,

So we are now Allies. It must seem strange to Americans to be
allied with us in a war. I hope that it may be a real alliance. We
two can be good friends. I wish that our nations might be. For a
moment my heart leaped, wondering if I could be put to any
liaison work, but I have been put to this now, & there is no chance
of the other, & probably no chance of my coming west again till a
year after the war.

The first part of my time here was pretty cold, with a good deal
of snow, & the billets were dirty & rather lousy, & there was some

danger, from shells & bombs, & I was sometimes in nasty places; but never in anything like such danger as during last autumn, when I was nearly killed in a strafe. In a way, there is danger still; not much of course, but some. A shell or a bomb may get anyone at any time within the area where I spend my days, but only possibly, not probably. If one gets me, I hope nobody will bother. It will be neither bad luck nor sad, but just Fate, whatever that may be, a rather strange & mysterious thing, the meaning of which I cannot fathom.

Anyway, the thing is not worth bothering about.

After the enemy was driven out of the district, I had to leave my billet & move back, & am now in clean quarters for every night, & have my little tub to wash in, & have killed all the many little beasts that pastured on me, "there were forty feeding like one" as Wordsworth puts it,[1] & as I am in the air all day & I am not racking myself silly with brain work, I am in better health than I have known for 23 years.

Harley got torpedoed coming home, but is in England safely.

I am anxious about you & yours in this troublous time. I hope that this war may spare all your circle & not bring too much suffering to your country. The enemy does a lot of dirty devilry, but his blows are mainly upon the weak & the helpless, upon prisoners & women & little children, & on the little nations. He has not done much against men in the four battles of the rivers & at Verdun. Lately, I've been seeing his cruelties to prisoners (who have escaped & come into our lines) & his wrecking of the districts he has been driven from. The prisoners have come in, starved, frostbitten, ragged, verminous & half dying, after months of labour in the gangs, under the whip, & the districts have been wrecked & fouled, as by a dirty criminal & mental degenerate.

Well. Bless you my dear Florence & I hope you & yours may be spared. Forgive a very dull letter. This robustious life makes one write like a hedger & ditcher. I keep wondering, in my cold & formal way, would it be correct to kiss an Ally. It would be nice, & beautiful, & all that, but then, if one began, there would be all these remorses, that one did not begin sooner.

Bless you

John.

You may have a chance of seeing the Somme & Ancre battle films. If so, do go to see them, for you will get from them some idea of the land I live in, & the places I pass my days in & the sights I

see every day, all day long. But I don't know that they will show
you much, really, of this league long desolation, destruction
death & manglement, & blasting of the face of the earth. That ha
really to be seen & trodden & smelt to be believed.

1. From William Wordsworth, 1770–1850, 'The Cock Is Crowing':
> The cattle are grazing,
> Their heads never raising;
> There are forty feeding like one!

> [France]
> May 2nd 1917.

Dear Florence,

I may have to leave this in about another month, & go to work
at the War Office. If that happens, I don't know quite what my
address will be, so if you write, will you address it to me at:
> Sandpits Hilltop,
> Boar's Hill,
> Oxford.

I am both anxious & sad about you, for no letter has come from
you for weeks now, & the worry of not knowing how & where you
are is making me thin. It is one of these d – – –d submarines that is
responsible no doubt, & as Mrs. Gamp says I wish it was in
Jonadge's belly.[1]

> O Florence, your note
> Is down the throat
> Of a codfish cold & clammy.
> The whelk & the shrimp
> Have made it all limp
> O dammy dammy dammy.

You see, living among these troops makes me speak like a
coarse soldier, & no longer like the man you once thought refined
enough to ask to dinner. (You see how my thoughts all run
towards food.)

I still pass my days walking the field. It is communing with the
dead in very truth; for I know hundreds of dead now by sight. I
have seen them in every attitude of agony, & as though sleeping,
& as though praying, & as though resting for a little while, & as
though all tense in one ghastly cry for life; & though I'm hardened
to all the sights & the horrors of war, the sight of all these fine men,

all so much finer & nobler than myself, often tears my heart across. Now that the battle has passed on, they are mostly covered now, but on the places where they fell I always think, "I was just up the hill when this man was killed. Why was not I killed & he left alive? I was in the valley here when this man caught it & I am still here, & the grass is growing on him."

Well. Goodbye dear Florence

from

John.

O for a letter from you soon, soonissimo.

1. Mrs Sairey Gamp, midwife, and a character addicted to drink in Charles Dickens' novel *Martin Chuzzlewit* (1844). She is widely regarded as one of his greatest comic characters.

France.

May 6. 1917.

Dear Florence,

Your letter (dated March 31 & posted April 6) has just come, when I was in the slough of despond about you. The mails get worse, & we are more than a month apart, & I'm afraid it is only too true that the man I sent in with the mails, when I was living near the line, never posted them; so you will not get my March letters. I feared he might not post them, but could not go in myself. Dear Florence, I hope he may be visited, if he never posted them.

I write every week, & latterly 2 or 3 times a week, so as to make it more likely that a letter will reach you. Latterly, I've been 3 weeks with no letter from you, & that is a heart-aching experience. It is very nice to have a great friend, but these wars wrench the affections daily & hourly, so one pays for it; though not as much as the love is worth, anything near.

You are a good friend to have, & may whatever guides this life of ours preserve you through this war & keep your boys from danger & bring them safely to you at the end.

You ask me how I am dressed & what I look like. I'm in my billet, which is a dark and rather dirty little room. It is very hot, & stinks of paraffin, from a filthy leaking lamp which has spilled all over the place. I am in my shirt & riding breeches (not that I ever ride, but it is my uniform) & I've taken off my boots & socks & my collar & my tie, & I'm as near the window as I can get. Some soldiers are singing "Stony Nat Tony" down below, & the battle is roaring in the distance. I've been out today near the recent fighting, in a league long wilderness quite indescribable by pen. There is no ground, only a collection of holes, with no blade of grass, nor tree nor shrub, nor home nor stable nor stye, nothing but desolation & smash & horror, with dead men everywhere, lying singly or in heaps, in the wire, or in shellholes, or headfirst in the mud which has now hardened into potter's biscuit. In one place there were two big bodies gripped together, & lying with their heads in the mud just as they fell when they killed each other. In another place, three hands were sticking out of the parapet of a trench, like the daughters of the horseleech, crying "Give. Give".

While I was there, a Boche aeroplane came over, as bold as brass, & instantly the little white clouds of shrapnel began to form all round him, like little dabs of cotton wool, & I saw the plane go up & up & up till I could no longer see him with my glasses. He must have gone up 3 or 4 miles, & at that height one of our aeroplanes attacked him with a machine gun, & I heard the guns in heaven as the Boche fled back to his lines.

I met Reedy[1] & Masters.[2] I agree with you. But what do you mean when you say you "couldn't bear to meet one of those poets again?" I am one of them, faute de mieux. O Florence, is this the boot?

> ? [Drawing of a boot] ?
> O gentle sea, protect the steamer
> That takes this letter from a dreamer
> And waft her, for the dreamer's sake,
> To one who is most wide awake.

Golly, I've got the lady & the steamer mixed! How can I think clearly when I've just had the first letter for 3 weeks?

May the good God guard you & yours in these sad days.

All blessings on you

from
John.

If this letter doesn't reek of paraffin it will be odd, so keep it clear of your new spring costume with the lovely feather.

---

1. William Marion Reedy, 1862–1920, St Louis editor and critic.
2. Edgar Lee Masters, 1869–1950, American poet and biographer. Author of the *Spoon River Anthology* (1915).

[France]
May 12. [1917]

My dear Florence,

You are a glorious good friend & what have I done to deserve it? You are an excellent lady. Thank you so very much. (This rings a little like the manner of King David.)

I've been out in the wilds again, & just as I was starting, your letter I came, unexpected & unhoped, so I took it out & read it in the wilds, in a scene wild enough & sad enough, & then again afterwards at night in my little cave by candlelight. After reading it I went out into the night, & looked away westwards towards you & wished you a safety from all this malice of war & a protection in the troubles of it. I was in a sort of camp of caves, with sentries & picketed horses, & it was a dark night with rain, & the sky was all one running blink of flashes from the guns, going right up to mid heaven from the big ones, & then very bright on the crest from the field guns, but no noise whatsoever, though the sky was all on fire. This land is like that, & I do not understand it, for we were within range. During the night the wind changed, & the roar brought me out to listen. Sometimes it is like the worst surf you ever heard; but when it is bad it is terrific & cannot be likened to anything. If one is near, when it is bad, it changes the nature in the heart into its impulses.

I hope that you & yours will never hear that noise of hell.

When I got back from the wilds this evening I found your II letter; & this was like manna in the desert or tea on the battlefield or some other special comfort. I had been anxious about you, thinking you & Eleanor were both much more ill than you let me think & I was so glad to think that you were both really better & away now from the tumult of New York in a happy place in the south. I shall send this to Asheville,¹ as perhaps you will be there a month. I hope that happy Asheville will heal the bone.

I may be back in Blighty when this reaches you, for my work here draws to a close, though I shall have to be out again, a good deal, probably, before it is finished. In many ways, one hates the thought of going, now that the operations are on; & lately I've been much with the Australians, with whom I was in Gallipoli, & that has brought back some of the romance of that time; though those old divisions are dead now, my God, & I walk on their dust daily & see the rags of their glorious clothes sticking out of the mud. There will never be such men again, nor such a battle as killed them here.

They went up a smooth glacis a thousand yards long in the face of a hundred machine guns, & then they held a thousand yards of ruin under a month of shell fire, & then they went over the ridge to a bowl or basin of hell in the middle of which was Monguet Farm.

I was there today, & walked over bodies & bones & feet & rags to the farm itself, which has done its worst now. It is a heap of rubble about as big as your sitting room, then a hundred yards of broken brick in holes, with another heap of rubble not quite so big, & some old shot iron banging about, & (fifty yards away) a few heaps of chalky earth as big as hazards in a golf course. There are some stumps of trees, for it had once 2 avenues of apple trees, and every inch in sight is blasted & bedevilled & broken & tossed on high & gouged & burnt & blown into hideous stinking holes, full of corpses, & of rats which eat the corpses, & all deathy & evil, with enemy grenades & rifles lying littered about among their rags & bodies, & a mile of desolation, deserted by every living soul, all round the place.

Down underneath is a narrow passage, 20 feet down perhaps, all full of dead enemy & as dark as pitch, where they fought with machine guns in the dark, so that the walls are all gouged with bullets.

Bless you & yours
John.

1. A town in North Carolina where the Lamonts frequently went for a winter vacation.

[France]
May 14, [1917]

Dear Florence,

This won't be a long letter, because, to tell the truth, I tore my one precious pair today, the only pair I have, on some wire, not even barbed, nor enemy, but simple English concertina-wire, that was lying about on the field, and it isn't a bad tear but very obvious & very jagged, & instead of writing to you I must go & try to mend it, & God knows, my dear Florence, if I'll be able to; for God, who gave me certain knacks & oddities, set also bounds to me, & it is difficult for me to say, straight off, till I look at the thing close, whether this comes within the bounds or not.

There is a chance, that by letting in a bit of collar or handker-chief it won't be noticed.

Yesterday, we saw a soldier who had been out on patrol, unable to get back to our lines for four days. An officer asked him why he didn't come back with the rest of the patrol on the first day. He said, "Too much shellfire, sir, all the first two days". The officer asked why he didn't come back on the third day? He said, "There was too much machine gun fire, sir". The officer said, "I wonder you came back at all, then". The man replied, "It came on to rain, sir".

Now I must go, & may the good Lord so guide my sewing that I won't be noticed.

Bless you & yours

John.

[France]
May 19. [1917]

Dear Florence,

Some lucky devils in the mess had an American mail today; so had I, a fine-looking foolscap envelope full of circulars. Well, however lucky the devils were they didn't have any letters from Florence, as I took care to see, so they aren't so lucky after all, & may go hang. But I, who was not lucky at all, what about me?

What a pity we didn't meet before the war, when one could have an answer to a letter in twelve days. It seems pretty long ago, doesn't it?

You asked me once about war books, & whether any are good (or if you did not ask this, I dreamed that you did) & I can't find any that are really good; though several are interesting. There is a Frenchman, Barbusse,[1] who wrote a book called Feu, or Le Feu, which is pretty good, & a young fellow, an artilleur, since killed, (his name was Lintier), wrote a journal, called Ma Pièce,[2] which is vivid, though a little too like Zola's Débacle, which he had read, no doubt. Your Mr. Hall's Kitchener's Mob[3] is vivid, for the life in the trenches.

But no writing can give any effect of it & no historian know (let alone tell) the truth of it. So much of it all is noise & smell & motion, & shocks to mind & sense, that it cannot go into words. You get some 1/2 sense of it from the cinemas, which were taken at incredible risk in some of the hottest spots on the front. You should go to see our Somme & Ancre films, if, as I think, they are in New York. They give you glimpses of it.

I hope you've all had a glorious holiday in the mountains, & that you & Eleanor are now hurraying on the peaks from what M. Bergson calls the élan vital.

All greetings & good wishes

John.

This is a secondary or submarine note in case the letters miscarry.

1. Henri Barbusse, 1874–1935, French author who wrote *Le Feu* (1917). Translated into English as *Under Fire* by Fitzwater Wray.
2. Paul Lintier, 1893–1916, who wrote *Ma Pièce, Souveniers d'un Canonnier* (1914).
3. James Norman Hall, 1887–1951, whose book *Kitchener's Mob* (1916) described the adventures of an American soldier in the British Army.

[France]
May 21, [1917]

Dear Florence,

Letters 1 & 2 & 4 have come (4 came today) but 3 is still en route. In a way, it is fine to think that there is one still on its road, & that it may turn up at any time, but I'm afraid there is some chance that it has been scuppered. It is these dirty Fritzes in their dirty submarines again.

I've seen a good many hundreds of Fritz prisoners, at one time or another, & I see four types in them, the sheep, the lout, the Jesuit & the homicide; & in all four types a kind of patient dirtiness, which I deny can ever inherit the world where so many golden souls have been lovely.

Yesterday I was away east, at Néstle, Estrées & Roye, where Fritz was thrust back in a hurry, before his dirty devilries were half done, but where you could see his mean & patient plannings laid bare on a large scale. At Roye, there was a very lovely old church with quite lovely old coloured glass in it. Of course, one may say, those things do not matter today, they belong to the middle ages, & in a way they do; but one is glad of one's old church in a town. The people there were married in it & christened their children there & saw their poor mothers buried there,

& had some sort of comfort from the singing & some sort of help from praying there; & people came to look at its beauty, & it was lovely enough, God knows, & beauty only comes by a kind of coming down of God. These dirty devils the Fritzes knew very well that they could not destroy the town, & that in any case we should not billet troops in the church; but they wanted to do some act of dirtiness to the place, so they mined the chancel & blew the roof clean off the walls & the glass out of its leads & left only the shell of the four walls standing. Then, on their way east, they cut down or hacked through every poor little cottage's apple-tree or pear, or plum tree, or little humble currant bush. I went for miles past little gardens & orchards, the possessions of poor men and women quite poor, many of them old, where the trees & bushes were cut in this way, & were lying in the grass, in blossom, but of course ruined.

I don't know what effect it has upon the French, but it made me feel that I would like to get down at the next gang of prisoners & cut all their throats.

There is a church on the battlefield in a very strongly fortified place which Fritz used to say was impregnable. (We took it this year with 5000 Fritzes in it).

Fritz made a latrine for his soldiers in front of the altar, & then in front of the latrine he built a big stone memorial to his own dead, & carved "iron crosses" over the lists of the killed. I have seen this incredible place many times, & it seems to explain Fritz & to give an image of his mind. It is exactly as I say; an altar with a latrine in front of it & a memorial to the kameraden gefallen in front of the latrine. There is not ten feet between the altar & the memorial.

I may be home in ten days from now, for my work here is finished, or very nearly, for the time, though of course I shall be out again a good deal before the end of the war. I don't think that the war will last long enough to bring your lad into any danger. I hope not.

All greetings

from
John.

[France]
May 22. 1917.
I hope to go back to
England about the 30th
of this month; or one week
hence.

Dear Florence,

Your third letter reached me today. Thank you so much for it. I have now safely received all your first four letters.

This third one was a long time on the way, because someone redirected it to three different places, one after the other; such is military zeal.

Perhaps most great changes come suddenly, because they come with great people & great passions; but I am not so sure that any profound change will come to us because of the war. We shall be changed in many ways, & in fact, are already changed & changing, but perhaps not fundamentally nor spiritually. War is not a spiritual thing, and I look, now, not for any spiritual change, but for one or two spiritual reactionaries, whom the world will crucify within the next ten or fifteen years. We shall have our Byron & our Shelley, & I hope to be young enough to recognize them & wise enough to stick up for them. I don't think we shall get more out of the welter than that, except some possibly sanity in this or that state department. Unluckily, it is early days to be prophesying, for the war is not over yet, by many months.

I have been wondering about America. What are you going to do? Are you going to get hold of Mr. Ford[1] & say, Mr. Ford, turn to and make any number of the most powerful possible aeroplane engines; and then mobilize some millions of skilled inventive mechanics to make amazing aeroplanes; & then pick out some 100,000 utterly fearless bold young athletic unmarried men to fly the same?

I always feel that a new country should have a new way of war. I keep dreaming of an American army which has nothing to do with these old vieux jeux of cannon & trenches & barbed wire & bombs, but just sails in the air, a kind of cavalry of the stars, some divisions strong, & doing the work of cavalry. Suppose 50,000 of these machines were to begin the work of cavalry here, scouting on ahead, & bombing hangars dumps & billets, with incendiary & gas bombs, & shooting troops on the move with machine guns. It

would mean, that in a week, no enemy battery would be able to
fire by day, & no enemy would be able to use a road in daylight, &
no enemy gunner would be able to correct his ranges in five cases
out of seven. The enemy would be blinded & harrassed & he
would droop & die. Meanwhile the bold squadrons would bomb
all his railway junctions & railheads & little light transport
railways, & all the waggons & carts that bring him up his stuff.
Then, going further afield, they would bomb his usines & factories
& shell-plants & send them all flying, & the fine chateaux where
his generals get drunk & go to bed in their boots. Then they would
have a field day & make a night of it & drop half a million cwt of
high explosive, in Baralong torpedoes (a kind of drainpipe full of
ammonal) right onto the top of Essen & send the Krupp
Gesellschaft to the devil of hell where it belongs. Then, after that,
they would see the lines of the enemy trenches, from the sea to
Switzerland, presenting the following odd appearance:

[Drawing of horizontal line with heads and raised arms showing
above]

and they would hear a long sigh of Kamerad going all the way
along.

Of course, all this is dreams of the earthly paradise; but it is not
all dreams, because aeroplanes must be the cavalry of the future.
The horse is nearly obsolete in war, even as a beast of burden; the
petrol-engine & the mule have beaten him.

The Fritzes have some very good anti-aircraft guns, but a good
quick fighting plane is hardly ever hit by them. It is the observing
planes, which come low to take photographs, that get hit. You see
the other little devils dodging about like flies, with every a-a gun in
range blazing away at them & never going anywhere near.

I am glad you are having a happy time in Asheville; but don't
talk of giving up New York, that city of orgies, walks & joys. You
would not be happy out of that swirl, & what should I do in
Central Park alone, & think of poor old Sherman.

You will have jolly good fun building & arranging your new
house; & I thank you (from my uncle James & Aunt Susan) for
your kind invitations to them. My aunt Susan (if that was her
name, or perhaps it was her maid's name) died when I was a boy;
& I never heard tell of my uncle James, but it was kind of you to

think of them. All this odd kind of folk that were about one when one was young seem very pathetic & far away & helpless:—

"Certes, ils doivent trouver les vivants bien ingrats."

All good wishes to you

John.

1. Henry Ford, 1863–1947, industrialist and founder in 1903 of the Ford Motor Company.

[France]
26 May. [1917]

Dear Florence,

I have finished the first part of my work & am hoping to go across to Blighty in 2 or 3 days time & shall then be in Blighty for some long while most probably. You will have received my new address probably, for I sent it in about 4 recent letters & the Fritzes can't have sunk them all.

The Fritzes are still very strong, & it would be wrong to expect a peace this year or next. At present there are only two ways of getting past a machine gun, in an aeroplane or in an armoured car, and both things need a small army of specialists, both to build & man. Modern defensive war is a slow business.

It is difficult to see an end to this war, but one knows, that in war as in life, it is the unexpected that happens, and the end that will come to this war may be quite simple, sudden & strange. I don't think that there will be a revolution in Germany till after the peace, say in perhaps five years from now. After that, she may become a very fine & enlightened nation.

You are so unlike anybody I ever met, with so much quick sudden intellect in your look, that people like H.B. & myself have simply no chance at all. It was no good for either of us to struggle, even had we wished to, for with one neat dart you had us both.

I must go. All blessings on you

John.

[France]
31 May. [1917]

My dear Florence,

This is to tell you that I am hoping to start for England tonight, & that if I am not scuppered on the way I may be at home late tomorrow sometime.

My last letter was not of much interest, as it was written in the town of Paris in great heat. I had to go there to see some archives, and in the intervals of archive searching I went to Versailles, & thought, "how excellent it is, to have a despot with a delight in splendour". It is a rare combination, for most despots are commonplace, & delight only in bigness; but in this place the King made a lasting beauty, which, like all real beauty, takes tone from time, & where the mind could wander for ever.

The archives, when found, were strange enough. Imagine living daily for some months in the corpsed & awful wreck of this battlefield, treading on holes in the ground & scraps of brick where the now historic villages stood, & learning (perhaps) only by the colour of brick dust on the earth that you stand within a village. Then imagine suddenly seeing pre-war photographs of these same villages, with the trees still standing & casting shadows, & the houses neat in their gardens, & the little pretty churches telling the time, & the people moving about or keeping still to have their pictures took. It is a strange experience.

There was one place, a chateau in a superb site, which was once evidently a very noble house of the 18th century, with perhaps painted panels on the walls, by famous hands, & a stately formal garden. Only last week I saw this very place in its present state, after the 3 or 4 attacks that have gone over it. The French tried for it, & got it, early in the war; then Fritz tried for it and got it; then we tried for it & got it; & then Fritz tried hard to get it back but couldn't. You couldn't tell that it was ever a house. It is just a formless, pitted kind of barrow of powdered brick, in a collection of enormous pits, some containing water & bits of men, others containing bits of men & broken woodwork. Imagine the owner being demobilisé & coming back to that.

Coming back, we passed a place where Fritz in the early days of the war may have seen the lights of Paris in the sky. He stole some horses there & burnt a few houses, & might have done much worse; only he thought he would have time for all that. Now the dirty ruffian is away past Bapaume.

I've had no letter from you this week, so perhaps, like the forethoughtful friend you are, you have already started writing to Oxford, & there may be one for me if & when I arrive. It is sad to be going, but not so sad as it would have been three months ago when the Boche was breaking back & the incredible muddy tumult of our advance was flooding up on all those roads. That was a thing to have seen, indeed.

Now, all greetings to you. Are you back in New York or still having a jolly time in Carolina?

John.

Reluctantly, Masefield returned to England from the trenches. His reporting project was finished and he looked forward to a summer and fall in his beloved Oxford before undertaking his next wartime assignment.

Oxford. England
June 7. 1917.

Dear Florence,

As you will see from the address, I did not get scuppered, coming across, but reached home safely; a home I had not really been in before, but which is now mine. You may have read a poet, Matthew Arnold, a poet rather in the Keats tradition of English, & one you may perhaps be not very tolerant of, but, in his best things, quite with Keats & Gray. He wrote two very beautiful poems, Thyrsis & the Scholar Gipsy, about the little hills & woodland here, & mentions a solitary elm tree, the Fyfield elm,[1] which is in front of me, as I write, a quarter of a mile away. It is a beautiful country, with hawthorn & deep grass & pink may & chestnut blossoms, very different from the downland, & old bare Lollingdon, where I was when the war broke out, though I can see old Lollingdon by going up another spur of the hill.

It is not a watered country, I suppose not many hills are except the hills of home, & this leads me to your question of what noise of water I like best.

I don't think any noise of water comes up to the heavenly noise hot tea made at tea time in the pannikins, at Anzac, in the summer, two years ago, when we were short of water. We used to sit around & listen to the tinkle, & watch the lovely little bubbles, & nudge each other, & notice how nice & wet it looked.

I like many of the noises of water, though not the great noises, which are often terrible. I like the trickle of little tiny brooks or springs far up in the hills, in glens & quiet places. I like the jolly run & babble of lively brooks which go (not too fast) over pebbles. But the brooks I like best are a very rare kind about a foot broad, & brim full, which run swiftly in grass meadows. One very seldom sees them, but their beauty, as they go by, swaying the grass of the meadow, makes a deep impression on me. I like quite silent water if it is not too vast, & I like fountains, & I like hill springs with a good gush on them, & I like watching the lashers of mills, & nearly all water is beautiful if you come to consider it; though I don't like the water in shell holes. I like the jolly noise of the sea when I dive, & the rush of the rivers in the hills of Ireland, & the noise a burn makes as it runs into the sea, & the noise of the sea on the Irish coast where Miss G K came to see us, tho she didn't add to the romance of it. Then when I'm thirsty I love the sizzle of a siphon, & the sort of rattling in the throat a soda water bottle makes when you first open it, & the happy gurgling glug of water-bottles & the splash of taps.

I am glad to think of you having a happy time in the mountains. I hope you won't go back to hot & feverish New York till the Fall. Who knows, there may be peace in the Fall, in which case we may be seeing each other. To have peace & then to see you; what should I have done to deserve it?

You ask me what is meant by strafing & if it means being wounded. It means "hating", & it doesn't always mean being wounded, but it always means that Fritz makes his level best attempt to wound you. A "strafe" is a bombardment by any kind of gun. He used to strafe my billet regularly with high velocity shells at 10 every night & morning. In a way, h.v. shells are better than the others for they come silently & you don't hear them till they bang, & of course if you are near you don't even hear that.

> Silently invisibly
> They take you with a sigh   (Blake.)[2]

But he has another beastly thing that howls like a cat, meeeeeeooow, & bursts with a Krrump, & this is the thing I hate so. The Krump I can stand, but the meow makes my blood run cold; you see, you may hear twenty in the air at the same time, & they are certainly the devil. Still, I expect ours are harder to bear. We have one which tears the air across as it goes along, just as

though the air were one vast rag, and you hear this kind singing as
it goes; "I'm the devil of hell. Listen to me tearing linen" and it
seems to tear the air right down to you & then to rend you through
the marrow; and when twenty of these are in the air at the same
time it is tremendous. You can see them going, if you stand behind
the gun when it is fired.

Now goodbye. All blessings on you & yours. I do hope little
Eleanor keeps well now.

John.

1. The famous Fyfield elm, which Matthew Arnold mentions in his poems, 'The
Scholar Gipsy' and especially 'Thyrsis', could be seen from the Masefield house
on Boar's Hill, near Oxford.
2. William Blake, 1757–1827, 'Never seek to tell thy love', Rossetti Mss.

Oxford.
June 9. 1917.

Dear Florence,

Your 5th letter reached me safely this afternoon. Thank you for
it, as for all your letters, which are great pleasures to me. One of
the many nice things about you is that you write awfully nice long
letters as though you really liked writing them & knew how much
they would be liked. It is very good to have good friends, & to have
made a friend like you is a great thing. I have lost enough in this
war, God knows, but as Wm says "when I think of you, good
friend, all losses are restored".[1]

You said you didn't agree quite about Fate. Well, I think fate
exists, but I don't think he shapes our ends, I think he rough hews
them; and I think in the main he is the big god & all other gods
knuckle down to him, though he is big & blind & underlying all
things more like a presence than a god. I think nations have gods,
which fight, just as they do in the Iliad, but Fate is stronger than
they are & darker. These things are hard to write of, because they
are matters of instinct & poetry & no more to be reasoned of than
joy in colour or sense of the beauty & mystery in things. So if you
draw the neat clean cutlery of your mind upon me I shall only say,
Well, go ahead; in your deepest moments you will agree with me.
The fashion of the brain passes but the passion of the spirit is
eternal.

Bless you, my good lady

John.

1. William Shakespeare: Sonnet XXX.

[Oxford]
June 11. 1917.

Dear Florence,

I wrote you a hasty scrap three days ago, but could not then reply to your questions about Dostoievsky.[1] The spelling is probably near enough, but it will save time to refer to him as D.

I do not know his books very well, but I know four, which are said to be his best.

There can be no doubt that he was a very great writer of the modern school, in fact, one of the very greatest.

He had a great, profound, simple mind, the artist's mind, which sees & feels rather than thinks. He had a great, profound & beautiful spirit.

At the age of 20 or 25 or 30 (I do not know the dates of his life) the damned Russian autocracy took hold of him & broke his mind & nature clean across by the foulest & most revolting spiritual cruelty. They warped the machine, & left one of the subtlest & most Christian brains of all time disordered so as to respond to agony rather than to joy & to look on life as a mental torture & nightmare. They could not make him a small man. He remained great, but instead of being what nature meant him to be, great in creative delight, like Chaucer, Cervantes & Shakespeare, he was great as a nerve specialist, with a wide knowledge of the damned.

I hold no brief for the modern school. They have all got a fever or an axe to grind, & I can't read much of them, but I think D had a power & a sympathy beyond the rest of them, and seeing what he was & what they made him suffer, I think his achievement tremendous & his vision of life a big one. I think he saw life as a welter of the most hideous devilries of poverty & wilful evil, with something simple & Christian trying to struggle through it & out of it.

All the same, the books are records of torture, and they will be read more by revolutionaries & by brains interested in questions of nerves & in quest of the savager truths of life than by the children & simple people for whom the eternal works are made. Future times will not read the books, but will say "This is what nineteenth century European autocracy did to its great mind".

This is hurriedly written, & I haven't got him rightly for you, but this is something of him. It is difficult to put him exactly into few words.

I know enough of writing to know that none but a very great power could have planned & carried through, at such a breathless

pitch, such things as Crime & Punishment & the Brother
Karamazov. It is all on a big scale, & every item is alive
screamingly alive, epileptically & insanely & awfully alive, they
are all shrieking & drunk & parricidal, & on the brink of madness
& on the verge of discovery. That is great power, my dear
Florence, & only the masters have such power, but only the insane
use it in such a way. There is a joy & a calm & the peace & the
terror of beauty in the masters. They give you a world as full & as
alive, but they do not leave you wanting to kill half the world & to
patronize the other half. They are like the sun & shine upon the
just & on the unjust, which is a jolly good job for most of us.

So, in a few words, D was a great man with broken nerves, &
broken nerves are very terrible, & when a great man has them the
result is terrible & tragic beyond all thinking.

Bless you
John.

1. Fyodor Dostoievsky, 1821–81, Russian novelist, author of *Crime and Punishment* (1866) and *The Brothers Karamazov* (1880).

Oxford.
July 2nd. 1917.

Dear Florence,

Your 10 letter has just come, telling me that you are still limp
from your operation. It is very hard not to know what operation.
The way these letters come reminds me of a reversed movey film,
first you see the corpse, then the dagger-thrust, then the quarrel,
then the pert hussey who made the quarrel, then the two friends
walking together before the pert hussey came into their lives.
Gradually I suppose I shall work back to your operation. I have
heard now of your recovery, then of your convalescence. My next
letter will say that you are at death's door & still too weak to write,
& after that I shall hear that the operation is to take place, & after
that of the symptoms which led to it.

You ought not to bother about the Jesus of History. There is no
Jesus of History. The only history of Jesus is Mark, & what a
wretched skimpy ill told tale it is & how next to impossible to
make out anything from it, & how simple a soul he was who wrote
it, & how little he could have known Christ. The law court part is
fairly full, but it always makes me feel that Mark only knew Christ

right at the end of his career. Matthew may have known Mark &
had some other material as well, & hated the Jews & gave them
some nasty jabs by the way. Luke was an educated man who
wanted to make the story palatable to the Romans. I don't think
he knew Christ at all, nor Matthew either for that matter. But
these are the only authorities we have for the Jesus of History. We
know more about Jack Sheppard & Dick Turpin.[1]

The Jesus of Faith is not much more real today. I have seen no
modern representation of him which did not make him an
anaemic imbecile. I saw the big Italian movey of him.[2] It made
him about as live as an elderly sheep that has been eating ivy. I
have more sympathy with a good old fire & brimstone Satan any
day. But when we come to the Jesus of the Imagination, then we
come to a tremendous figure; & by thought & brooding over the
poor skimpy ill-told gospels this figure, comes up & is heroic, &
you see a swift keen Jew, with the clearest & quickest kind of
mind, great courage, great wit, & a kind of extraordinary rightness of conduct such as only comes from a clear & swift & big
imagination. With this figure in one's heart, the greasy, servile,
white lamb & tortured gentleman idea of him becomes most
loathsome & awful. Jesus in his wit & in his anger would have
shrivelled up such a creature with one glance. So burn your new
book, my good lady, or better still sell it & buy some nice little
blasphemy by Voltaire or Anatole France with the large sums you
will surely receive in its stead.

Do you know: There is a faint chance that I may come to
America this coming winter.

But my ink is even out of my pen & my pen is – Look at the
beastly thing it has just given me the lie by squirting this blob out
– There is, as I say, a chance, but do not think nor speak of it. If it
should come off – well, – if not, if we do not think of it we shall not
be disappointed.

I do hope that you are really well again & not too much
harrassed by the war & the hot weather.

All greetings to you & the best of wishes

John.

---

1. Jack Sheppard, 1702–24, and Dick Turpin, 1706–39, were famous, or
infamous, highwaymen.
2. 'Christus', a film dealing with the life of Christ, based on a poem by Frank
Salvatori, an Italian author. Shown in New York City in May, 1917.

[Oxford]
July 4. 1917.

Dear Florence,

Today I had your 9th & 12th letters. 7 & 8 are still missing. God knows what has become of them. They may be puzzling some hungry haddock in the wine dark ocean stream, or the Censor may have stopped them, or the post office may have lost them, or some thief, either eager for booty (in which case he was sold) or anxious to improve his literary style, may have bagged them. On the other hand, they may still turn up, & I hope still to see them. Anyhow, 9 & 12 are here; please God the Censor won't take this for code; & it is a jolly good thing that your operation is safely over, & that now I hear something about it. I hope it has left no sort of ill effect & that it was what the surgeons call a complete success. It will be a famous thing for you to have to rest for a time & be out of the whirl of the war.

The recent fighting was the most terrific thing. The Fritzes were a little on the alert the night of the attack & kept up a heavy & continuous fire of gas-shells, which don't bang, but make a mean kind of a patty-ping. The attack was to be at 3:20 a.m. & the troops had to be ready an hour before, so for that hour we were all on pins & needles lest the Fritzes should see something & shell our front lines all to pieces. Our hearts were in our mouths every time a flare went up, but they were only cautionary flares, & the fire didn't come, though it was expected. Towards three o'clock they turned on their machine guns for all they were worth, & our hearts sank, for we knew that that could only mean that they saw something; but it died down; & the flares went up from time to time & the gas shells came patting & pinging; but nothing to count. Then, at the appointed time there came a roar like a damned volcano breaking in half & the first of the mines went up like a sort of big bubble of dry blood as big as St. Peters at Rome. There was a sort of gasp of "Golly" all down the line, & then there came another mine, & another, & another, & another, & all our guns came down on the instant & about a thousand machine guns with them, & the whole landscape disappeared into a night of smoke & dust & one saw nothing but this darkness for two solid hours, and all in a racket that struck one sick and dizzy. Then after two hours the darkness lifted a little & one could see our men picking up souvenirs on what was left of Fritz's position.

You ask me to tell you of some French books. You would like the stories of Guy de Maupassant (not the novels, which are mainly ɔunk) but the short stories, gay, grisly & terrible. Read them all, & if any are too terrible, turn to the next, & so go through them all. He is one of the best short story writers.

I am very fond of Prosper Merimée's[1] Carmen, & some of his other tales.

I admire the writer Fromentin,[2] who wrote Un été dans le Sahara, & the novel Domenique.

I admire Stendhal (Henri Beyle) who wrote La Chartreuse de Parme and Rouge et Noir. The Chartreuse is splendid. Did you never try any of Balzac's Novels? You might like a lot of those. Flaubert was a fine writer. Do you know his Trois Contes? Then there are some topping Memoirs. Old de Ségur,[3] who was at the Court of Empress Catherine of Russia (that very brazen hussy) wrote a fine old book, & his son,[4] who was on Napoleon's staff, wrote an even better one. There are 10 vols to begin with. Then, there is Marbot,[5] & good old Dumas, with all the Musketeers, & then Tartarin of Tarascon.[6] Golly, you have enough before you.

All blessings on you. I do hope you're well again
John.

Old Racine was a jolly fine writer, for all your talk.

1. Prosper Mérimée, 1803–70, French author.
2. Eugène Fromentin, 1820–76, French painter and critic.
3. Count Louis Philippe de Ségur, 1753–1830, French general and diplomat. Ambassador to Russia.
4. Count Philippe Paul de Ségur, 1780–1873, son of Count Louis Philippe, was a French general who wrote a book about Napoleon's disastrous campaign in Russia in 1812.
5. Antoine A. M. de Marbot, 1782–1864, French soldier and author of *Memories of His Life and Campaigns* (Paris, 1891).
6. *Tartarin de Tarascon* (1872), by Alphonse Daudet, 1840–97.

[Oxford]
Aug. 1. 1917.

Dear friend Florence,

You ask me a very difficult thing in your letter of July 16. I want to stick up for my own land & to be just to France, & to be both is difficult.

First, as I know America fairly well, I may say, that the American mind is naturally more drawn to the French mind than to the English. You are more drawn to the French.

Secondly, the French can explain themselves much more fluently, readily & clearly than we can. They are easier to know.

Thirdly, in thinking of the French, you have not to overcome a century & a half of hostility & misunderstanding.

Fourthly, the word spiritual, as used at present, may mean anything, from excitement to charlatanry, & from inner life to inner death.

I don't know what the word means. I know a spiritual person when I meet one. I have met two, in my life, and have seen the photograph of a third. One of the two whom I have met was a French nun, the other was the warden of an English college. So far the honours are even. The photograph of the third was of another nun; she died in a French convent; but was not certainly French; she may have been Scotch. I think they said she was Scotch, tho' her name, "in religion", was French. Thinking over these people, I know that they lived on & by whatsoever things are pure & lovely & of good report, "love, mercy, pity, peace," truth, cleanness, braveness, all noble things, I've met lovely people & have more beautiful friends than I ever deserved, but I knew at once, that those two people were apart, that they were "spiritual", & the others weren't, or not nearly so much.

I am not spiritual myself, nor nearly so good as any of my dear friends & I love the muddy soul & am sorry for the sad one & am glad of the merry one. C'est mon métier à moi.

Now it seems to me, that the really "spiritual" is the really beautiful, the really noble, clean, brave & merciful, the really excellent.

Excellent is supreme but very rare.

The question therefore comes down to this, is excellence more common among the French than among the English, & do the French seek for it more than the English?

I don't think so, Florence. I think that excellence is rare, the rarest of all things, & that men & women in civilized countries have their national aptitudes & clevernesses, but are otherwise very much alike, worse than their thoughts, better than their acts, but not worse or better than each other, only cleverer in certain things & duller at other things. The rare souls of all nations are admittedly rare & excellent, & the spiritual of a nation comes to a nation only once. There is only one "spirit" to a nation: to Spain, Teresa, to France, Jeanne, to us, Shakespeare, to you, Lincoln

Then as to behaviour in this war, all the nations involved have been heroical & noble & wonderful. Whatever can be said of the French, must be said also of the Belgians & of the Serbs, the Russians, the Roumanians, &, God knows, the enemy, too. Whoever has faced modern fire in the mud, in the early dawn, after nights & days of defeat, has been spiritual; so I say, in the English soldier's song, "we'll all go the same way home" & God won't be hard on any.

God bless you my dear friend.

[John]

[Oxford]
Oct 28. [1917]

My dear Florence,

I've just had your letter of 25 Sept, about the poor lad who had the flying accident. One does not know what to say about these things, for one does not know the purpose of life. But life can be very full, even on a sick bed, if the mind is generous enough & the pain not too inhuman. Kindness & courage are, roughly, the big things in life, perhaps; feeling for the world & facing it; & one knows so many who have been bigger in suffering than one had thought possible; & yet God knows it is not what one wants, or feels to be fitting, to have the young maimed, & to lie in bed all the time. All that one can say is, that to the giving mind much is given, & that there are compensations in all things, & for all things.

There is a sailor here who has been torpedoed in 6 different ships, & is now working on the land; but he wants to go back to sea, because of the compensations; easier work & more tobacco. I think that it is false to say that God tempers the wind to the shorn lamb; but true to say that the lamb gets something from being shorn; a better chance of pneumonia, certainly, but a greater freedom of motion, & a sense, perhaps, that now indeed he faces the world.

It is pelting with rain, & the poor bloody infantry are lying out in the mud, & I am trying to get my speech "square with the lifts & braces", & it is a hard job. I want to get something said about the future, & working together, & the rest of it, & every time I get going, the memory of the past, 1776–1783, & 1812–1814, & all these other damned & evil spectres, rise up & take me by the throat & mock my endeavor.

Poor Robert Fitzsimmons[1] is dead. Do you remember that terrific St. Patrick's day, 1897, when the wires flashed the news, "Fitzsimmons, in the 14th"? Where were you then? Were you at Englewood?[2] I was at Yonkers,[3] in the mill, but what was the mill on such a day?

I can't write, for thinking of the poor bloody infantry lying out in the mud & not being there myself.

Bless you dear Florence

John.

1. Robert Fitzsimmons, 1863–1918, British boxer who won the world's heavyweight championship over James J. Corbett in 1897 in Nevada.
2. The Lamonts lived in Englewood, New Jersey, from the time of their marriage in 1895 until 1929.
3. Starting in the fall of 1895 at the age of 17, Masefield worked in a carpet factory in Yonkers, New York, for almost two years. In 1941 he wrote a book about it, *In The Mill.*

Masefield returned to the United States early in 1918 for a ten weeks' tour to promote America's war effort in the Allied cause.

In St. Louis, Mo.
25 Feb, 1918.

Dear Florence,

I shall be leaving this place this evening by the 11 train to Kansas City. Tomorrow I hope to start from Kansas for Denton, Texas, in the beginning of my journey to the West. I hope to be in Los Angeles about the 8th or 9th March, & to be there for 5 days or so, at the Hotel Alexandria. After that, I dodge about, to & from that hotel, for some days, till the 18th. On the 20th, I am to be at Palace Hotel, San Francisco.

I am to be back in New York on the 14th April, if not a casualty by that time. That is, this Monday 7 weeks. If you will keep that week fairly clear, of evening engagements anyhow; we might meet & talk, if you would.

Some of the travelling has been trying, but only when the trains are many hours late, & give me anxiety, lest I miss my engagements. It seems an interminable time since I left New York. Time drags along on leaden wings, O haste, dull-footed time, this drowsy way of doing things, it is not worth a dime, three weary weeks like weary years and seven more to come would drive a female saint to tears & a manly saint to rum.

O heaven, I never thanked you, but I do now most warmly for your great kindness in sending the dixonaries. Thank you ever so much. The red one is very good indeed. It was most kind of you to get them for me.

All greetings to you & to your household
John.

Austin [Texas]
5 March, [1918]

Dear Florence,

So many thanks for your nice letter.

It is curiously like Italy down here, & the light & the landscape are exactly like those of Pisa, so that often I look up to see the Campo Santo & the tower, which might be up the street, from the feel of things.

All things come from the sun, & I am sure that in a few years there will come a fire for beauty here, & the light & the air will drive a beauty through the life of this land such as Italy never saw in the Renaissance.

It is pretty hot here already, after icy Chicago & bleak Missouri, but the sun is good to have:—

> "He is the lord of us
> He will unconquered sink
> Red but victorious
> And smoking to the brink."

Violets were in blossom in Georgetown, & here the peach-blossom is out, & the pear blossom, & a white-blossomed plum, like our wild plum.

They haven't shot at my feet yet, to make me dance, as I expected they would, nor tried for my poor scalp yet.

I am trying to fix a lecture for Aeolian Hall,[1] on April 23rd, & think of speaking *solely* of England's share in this war. Do you think that this would be wise, as well as acceptable? You see, it is St. George's Day, which gives an excuse; but I don't want to do an unwise thing. Will you consider this?

It is very good of you to write to me & to bother for me in the

way you do. Thank God, I may be east again in less than 6 weeks.
Joy, joy.

All greetings to you & to your household

John.

Note.

About those throat lozenges of mine. I am now used to them, &
think them splendid, I eat them all the time, & am a lozenge-
fiend.

Please greet the Morrows² from me, if they have not sailed yet.

1. Aeolian Hall on West 57th Street, New York City, was frequently used for
recitals and readings. It is no longer in existence.
2. Dwight W. Morrow, 1873–1931, partner in J. P. Morgan & Co. and later
United States Ambassador to Mexico, and his wife.

In the train, going n.
[Portland]
27 March, 1918

Dear Florence,

I am suffering from train sickness, but in the intervals I mean to
write to you. Train-s is very like sea-s, only worse, for I didn't
expect it.

I want your advice very much on this matter of my talk, & of
propaganda generally.

At present, I plan to sail about May 4th, & speak for a few
weeks about America, in English cities, before going to France.
But I am not sure that I could not do this better after making
another journey here on different lines.

Do you think it would be acceptable if I were to go to the camps
here, in the east & middlewest, to speak on England's achievement in the war, free, to the men, & everyone who cared to come?
I daresay they would wish me at the devil, me & my England, tho
I would try to make it a pleasant talk.

I am much torn about it; for I long to be back in France; in the
trenches if they will take me; for I don't feel that I have done any
good here, talking to special audiences, instead of to colleges & all
comers, free of charge, & if I'm to be wasted I'd like to be wasted

...roperly, & yet this other thing might do good. It is hard for me to ...ell.

Perhaps it would be well to go back to England as planned, on ...ay 4th. It doesn't seem right for me to be out here, doing ...othing but speak.

But if you (& perhaps you would ask your husband to give me ...is advice, too.) think I could do good to this cause of ...nglo–American friendship by talking on as I suggest, then I ...hink my people would let me go, & I would try to arrange it ...erhaps.

San Francisco upset me, & I'm tired & trainsick.

This may not reach you till New York. All blessings on you ...herever it may find you.

                                    John.

I send this from Portland. I'm sick & giddy from the train, & ...eel as though I must cut my engagements & go back to Neville[1] at ...ny cost.

---

[1]. Neville Lytton (3rd Earl of Lytton), 1879–1951, English artist. A Major in ...he British Army when J. M. first met him in France in 1917.

                              Seattle, Washington.
                              April 2. [1918]
Dear Florence,

Thank you for your letter. It is a great pleasure to have a letter from you. In this scattered worrying life of mine, it is a great pleasure to find, on coming to a place, that some fixed affection has taken thought for me beforehand, & seen to it, that a message greets me on arrival. I cannot tell you what a difference all your kindness has made to this trip of mine, nor how deeply I have been touched by your so gentle thought & care.

As to the war, one must live it through with courage. They are standing up to it in France. We here must build up behind them such a wall of love & courage as they can lean on & get strength from.

I would to God I were out with Neville again. I am not sure that I ought to stay here even to finish my tour, except that I am under orders. Twelve more days. It seems like twelve dreary eternities.

And then, I suppose, if the train's not late, you will come along th
avenue to Voisin's corner, and Golly, my dear Florence, neve
mind the new hat, but just be there yourself.

    All greetings & blessings

                John.

    Gilberto[1] won't find it so easy to supplant me. I have a penknife
(& some very poisonous throat lozenges.)

1. Nickname for Gilbert Murray.

                          Petersburg, Va.

                          May 23. 1918.

Dear Florence,

    I still wonder, if it would have been a melon. There are so many
lovely fruits to begin a day with. Did you ever have an English
melon, with white castings on the outer rind, or English white
muscatelles, as big as greengages? Or did you ever have English
white & red currants, mixed in a bowl with red & white raspber-
ries & cool pale blobs of Devonshire cream? Or did you ever eat
great sweet English whiteheart cherries picked that morning, with
the blackbird's peck still on them? Or did you eat mulberries ever
off an English Dean's tree, in a cathedral close? Or did some
Warden or Provost of an Oxford College ever give you strawberries with a silver ladle out of a Worcester Bowl when the June bells
were chiming five?

    Or did you ever crush a mango into a cup of snow & put out
your tongue & lick the same?

    All these things would have become your tongue as well as a
melon. So think it over.

    I hope you are well & happy & having a good time, & a rest, at
Englewood. It was splendid to speak with you last night.

    Good night, & bless you

                    from John.

In Newport News, Va. (Till
26th)
24 May [1918]

Dear Florence,

> I've had your lovely letter here
> Hurray hurray hurray
> You make an April trebly dear
> And give a spice to May
> You give a beauty to July
> A loveliness to June
> A dew to Augusts that are dry
> And light the harvest moon
>
> And nothing half so nice as you,
> Nor so pleasant to remember,
> Was ever seen in Sept or Oct
> or November or December.

But this is the kind of poem I send in the camps. I write much nicer ones for real friends, as you know.

What I wanted to say, when I began, was this.

I may be in N.Y. on the 15th June, or 2 or 3 days earlier than I thought. Will you be in the neighbourhood then, or shall I, as Shakespeare says,

"Shall I on, & not depend on you?"

If you are not to be there, I might go into the country for 2 days perhaps. But it is for you to order the 2 days as you prefer, as you know.

Bless you, my kind & thoughtful friend

John.

I think I can really hold & thrill the men now. I had a succès fou yesterday. I love these men, & I think I can do good now. I love speaking to them.

Atlanta, Ga.
3rd June. 1918.

Dear Florence,

In that matter of the fruit:—

Figs are all very well, & so are melons, but both can be had, far better, in England, than in any part of Italy, so I think you are wise to plump for England. Of course, with enough slaves, one could have these English things in sight of the sea & the snowy mountains, & that might be better than all.

The mango you have to undress to eat. You eat mangoes in your bath. They are too juicy for clothes & the dry land.

The mulberry grows on a big tree, & is like a blackberry to look at, but is as big as a strawberry. Poets, like W.S., plant mulberries in their gardens.¹ Deans & Wardens of Colleges have mulberries in their Closes. Mulberries taste like poetry & college closes mixed, a sort of flavour of loveliness & the beauty of learning blended.

Some wise men plump for the English wild strawberry, which is a little red thing, as red as the love of God & as subtle in his taste as the holy wit.

"But, better a dish of herbs, where love is, (I think it is the Bible says this) than a melon & a fig & wrangling therewith";² so we will not quarrel on the matter.

Blessings on you.

I hope the ankle & head are cured.

John.

1. Shakespeare is reported to have planted a mulberry tree in the garden of his final home, New Place, Stratford-on-Avon.
2. *Proverbs* XV 17.

San Antonio, Texas.
30 June 1918.

Dear Florence,

Thank you very much for your most charming long letter. I'm so glad that you like the house & coast. I hope you'll have a lovely long rest, & that the earache won't recur. I used to be scared at the thought that an earwig would get down my ear someday & eat my brain (this in the early days of course when I still thought I had a brain) & whenever I had an earache, I used to think, Now it has happened. This is how he begins.

About a negotiated peace: we all felt, that a year ago, before Russia collapsed, & while France was panicky, as I know, from being there, that she was, a peace might have been negotiated on tolerable terms. But that time passed, & Russia collapsed, & some damned short-sighted leaders let her collapse, & the Boche, who were in a tight corner, & not liking the war, suddenly found half their enemies gone, & the prospect of *unlimited* booty right in front of them. At once, they stiffened, all prospect of peace vanished, & by autumn 1917 we knew that no tolerable terms could be had.

At the same time, we generally felt, at the end of 1917, that this war is such a burden (you cannot understand just what a burden it is) on the belligerent peoples, that Russia would not be the only nation to break under it, & that by the end of this year other nations would have broken rather than bear the burden longer. This is a possibility in all the belligerent countries still, but of course the Boche's cynical devilry (with regard to Russia & the Russian peace) has roused up a dying anger, & this fury against her is now exceedingly bitter, & stiffens the nations against her.

Of course, the Boche don't mind being hated; they probably quote Christ, & say "marvel not if the world hate you, for ye are the salt of the earth".[1]

They know that they have had a big success in the west, & that this success has probably caused much bitterness among the Allies, a bitterness of fault-finding & blaming, each for the short-comings of the other, & that if they can repeat the success, they may make this supposed bitterness too acute. They probably disregard America still, & they certainly still trust the U-boat.

In any case, they have the booty of Russia, a prize so great that they can almost neglect the other issues at stake; a prize so important that probably its possibilities are only just beginning to unfold themselves. They have, there, slaves & lands more than they had ever dreamed of as possible, even to the Boche.

That prize is so important, that perhaps they may *even now* be preparing to offer tolerable peace terms so that they may go home & have that prize.

They will try a furious & awful drive in the West, which I hope I may see, & then, if that should fail, they will know that they can never win, & then they will offer tolerable terms, or even generous terms, to France, so that they may nobble Russia at their leisure.

Probably they feel, just now, that in any case they can nobble
Russia, & that a very little more will let them nobble France, too.
    Best greetings to you
                              John.

1. I John III 13.

                              Los Angeles. Cal.
                              July 5. [1918]
Dear Florence,
    I arrived here late last night, & find I have 2 big speeches today
1 big one tomorrow, & then go away to S. California where they
are going to put me through the mill in form.
    I hope you are well & happy & having lovely times by the sea. I
write Chaucerian poems about you most of the time, thus:—

    This wysë fresshë Florence as I say
    Down by the saltë sea is gon to play
    Ther as the grenë grassë is al broun.
    Ther is no nay hir liketh nat the toun,
    For tounës ben so hot and so unclene
    Her liketh nat the tounë worth a bene
    She likth the sea with brightë fissche therein.
    Ful many a herring with a bentë pin
    She hath i-nome for soper I dare wel say.
    She is as brighte & fresshë as the may
    This Florence lady bright of whom I tell.
    Of all Black Point[1] she berth away the bel
    For beauteë & for high discrecioun,
    And for her gost, as in discussioun.
    Her wit is lyke the newë sharpë pyn
    It is so sharp ther is no dul therein.
    But "sale that savours al" as Senek saith.
                    Blessings on you
                              John.

1. A small summer colony with a bathing beach on Long Island Sound and near
New London, Conn. The Lamonts spent several summers there.

[Los Angeles]
July 7. [1918]

)ear Florence,

Thank you ever so much for your nice letters about the
Volsunga.[1] I'm so glad that that was a success.

Brynhild is the big thing in the saga, but you see, that there are
many versions of the tale, & that in some, Brynhild has a child by
Sigurd. Your version hints at this, & even mentions the child. The
invention of idea of Brynhild is superb; but as a lyrical poem, the
ay of Gudrun is in the same class.

There is something about the awakening of Sigurd to manhood,
after he has killed Fafnir & awakened Brynhild, which makes
everything else seem so small & feeble.

How anyone can consider Wagner a great poet after seeing
what he did to this tale.

To go on with Chaucer:

This lady Florence whereof I yow telle
She dwellth adoun besyd the wavës grene
Of al the ladies ther she berth the belle
Even as the may is of al floures quene.
She rakketh of the poets nat a bene
They ben but sory dokës that go quakke.
As nedë most, she giveth hem the sakke.
For certes, poets ben nat worth a flye,
They ben so sory, with ther lenë throtes.
O wysë Florence, thou hast the maistry,
Scorning these men that pipen in thin oats.
Let put thise poets into oldë boats
And let hem sayl the see, as Cato saith.
These brightë ladies get of hem gret scaith.

I go on today to San Diego, which is beside Camp Kearny, &
there I start north again.

I've seen Marion & her mother & her sister.

Best greetings.
John.

---

1. *Volsunga Saga* relating the legend of Sigurd and the Nibelungs. The Germanic
version is the *Nibelungenlied*.

San Diego.
July 12. [1918]

Dear Florence,

You ought to have heard me last night. You may have seen the Exposition Buildings here, of 1915. They are quite lovely things in the Spanish style, & all beautifully laid out among ilex, acacia, orange & myrtle trees, and there is a patio where all the doves of heaven sidle and coo. I spoke in the patio, from the steps of a palace, & had the sunset & the sea in front, & the patio (with the doves) all full of navy men, & gradually the light faded, & I had simply the patio & the audience, & my voice never sounded so attractive to me in all my days. If you had been there, you would have been bowled clean over, & the Navy men would have said "Poor thing, I don't wonder its been too much for her. He oughtn't to be allowed to do it. People aren't strong enough to stand such strains." Then they would have given you a tot of Navy Rum in their rough way & promised you a parrot their next voyage.

The only improvement in the setting of the speech would have been a moon after the sunset, & then the sight of a good friend & heeler like Florence laughing at all my feeblest jokes. Then afterwards we would have eaten a grapefruit together & read some jolly poems.

How are the sagas shaping? Do you still think of the Volsunge? There is a quite lovely tale in the 3 N Love tales. I think its called Frithiof the Bold. It is most beautiful.

Now blessings surround you & mind you catch a lot of fissche for your soper.

John.

Plaza Hotel. S.F.
July 15. [1918]

Dear Florence,

The people here want me to cut my northern tour, & to stay on till Saturday, the 20th, in S.F. so as to reach the Navy men round the harbour & the other bodies of men near the city. There are many thousands of people here of course & if I stay I should save the long & sickly journey north, & reach at least 3000 more men than I should by going.

They are going to let me know as soon as they can (so they say).

I went out yesterday to Palo Alto, to dine with Geneva Feliger & her sister, & then I spoke at the Camp, & so back by moonlight in a cold divinely lovely night, talking with an old gold-miner, who was a fine old scout. Tonight I shall be doing the same thing, dining with G F & sister, talking at the Camp, & then back with the gold miner.

You never rode with a gold miner, & so you don't know what a life he leads. He scoops up a pan of water from a gulch & puts it on the fire to boil, so as to make him some shaving water, then he notices some little glittering grains in the boiling water, & his heart stands still, & then he runs to the gulch & sees a yellow streak in the water, just as they did in you at Black Point, & then he foams at the mouth & shouts out Eureka Eureka. Then he stops being a miner, & stops calling a gulch a gulch, & draws his shaving water from a tap, & works for the Y.M.C.A.

Best greetings to you & all sorts of bright thoughts & wishes.
from John.

Dear Florence,
It is too maddening. I've got to fly off, right now, to some devilish navy yard, 3 hours in a seasick steamer, & after being heartily sick, I'll have to speak 3 times, & then be sick coming home.

Still, who would not be sick for England?
Bless you.
John.

July 18, 1918   O captain stop this misery.

[San Francisco, Calif.]
20 July. [1918]
Dear Florence,
I finish my speaking to the men tonight, & then shall have only 2 or 3 unofficial talks to give, possibly 1 in Detroit, & certainly 1 in Rochester, & perhaps one in Connecticut, & then thank God, my play will be done, & my cushy job brought to an end. I do hope that they will think I have done a little good. I don't suppose they will.

I've various schemes to suggest to them, but they aren't likely to be approved, so I hope they'll just ship me off to Neville as soon as may be & leave me there for the duration.

> Joy, joy, joy, to be going back to the front
> To lie inside a hole & try to see a stunt
> With a gasmask on your face & a helmet on your head
> Above you, stinks of shells, beneath you, stinks of dead,
> Around you howls & bangs & little flitting rats
> And clods & flying shards to hit you heavy bats,
> And roars & dust & glimmers & curses loud & deep,
> And little tickling things which keep you from your sleep.
> Well, bless you, dear friend, & thank you for so much.
> > John.

His second American tour done, Masefield returned to England, still hoping for another visit to the Western Front. But events overtook him.

> Boar's Hill, Oxford.
> Aug 31. 1918.

Dear Florence,

I hope in a few days to give a letter of introduction to you to Mr. Robert Nichols,[1] the young poet of whom I told you, whose *Ardours & Endurances* I probably gave you.

He is going to speak in America, & I am anxious about him, as he is a young man of real talent – W.W.G.[2] is simply a goose beside him – & he has been badly shell-shocked, & may break down under the strain of speaking & the excitement of your climate.

So I am taking the liberty you have so often let me take, of asking you to keep an eye on this young friend, so that if he goes Kapoot you may see that he isn't killed, either by kindness or neglect. Will you do this? You are so kind that I am always taking advantage of it, but in this case there will be some sort of return, for he is a very nice lad, very like my young friend Peter Warren, & a real genius. He is much cleverer than myself, & I am sure you will like him for that, & it will be most helpful to me to think that you will have a sort of eye over him. He really wants a rest-cure, so they send him to New York, & I send him to you. Well, I couldn't send him to anyone kinder, nicer or more thoughtful in all America.

Thys litel poet, with his wysë gost
To you & to your philosophical mind
I do entruste, because you are the most
Thoughtful of allë & the mostë kind
And of your godenesse he wol nat be blynde
But heretely in sonets give yow praise.
God Sheeldë yow & give you mery days.

Now goodbye & blessings & greetings – remembrances to you.
A very live sense of your kindness is always with me.
                    Greetings
                    from
                    John.

1. Robert Nichols, 1893–1944, English poet and dramatist. A close friend of J.M.
and F.C.L., he often stayed at the Lamont's residence in New York City when he
was visiting the United States.
2. Wilfrid Wilson Gibson.

[London]
Sept. 16. 1918.
Dear Florence,

I've had rather a racketing ten days or so, without much time
for reading or writing, but I have read some rather interesting &
strange books about spiritualism. You ought to read them. There
is a book called The Reality of Psychic Phenomena,[1] by a man who
has thoroughly tested the usual psychical exhibitions, such as
levitation, table-rapping, & pressure of spirit fingers. He has
found that mediums engaged in levitation lose weight, & he has
discovered that the psychic power which causes the levitation acts
on the system of the cantilever, & can be felt, as a rather cold &
rather clammy thing proceeding from the medium. He has taken
gramophone records of the knocks & tappings of the spirits, &
waxen prints of the spirit fingers. All of this work is scientific &
exact, & deeply interesting.

Even more interesting, & very much stranger, is a book called
The Gateway of Remembrance,[2] by some people living at Glaston-
bury. G, as you may know, is a sort of holy ruin of an abbey, in the
west of England. The people who wrote the book are anti-
quarians. They wanted to know where some of the lesser chapels
of the abbey were; & they tried automatic writing, & received

(from the spirits of the dead monks) information as to where the chapels had been, and how big they were etc. Then they dug where the writing bade & discovered the traces of the chapels.

I hope the cats have been "eliminated" by this time. There is nothing like a sack, a good brick, & a neighbour's well, for a superfluous cat.

Greetings & thoughts & good wishes to you
from
John.

1. *The Reality of Psychic Phenomena*, by W. J. Crawford, 1916.
2. *The Gate of Remembrance*, by F. B. Bond, Oxford, 1921.

The Armistice bringing the First World War to an end was declared on 11 November 1918.

[London]
Nov. 13. [1918]

Dear Florence,

It is over now (has been over for two days), so now we have peace, & some prospect of unwinding the accursed chain to some purpose. The day of peace was dark, with a lowering sky & rain, so much rain, that the tumults were kept within bounds. Flags, yells, a little gunfire & a little drunkenness saw the day through. Yesterday, being fine, they went further & burnt a bonfire in Piccadilly Circus. Tonight, being fine, & the streets lighter, I expect something rowdier & more drunken. But it has been a happy time of deliverance, a setting free from death, a loosing of bonds. "Damn braces, bless relaxes", Blake said,[1] & as long as the relaxes do not mean chaos & formlessness he meant what he said. But God save us from chaos, I say, & may this great, kind, generous & truly noble people find its reward in beauty & happiness after all these years of death & hell.

You will be glad to hear that I have gotten a gilet jaune, to take the place of the famous green shirt. It is of a very lovely yellow, like the sound of a flute, or ripe grapes at Canary, or a lemon in the grove. People say "Tiens" as I go by. Somehow, this bright colour of yellow seems significant of the ending of the war. Curiously a zest & joy in yellow is everywhere. It is is the colour of so many of our spring flowers, & of the rising sun, that it may well be the colour of a beginning world.

In a few months now there will be passenger services again, & you will be here for a visit. Think of that.

All greetings & good wishes to you & all your household.

Blessings on you.

John.

1. William Blake, *The Marriage of Heaven and Hell*, Proverbs of Hell.

Boar's Hill, Oxford.

24 Jan. 1919.

Sitting in my shack here, I used to hear the guns in France all day long, & now they are all silent. They must have been over 100 miles distant.

Dear Florence,

For the first time in 4 1/2 years Oxford looks normal or nearly normal.

Of course, it has the look of a Venus with a tooth gone (& some measure of skin disease on both cheeks), but that is only the brick & stone side of it; I mean the life of the place.

Nearly all the cadets, who used to live in the colleges & wear one's arms out, returning salutes, when one walked the town in uniform, are gone, & a lot of undergrads are in their places. The hospitals are fast emptying, the streets are no longer crowded with "walking wounded", & one no longer sees hundreds of stretcher cases arriving daily with the mud of the stunt still on them. The fliers are gone or going. One sees bareheaded cheery boys going to lecture, as of old, with the menace of the front removed from them, & "soon will the high midsummer pomps come on", a jolly bonfire in the quad, & dance under the Dean's window, & then more punch from the bowl.

Then there are other tokens of peace, one may buy oranges. Sweets are coming back, or as you would say, "candies will soon be vendible"; it is said that one may buy flour by the sack again. Horses & poultry may soon be properly fed again, & it is thought that beer may soon be made stronger; at present only colonial soldiers can get drunk on it.

So much for peace.

Now will you please find out & let me know what duty a model ship would have to pay on arrival at the U.S.? It is a work of art, & as such would, I suppose, have to pay a swingeing duty. Will you please find out what the duty would be?

Your picture of me was very unlike me. That was a naval sailor, a very inferior, trifling sort of person; I belonged to the great M.M.S.[1] who are all good friends & write to their friends most faithfully & with tender thoughts.

from

John.

1. M.M.S.:Merchant Marine Service.

Boar's Hill, Oxford.

April 4, 1919.

Dear Florence,

I've been having a most harrassing time this week & I'm sorry to say I've not written you a word. It is the devil when the world suddenly falls down on one's head & then leaves one to climb out.

I'm glad you went up to the salient, & to the sweet fields of the Somme. It will give you a picture of war such as you can get nowhere else. You must not worry too much about the horror. You only see the horror now, but when the war was there you could see the courage & devotion & good temper & friendliness; all big things.

How does the Conference go?[1]

It was a great error of you, to go away before our Entertainment. It was a wild success. Walpole & N.L. were at their best, & we ate honey & eggs afterwards till we were all sticky all over. You didn't have so good a time I know.

Now best greetings from us all.

John.

1. T.W.L. was a representative of the United States Treasury on the American Commission to the Paris Peace Conference held after the conclusion of the First World War from January 1919, through June.

Boar's Hill, Oxford.
April 22. [1919]

Dear Florence,

Next time you come here, if the weather makes amends to you, you must come on the river. I've just been punting up the Char with Nevinson, & I think it is the kind of rest-cure that would be good for you. So when you come, we'll go down to Iffley or up to Bablockhithe, & fleet the time carelessly as they did in the golden age.

I hope that you are rested now. One reason Paris is so tiring is that there is no amusement there. They don't go on the river, or have merry-go-rounds, or shove hapenny like we do.

When you come to London, you must not miss the Lincoln play.[1] You are quite wrong about it.

Yesterday to my great joy, though not to my satisfaction, I finished the draft of my new ditty. It is like being sunk in a ship to write anything long. You go down & down & think you'll never come up, & then when you are blind & gasping, you see the light, & there you are, floundering but happy, with most of the sea underneath you.

Now, greetings & blessings to you, & all gentle thoughts & prayers.

from
John.

1. *Abraham Lincoln* by John Drinkwater, 1882–1937.

Cushendun.
[July 1919]

Dear Florence,

I've been thinking of you night & day. Even at meal-times your face swims up between me & the butter.

H.W.N.[1] will be here in 2 or 3 days & he will give me the latest news of you, but I want to hear about you & W.W.[2] afloat on the western ocean in a battleship. Did you flirt behind the big guns, did you talk about literature, and did you have a chance of telling him that he is but a little thing to the skating at Hennikeys?

Here we have no skating, but it is nearly cold enough, & I have chilblains on hands & feet, & this in mid July. But though we have no skating, we have circuses. Every week a god-like troupe rolls by, & pitches a tent, & spotted horses wander around, & a band plays The Boys of Wexford, & then the marvellous riders ride, & the clown with the rough cast on his face comes in & says it's a good morning this evening. Do you have circuses? I think you have, but I doubt their being so good as ours. Yours are probably too good; ours are humble & of the people, & they move me to the bone.

Many years ago, I went to many, & I thought, when these came, it will be no good going to these now, I am a blasé old rangée realist, & they won't delight me now; but it was not so; they are still of the heart of romance & unspeakably beautiful.

> "No great First Cause inspires the happy plot
> But all is matter, & no matter what."

It is a hard life they lead; but they are artists, content with any hardship, so that they may have their art & the proud privilege of being themselves, even in a world all ranged against them, the movey & the music hall, & the price of hay, like 3 lions in their path.

Blessings & greetings to you from us all & from me.

John.

1. Henry W. Nevinson, 1856–1941, English journalist, essayist and historian.
2. President Woodrow Wilson, 1856–1924.

Boar's Hill, Oxford.
Augt 23. 1919.

Dear Florence,

I expect that Maine is by much more lovely than Antrim. For several years I thought Antrim[1] beautiful but now I do not. There is something sodden & savage & raw & rained on about it. Then the people are too foreign; and the question arises, why go abroad to an inferior climate & a less compelling landskip? You may answer, the natural madness of man; but that is no answer, now that I'm old. Madness is unnatural in the old; think how shockt we are at Lear.

Summing it up, I think I hated being in Ireland, this year. It seemed to be back in 1913, or 1813, brooding on the same false

history without any more enlightenment. It seemed to have
forgotten nothing, forgiven nothing, learned nothing, seen nothing & done nothing (except grow rich automatically), & so it
seemed a different world to us, & one we were very glad to leave.

It is now time for me to go to rob the bees of their honey.

On 2nd thought, I cannot do this, for it is raining, & all the bees
would be at home & would resent my presence. I will wait till it is
fine.

It seems, that in the peace conference, some typed sheets about
the state of Austria were handed round to people, describing the
miseries of the people. One of the statements was that "the priests
are violating their vows". A careless typist mis-wrote this on one
sheet, so that it read "the priests are violating their cows", & a
man wrote in the margin "I see now what is meant by a Papal
bull", & by some accident this sheet & marginal note were
printed as a State paper, & then distributed abroad. The Italians
are now very indignant about it.

Gilberto[2] lives near us now, & we see him fairly often.

Your young friend Robert N[3] is a worshipper of yours. He wrote
me a long letter about your kindness & justice & niceness &
beautifulness & sereneness & loveliness & attractiveness. You
evidently saved his life by your kindness to him & he is most
deeply grateful & attached to you.

Best greetings

from

John.

1. Antrim is a county in Northern Ireland (Ulster).
2. Gilbert Murray had moved to a house about a mile from the Masefields on
Boar's Hill, Oxford.
3. Robert Nichols.

Boar's Hill, Oxford.

4. IX. 1919.

Dear Florence,

I suppose by this time you are back in New York, or just at point
to go there. You ought to be within hail of N.Y. for I don't think
you can get along without the electric whirlwind close by.

You feel most lonely & alone
Without the clanging telephone
It chills you to the very bone
To be without your dictophone
You feel inclined to stop & die
Without the loud Victrola's cry
You feel so sad it makes you ache
To be without a jarring brake
A dozen jarring brakes at once
Put on by hefty Adam's sons
With oaths, a long shrill gritting
          Skirrrrrr
You like to hear the genial whir
Of aeroplanes & zeppelins
And little boys with stones in tins
And bigger boys with college yells
And megaphones & Liberty bells.
O hi-yi-hi, & Siss Boom Bah
That is the quiet soul you are.

The general strike was avoided for the time, as you must have seen, so we go on again. There will pretty surely be some troublous years in the world between now & 1930.

Ransome's¹ book upon Russia is not likely to be very sound. He used to be without much judgement, tho' a nice lad enough. He probably liked much of the friendliness of the revolutionary spirit, & that, I should judge, would be all he would be qualified to judge, in the turmoil there. There was something of the happy child in him that prevented him from doing much.

I'm now planning out my big model ship

Best greetings & thoughts to you.
          John.

1. Arthur Ransome, 1884–1967, English journalist and author of *Six Weeks in Russia*, 1919. He is well known today as the author of numerous children's books, beginning with *Swallows and Amazons*, 1930.

> Boar's Hill, Oxford.
> Sept 11th. 1919.

Dear Florence,

Just a line to say that Charles Hopkinson[1] has now finished my portrait & plans to go off with it to Boston. It is like this, the portrait is:—

I am sitting at a table reading, & at the same time dancing with inspiration. The stars above are my horoscope. I wanted him to do me like this:—

But he said he hadn't enough paint for the audience, & anyway it was too hot. Judith[2] wanted him to do me like this

but he would have his own way, & so if you see the result you'll know how it came to pass.

Best greetings from us all.

John.

1. Charles Hopkinson, 1869–1962, American portrait painter of New England, noted for his paintings of cultural, educational and political leaders.
2. Judith Masefield, J.M.'s daughter.

Boar's Hill, Oxford.
Sept 18. [1919]

Dear Florence,

You need a hauling over the coals for what you say about the books of J.G.

As Shelley says, "the laws (or causes) of poetical compostion (or which govern the brain during it) are very imperfectly understood".

As I say, "they aren't understood at all".

But I add this, that they are mainly independent of the composer. He can control the shape but not the quality of the thing composed. A man may write "well" & interest people for 10 books in succession; then write seemingly not less "well", but yet without interest to others. Then after another 10 books he may write "well" again & interest people again.

Galsworthy has written a great deal in the last 12 years. No man can be always at his best. You don't know what a strain writing is. You pour quarts of blood out each time. When a man is bled white for a while you complain that the latest gush of blood isn't red enough. I say that it is blood, & that it is the blood of a jolly good vein, & interesting as such, even if it isn't as red as some.

You try writing 12 or 15 books & plays in 12 years & see how much quality you can command at the end. You cannot command it at any time.

To hear these critics, one would think that the diviner qualities of art were within the reach of all, for the taking. Let them try it. That may teach them a little humility; but they know better than to try it. They know that it is a good deal easier to praise or blame than to understand.

However, we will save up this discourse for a merry quarrel at Voisins the next time we lunch together.

We aren't in the house yet, but it does draw nearer to a kind of completion, & 2 more weeks ought to see it done.

How are you now & where are you & how is poor Corliss? You left the most golden opinions in all hearts here, Neville, H.W.N., Nichols, all your devoted slaves.

Blessings on you.

John.

Boar's Hill, Oxford.
Oct. 7. [1919]

Dear Florence,

Your letter about the police strike came when we were in the throes of the railway strike. It was no good answering at once, for the mails were imperfect during the strike & aren't quite settled yet.

I don't think that your police strike was as serious as ours at Liverpool, though it seems to have been more criminal & less good tempered. At Liverpool the streets ran beer for a while, & you could buy diamond rings & watches from children at sixpence cash; but it was quite cheery & good humoured, though one bit of the town was sacked.

The railway strike was also cheery & good humoured, but wouldn't long have stayed so. One soldier got a bat on the head & two or three men were fired at, but the head was hard & didn't cave in under the bat & the shots all missed, luckily, & that is a jolly good record for a 10-days strike of 1/2 a million men. In another week there would have been trouble, but it was settled in time.

I feel more & more strongly the wisdom of your husband, who gains his points without fighting. We've been thinking how much better it is to win your adversary by generosity rather than by batting him out. It seems likely that after this the relations between Govt & labour here will be ever so much better.

The poor old Fox hasn't begun to run yet, owing to the strike.

We are now living in the new house & the workmen finish today & go elsewhere. It is jolly to have room to turn. It is a pity you can't turn up to see me in your green dressing gown reading poetry by the fire, or thinking of you, which comes to the same thing.

R. Graves[1] is coming to be our tenant at our cottage, he & his wife & babe. It is very sweet (but not very usual) as St Paul says, to see poets dwelling together in unison.

How do you get along with the Arabian Nights?

We were delighted to have a jolly letter from your husband last week.

My greetings & thoughts to you.

from

John.

1. Robert Graves, 1895–, English poet and novelist. Author of *Goodbye to All That*, 1929. He delivered the main address at the Memorial Service for Masefield in Westminster Abbey on 20 June 1967. (Masefield died on 12 June.)

Boar's Hill, Oxford.
Oct 24. [1919?]

Dear Florence,

You ask about the Russian railway story. It is as follows. It is probably as true as most Russian stories.

A party of strangers were travelling by train in Russia recently. They were in a compartment together. They were: a lady, two merchants, and a Russian soldier.

Presently the lady missed her purse & cried out that she had been robbed. The merchants said, "the soldier was sitting next to you, he robbed you". "I didn't", said the soldier. "Yes, you did", they said; so they called the guard. When the guard came, the lady said, "This soldier robbed me".

So the guard shot the soldier dead.

While they were heaving the soldier out of the window, the train stopt at a station crowded with soldiers.

"Who in hell shot this soldier?" said the soldiers.

"The guard did", said the merchants.

So the soldiers shot the guard dead.

Presently the train went on, & the lady took out her handkerchief to mop her brow. As she did so, she dropped her purse.

"Why here's my purse after all", she said. "I wasn't robbed, after all. Fancy that."

So the merchants shot the lady dead.

There was nothing in the purse except a powderpuff, so they hove it out of the window & continued their conversation.

This is a good illustration of the "attitude towards life" of after the war in Europe. Nearly all the young men have killed people at short notice, & think no more of it than of pressing a button to ring a bell.

Your lovely gift, the desk, has come, & is a great delight to us in the new house. I wish you could come in to tea tonight to see it in its new setting.

We have such a lot of jovial poets here now that you would like coming to tea.

Best greetings to you & many gentle & happy thoughts.

from
John.

Boar's Hill, Oxford.
[12 Jan 1920]

Dear Florence,

The mail is going out tomorrow, so I send this, to say, that S. Sassoon[1] is going to N. York on the 24th, by the Megantic, a sort of 12-day ship, which should turn up about the 6th Feb.

I believe you already know S.S. so I am going to ask him to bring you the little model.[2] It will be a *very* little model because of the difficulty of packing a big one, & if the thing gets smasht on the way, as it may, I'm afraid the repairing it will be a problem.

One of the greatest of all American books is Dana's 2 Years Before the Mast,[3] so I am making the model a model of a brig, like Dana's brig, so that you may hoist American colours on her & use her to look at while you read Dana's matchless pages; which I hope you will often do.

When I can get my carpenter's vice, I may be able to do bigger models.

Bless you, the best of thoughts & greetings to you. It is such fun doing this for you, & I hope it will look nice when done & please you.

John

---

1. Siegfried Sassoon, 1886–1967. English poet and prose writer. Served in the trenches in the First World War. His poems of protest, *Counter-Attack*, were published in 1918.
2. J.M.'s special hobby was the modelling of small sailing ships. He sent several such models to F.C.L. during the years of their friendship.

3. *Two Years Before the Mast* (1840), by Richard Henry Dana, 1815–82, an
account of this American writer's voyage as a common sailor around Cape Horn
to California. The book was written to secure decent treatment and justice for the
sailor.

Boar's Hill, Oxford.
3rd March. [1920]

Dear Florence,

A word reached me from St. Paul; so many thanks for it & for
the cutting about poor Joe Gavit.[1]

By this time you must be on the seas, starting from Seattle or
San Francisco, you don't even say which, for some strange
pigtailed port where prohibition is unknown. You will be in the
Pacific Ocean, somewhere on a red line on the chart, marked
"Seattle to Honolulu 45000 miles" or whatever the distance is. It
seems far more than that, in thought.

One thing about the Pacific is, that it is an ocean which has not
yet made me seasick. I hope it is similarly nice to you. God bless
all oceans that let one "enjoy one's private", instead of thrusting
their d----d bolshevism into everybody's gizzard.

They say the Dead Sea is nice & still. They ought to call it the
Peaceful Sea, or the proper Sea, or the Right Kind of Sea, instead
of just dead.

> It lies above Gomorrah & Old Sodom
> In silence & in saltness aye unshaken,
> And crumbs of Lot's wife, sunken to the boddom,
> Are gathered by the tribes for curing bacon.

Will you come back by way of the Dead Sea? It wd be a long
way round, but there are few more interesting places than it. If
you get a goat there, you can put your sins on it, & shoo it away
into the desert, & then away it goes, as red as scarlet & leaves you
as white as snow.[2] This would not be any good to you of course for
you are so good & kind you would not want a goat not even a kid,
but would have absolution on your look alone. To a fellow like me
it would be a blessing.

Best greetings & good wishes

from
John

1. Joseph Lamont Gavit, 1899–1920, nephew of the Lamonts, who died of typhoid fever in January 1920.
2. The scapegoat which carried the sins of the children of Israel into the wilderness is described in Leviticus, Chapter 16.

Boar's Hill, Oxford.
June 11th, 1920.

Dear Florence,

A letter from Peking & 2 from Japan[1] reach me today together after a month of silence. Your letters are splendid & make one see the East. Thank you so much for writing so fully. It has been a great pleasure to hear of your doings, & your success. Congratulations on your success. I expect the Chancelleries of Japan are making up your Dossiers: "F.C. Lamont, mariée, Americaine, brunette, aux yeux magnifiques; prenez garde à cette femme. Elle a bonté du coeur, mais elle est bien dangereuse pour les diplomates. C'est impossible de lui refuser. Elle a bien joué notre bon Mikado," etc.

What a wonderful thought for you to have helped in making the future of the East.

Your Pekin letter was the best you've ever written, even you, the great letter writer, surpassed yourself, colour, style, interpretation. But don't be puffed up as St Paul says, "be not puffed up",[2] for some others can write too, though they haven't those other qualifications, which you have, of good-ness of heart.

You ask what I am doing in the way of writing. I'm in the throes of a sort of nightmare of a poem, which I expect will be my last. I hoped to have it done by this time, but Sir W. Raleigh[3] asked me to lecture for him this term in the University, so I took 2 of his 6 lectures, not out of goodness of heart, but imbecility of mind, & gave them last month & they took about a month to prepare. One was about the technical side of story writing, the other about the art of writing plays, the latter was very technical & I should think helpful at any rate to me, the 1st wasn't much.

I'd never lectured in the Univy Schools before. We had about 1100 students. One of them took notes. She was a lady. Her notes were afterwards brought to me. This was what she made of my remarks.

Potry is the same as Danseing.

after getting that much preserved, I suppose she was spell bound.

By the way have you heard what Lenin is up to? He is declaring that Russia is really an Oriental country, & is bringing about a rapprochement between Russia & Islam.[4] Russia is going to go Moslem. Lenin is declaring now throughout the Moslem World that he is Mohammed come again to reinterpret the Koran, & now throughout the Moslem world pictures of Lenin are appearing thus.

[Drawing of a man]

Lenin. (That is) Mohammed.

This is causing a ferment throughout Islam. It opens up so many possibilities of change that one likes to think what might come of it, & how Christianity would stand a big religious revival outside her borders.

The yellow coat with blue facings suits me charmingly. I wear it now instead of my Doctor's robe when I want people to be impresst, such as interviewers & the clergyman.

The little ship,[5] if she be dry, ought to be posted to you tomorrow. I hope that she will stand the Atlantic all right, She is a brigantine. [Drawing] She will be screwed to a batten which will be screwed into a box, and she ought not to mind if the post people toss her from hand to hand all the way from me to Maine. She is not much of a gift, but she's the best I've been able to make all by myself & I wd like you to have her on your desk.

This photograph dates from the beginning of the war. It is me clearing away lunch from some wounded men. I wore gloves in the hospital because it was a septic place & I had had both hands badly poisoned a few days before the photograph was taken.

Your letters still turn up from the far East. Perhaps they come by way of Suez. I think I've had them all, & thank you ever so much for them all.

Blessings & greetings to you, & I hope you'll have a jolly time in Maine, with those live wires, your family.

My greetings to Mr & Mrs Gavit.[6] Special greetings, for I think so much of them both, every day.

Blessings & greetings to you, & many thoughts & good wishes.

from
John.

1. In 1920 the Lamonts took a two months' trip to Japan and China, in both of which countries T.W.L. was carrying on business negotiations.

2. I Corinthians XIII.
3. Sir Walter Raleigh, 1861–1922. Professor of English at the University of
Oxford. Author of *The English Novel*, 1894.
4. In 1917 a declaration promising religious and national freedom to the Muslim
peoples in the Russian territories had been issued by the Bolsheviks, with the
signatures of Lenin and Stalin. In June 1920 a communist republic of Gilan was
temporarily set up in Persia. J.M.'s comments may have these events in mind.
5. Another small ship modelled by J.M. and sent to F.C.L.
6. Mr and Mrs John Palmer Gavit, parents of Joseph Lamont Gavit. Mrs Gavit
was the sister of Thomas W. Lamont.

Boar's Hill, Oxford.
July 12. 1920.

Dear Florence,

Very many thanks for your letter from home, & for all this store
of lovely gifts, so thoughtfully chosen & so charming in themselves. Miss Plague sent them on to us on her arrival in England. I
thought, when I saw the package, O God, I thought, this is the
manuscript novel of an elderly single lady who wants my candid
opinion & will write a bitter letter when she gets it, or if it isn't
that, for I now know all the kinds of package that come to me, then
it is a lot of specimen needlework by a decayed lady who would be
glad if I would buy a piece; or if not that, then it is a collection of
water colour drawings, by a lady, who would be so much encouraged, if I would buy some at the very beginning of her career, or, if
I couldn't do that, would I recommend her work among some of
my clever friends. So my heart was in the dumps when I cut the
strings, & lo, the packet was from Florence, & contained all these
beautiful things & so much thought from her. We were all
charmed & delighted & enchanted. Leprosy never entered our
thoughts. We thought that we had never had so many lovely
things together nor any so generous a friend.

Thank you again for all your lovely thoughts for us all.

from
John.

K. Cate may bring me news of you, & Nevi[1] will be coming soon
& he certainly will.

1. Henry W. Nevinson.

Boar's Hill, Oxford.

[22 Sept 1920]

Dear Florence,

I'm writing this in a hurry, just to say how concerned we all feel for you & your husband in this damnable bomb outrage.[1]

It must be a hideous time for you. We all send you our heartiest & warmest sympathy.

It was a huge relief to find by this morning's papers that your husband was not seriously hurt.

Nothing American has stirred this country so deeply for years. There is a most wide-spread rage & indignation against the bombers. I meet it everywhere, among all classes; a feeling of fury against men who would commit a crime so dastardly & haphazard. I was talking to a carter about it, & he was white hot on the subject. "The brute ran away", he said, "and left his poor horse to be blowed up".

However, it is over, & your husband is safe, & I don't think for a moment that any plot of the sort will be repeated. I don't write this only to comfort you, but from the feeling that the snakes have spat their venom. I hope that you will think this & not go worrying & worrying.

We all send our messages of sympathy & respect to your husband & of greetings to you.

We here are on the brink of another big strike, which may or may not come off.[2] If it does come off, then I feel that it will be a serious thing, not likely to end without bloodshed. However, I think we are "disposed" by powers wiser than ourselves, "that make the seven stars & Orion & turn the shadow of death into the morning", so we must be of good courage & abide their measuring out.

Many thoughts & greetings.

from

John.

1. In September 1920 a powerful bomb in a horse-drawn cart exploded on Wall Street, New York City, in front of the main office of J. P. Morgan & Co. The explosion shattered many windows and the glass dome of the bank. Two bank employees were killed as well as 38 people outside, while more than 300 individuals were injured. The perpetrator or perpetrators of the outrage were never apprehended, in spite of extensive detective work.

2. Industrial unrest had been increasing in the summer of 1920, and was taking a

strongly political character. On May 10th London dockers had refused to load munitions designed to help the right-wing Polish government in its war with Russia; and following the rout of Polish armies a general strike was threatened by Labour leaders if support for Poland were continued.

[Boar's Hill, Oxford]
[23 Oct 1920]

Dear Florence,

I have just seen R.N.[1] who is now fairly certainly going to Japan to take up a Professorship of English, the Chair once held by L. Hearn.[2] He expects to start about January, & to be away for 3 years.

He was in sad gloom over the following. He pinched a gramophone from a friend, with great success, some months ago, & was then as happy as the day is long, playing the thing & buying records for it. Now the friend has pinched it back, with even greater success, & life seems to hold nothing further.

If you want to relieve the gloom, a gramophone would be the thing. Music is the one thing which seems to calm him at once, from his wild moods to something like peace.

We are in the coal strike, in the 1st week of it, & of course at present miners look on it as a holiday. It happens to be fine weather, too. It is not yet certain what other sympathetic strikes will follow: the railway men will probably strike, half-heartedly, in a day or two, & the carters and transport workers, thoroughly, with them. Unemployment is already pretty bad, & there is plenty of "loose revolution" lying around, ready to cut loose & pillage. One must just trust in God's providence & our own good sense inspired by the same. Out of it all may come a better state than there has been here this 150 years.

It is queer to see the revolutionary look in people's eyes everywhere in the cities. I was in Birmingham & Shrewsbury this week, & noticed it in both cities; a kind of anger screwed up to spitting point. So little would set both sides spitting, or biting the thumb. Well, God will dawn etc. Something will survive, & the ashes of what is burnt may manure the rest.

I had not been in Shropshire for 18 years. It was glorious to see the Wrekin again, & to eat a Shrewsbury cake again. The Wrekin is a volcanic hill, it is supposed that anybody living near it must be friendly to his neighbours, & as the staple diet there is Shrewsbury cake, this is an actual fact. It is my family's county. We were yeomen farmers there (they say) & that is why I like hills & am so fond of cake.

But you, most kind of friends & thoughtful of women, have ice-cream sodas & nut sundaes at command, so what can you care for Shrewsbury Cake & Severn, rivers of Damascus; not one single darn.

Bless you & all thoughts & greetings to you
from
John.

1. Robert Nichols.
2. Lafcadio Hearn, 1850–1904, American author who spent the last part of his life in Japan and became an expert on that country.

Boar's Hill, Oxford.
Dec. 1. [1920]

Dear Florence,

Thank you so much for two letters, one of 2 days ago, & 1 of today, by the Aquitania.

About J.G.[1] I have tried more than once to thrust an introduction to you upon him, but he is rather coy about it, because he is given rather a rushing & tempestuous life in N.Y., by friends & journalists & doers of good works, & dreads making more engagements than he already has. Then, too, he left here expecting to be in N.Y. only a day or two, & then flying to the west, & so, what with coyness & lack of time, he seemed to me to fight shy of the heavenly privilege of being acquainted with you, & so I said to myself, "well, your blood be on your own head, then; if you won't you won't; you must just suffer accordingly, & take the natural consequences, by continuing in your present warped & cramped condition". And so I left him, as I'm sure you will for the time, more in sorrow than in anger; yet hoping, that presently, wisdom would yet prevail, & gather him into your circle. When he knows what he has missed, his repentance will make you amends.

I have been remiss about writing, in these last 10 days, but that has not been my fault, but fate's. I have had more than much to do. It has been like being in America. We have been giving a Concert in the village, & that has taken much time. Nevil[2] came & danced his morris jig, with bells on his knees, & quite lovely grace of movement. He also fluted to us, with singular beauty, from Gluck³ the divine musician. Miss Draper,⁴ your country-woman, gave a recital of some half dozen humourous characterizations, all very skilful. Na & other dancers danced, I read, & a lady gave a lantern lecture. It was rather a great success, aesthetically & in money.

Then Nevil drew me in charcoal, & when he had done, I had to go for 2 days to Sir Walter's⁵ to be drawn in charcoal by Mrs. Bell,⁶ whom I had not seen for 16 years. She did a very nice drawing, thus; [Drawing] Sir W was very gay with some new rhymes he'd been making. They were as follows, or nearly;

> "Pity the artist & his wife
> They live a horrid haunted life
> They live with all the things they made
> That are not wanted by the trade."

It is only too true, they do. How many artists have I seen, whose studio walls are stackt with duds, whose only fate will be, to be painted over. Full many a glorious landscape have I seen, that in time had to become a portrait of an alderman.

You must tell me more about your house. Is it really so far advanced as that? Are you moving in to it, or beginning to furnish it? My heart yearns for anybody moving house; when I see a furniture van I say "There but for the grace of God go I". May the kind fates make the move easy.

Coming home from Hinksey yesterday I saw the little currant jelly dogs in full cry from Cumnor; a most stirring sight & sound. Currant jelly dogs, are beagles, which hunt the hare, & hares are eaten with currant jelly. In fact, without the currant jelly, or a famine, no-one would ever eat hare.

I hope that this letter will go to you by the Aquitania, & reach you in a week. I hope that Asheville has done you good.

The Irish news is still horrible, but the horrible thing to me is the skill with which evil men present us as the sole offenders & the Irish as lambs & martyrs. The reprisals came because men were barbarously & beastlyly murdered by Irish assassins, & not in one or two cases, but in over a hundred.⁷

Best greetings & remembrances
from
John.

1. John Galsworthy.
2. Neville Lytton.
3. Christoph Gluck, 1714–87, German composer.
4. Ruth Draper, 1884–1956, American monologist.
5. Sir Walter Raleigh.
6. Vanessa (Stephen) Bell, 1879–1961, artist, portrait painter. Wife of Clive Bell and sister of Virginia Woolf.
7. The Irish Republican Army had been constituted in January 1919 out of the old National Volunteers. At the time of J.M.'s letter the English had an army of 50,000 in Ireland, but although the Irish parliament was already in existence pending the establishment of the Irish Free State, a condition of near civil war obtained.

> Boar's Hill, Oxford.
> Dec. 2. 1920.

Dear Florence,

I am glad you are bored by Freud.

Like most men of energy he insists on jumping every fence with his own stolid legs, whether the gates are open or not. Most of his hops are absurd. I don't think the soul can be explained by mucous membranes. His book seems so like modern Germany, all energy & hard work & mental power, without any glimmer of illumination.

By whom is man the marvellous most cloyed?
                Freud.
By whom are weary students most annoyed?
                Freud.
Whose flouting would make students overjoyed?
                Freud.
Whose central teaching is a hollow void?
Who rattles like a pea in celluloid?
Who ought to be ungummed and unemployed
Or fatted up with extracts of thy-roid.
                Freud.
But though I thus hard-scrubbing-brush and sand him
I do not read, & hardly understand him

Good night Good night.
                John.

Boar's Hill, Oxford.
2nd March. 1921.

Dear Florence,

Thank you for your letter. But, as the lady in the poem says,

"may I live upon trust,
If I know to which question to answer you fust."

I have met the Berensons,[1] & their daughter, Mrs. Strachey, & Mr. Pearsall Smith.[2] I have looked at Trivia with pleasure. As to have I read Moby Dick, if you were in range, I'd fling something at you for that.

I read Moby Dick before I was 18 years old. I wrote an article on it before I was 25, & had it printed. I was directly responsible for its (the book's) being reprinted in this country on one occasion, & I have twice or three times written about Melville so as to make him known here.[3] Now do you know Herman Melville's Redburn? That is a fine little book, about little old New York & little old Liverpool, & I think its a lot nicer than Moby Dick. Then, do you know H.M.'s Typee or Omoo & White Jacket & poems?

I don't like whales much. They have too much bulk & too little brain, & they are greasy when opened & left about. I don't like anythings that live in the sea except those that are easy to catch & good to eat. A good herring is more use to me than a whale. Prof Thomson[4] says that herrings are very highly strung & have a passion for liberty.

You may say that whales respect prophesy; & bring in the tale of Jonah as evidence. That was one good whale in all history. He was the exception whale to prove the rule.

When I see a whale I look the other way. They are like jovial boys who have learned how to spout water like pugilists do when they are acting as seconds. It is a disgusting trick. I could do it, but I wd scorn to.

Whale is a good rhyme to tale & flail etc. There aren't any rhymes to herring and salmon. There is no fun writing poems about whales. There are too many rhymes to them.

Clergymen seldom preach about whales.

Our present government is headed by a man from whales.

People can't tame whales like they do dogs and to some extent cows.

It is cold, thinking about whales.

God bless you. All our greetings to you.

John.

1. Bernard Berenson, 1865–1959, American art critic, and his wife.
2. Logan Pearsall Smith, 1865–1946. Essayist and critic, whose sister Mary married Bernard Berenson. A collected edition of his miniature essays, *All Trivia*, was published in 1933.
3. Herman Melville, 1819–91. American novelist, author of *Typee* (1846), *Omoo* (1847), *White Jacket* (1850) and *Moby Dick* (1851). *Redburn* (1849) describes a voyage of ten years earlier, when the author travelled to Liverpool as a cabin boy.
4. Professor J. Arthur Thomson, 1861–1933. Professor of Natural History at the University of Aberdeen.

Boar's Hill, Oxford.
[5 Mar 1921]

Dear Florence,

The other day I wrote you a letter taking a mean view of whales. I have just been reading a scientific book about whales, & now hasten to retract anything I said against them.

A scientific prince used to go about in a big yacht dredging up strange beasts from the bottom of the ocean. One day he noticed how the whales used to come round to eat what things he caught & did not want to keep. So one day he tamed a whale & taught it to go down to catch things for him. He did this by suggestion & the dalcroze method.[1] Then when the whale came up all deeply laden, he tried to get the whale to disgorge, but the whale didn't wish to, so he fired a gun over the whale's head, & that upset the whale, so that he kind of Church-of-Laodicea-d the catch into the sea.[2] So then the prince took the catch & found it contained amazing things, bits of icthyosaurs & dinosaurs, all fresh & newly chawed off, such as no-one had suspected still lived. After that, he never went dredging any more, but always fished by his whale, & now he is more famous than probably any scientist, & he goes around singing Isaiah to his whale "the abundance of the sea shall be converted into thee". He does this in a tenor voice.

Best greetings & thoughts
from
John

1. Emile Jacques-Dalcroze, 1865–1950. Swiss music teacher and composer who originated eurythmics.
2. For the equation of Laodicea with spewing out, see Revelations XXX 14–16.

[n.p.]
[May? 1921]

Dear Florence,

We were not home till after the going of the post last night, so that I could not write to you at once, though I wanted to.

I think I was horrid to you about Othello. May I just explain, that the prejudice most English acting of Shakespeare rouses in me is due to this:— W.S. wrote at a time when people were less restrained than now. A man then had to be his own police-force, his own newspaper, & his own helper. He (W.S.) wrote from his own observation of men being these things. Men were laid bare in their inner selves in ordinary daily life then, as today they are only laid bare in excessive occasional calamity, a war, a murder, or a bursting boiler, etc.

Well. As life calmed down, actors ceased to see in daily life the passions they were imitating. They substituted for observation & knowledge a *tradition* of acting, which became less real year by year, as the original passion which founded it grew dimmer in the mind.

Today, Shakespearean acting is often a soul-less passing on of a weak and bad tradition. It is not a living study of passionate natures. I thought that the Court people had done much to give a good rendering of the play, but had not done enough to give a good rendering of the passions. They had not gone where the passions may be watched, but had learned what other actors had done at particular points, & had made their performance rather a museum, than an explosion blowing many bright & dark souls violently out of life after long & slow preparation.

I was really so happy to be at the dear old lovely little Court theatre with you.[1] It is a sacred building to me (One of the few places in London that I feel tenderly towards) & I'm glad to have been there with you. They've redecorated it (& very hideously) but it is still the Court, & I say of it as Shakespeare does,

> "Was't never at the Court, shepherd?
> No? Then thou art damned." [2]

One of the few places I'd like to be buried in would be the Court theatre.

Blessings & greetings to you
from
John.

You should have seen the lovely things Geoffroy[3] wrote of you in his letter.

1. The Royal Court Theatre in Sloane Square, London, was built in 1888, and destroyed by bombing in 1940. It has since been rebuilt.
2. *As You Like It*, Act III, Scene 2.
3. Charles Geoffroi Dechaine, French painter and close friend of J.M. When in New York City, he was often a house guest of the Lamonts.

[Boar's Hill, Oxford]
[May 1921]

My dear Florence,

(This is the English form of address, not the American). We are most sad to think of your forlorn state alone in London. I am sending you this little word, to bid you be of good cheer, & to say I wish I could be at breakfast with you to see you read it in your pink Babette cap.

The thought, that you bade us think, about the car journey, has been thought, or rather, since you say there is no such thing as time, is being still thought, or exists in thinkingness. We would like you to see Blown Hilcote copse, where Reynard lives; and the downs where Right Royal canters;[1] & then Morris's tomb.[2]

> Let us be happy in our gloom
> And drop a tear on Morris' tomb
> And hang a wreath on Kelmscott manor
> And then have tea & sing Hosannor. .
> And coming home we well might pass
> The White Horse cut in chalk through grass
> And whiz like water through a sieve
> Through where King Alfred used to live
> And pass Tar Wood where once (they say)
> Men found a fox that ran all day
> Full 50 miles in 7 hours
> For Ananias keeps his powers
> He is a genius at a story
> May happiness and joy & glory
> Be ever yours my valued friend.
> I say Amen. (You'll say Amend.)
>   [John]

1. This refers to J.M.'s poems *Reynard The Fox* (1919) and *Right Royal* (1920). The subsequent poem refers to the prehistoric figure cut in chalk on White Horse Hill

on the Berkshire Downs near Wantage, where King Alfred had his court. Tar
Wood is referred to in *Reynard The Fox*.
2. William Morris, 1834–96. English poet, prose writer and designer. He lived at
Kelmscott in Oxfordshire from 1871 until his death, and is buried in the nearby
churchyard.

[Boar's Hill, Oxford]
[3 Aug 1921]

Dear Florence,

You want to know about my 1st long motor drive. I have since
then had my 2nd, which quite puts it in the shade, but about my
first.

Rising at 3.30 a.m, I started at 4.30 a.m, through deserted
Abingdon, across the empty Downs, to Newbury, where the battle
was. Newbury was just waking up when I got to it, but I did not
linger in it, but went on, over the battlefield, where Charles I tried
to force his way to London, & was barred by the Parliament
Army. Some think that Cromwell might have finished the war at
that battle had he had a free hand. It was a most bloody fight, with
over 4000 killed, as will happen in battles when the only general
with any intelligence has his hands tied by superior officers.[1]

After Andover, we made the very unpleasant town of Salisbury,
which is a city I dislike more than most. Like Sir Andrew, I have
no most exquisite reason for disliking it, but I have reason good
enough.[2] I think that hell has probably got 2 suburbs, one exactly
like Winchester & the other exactly like Salisbury, or perhaps the
east end in hell is called Salchester or Winshisbury & is modelled
on the two.

There were a lot of sons of Belial on the side walks in Salisbury;
also daughters of Belial, with aprons on, standing at doors of
beershops.

Presently we were as it were purged of the taint of Salisbury &
were up in the lovely downs that go on forever and forever, &
nobody on them except gipsies & shepherds, & that I liked well
enough.

Coming back, I came through a divine downland further to the
west, & went faster & faster & faster, 25–30–35–40–45 per hour,
children were crushed into pulp, wives were left widows &
husbands widowers; as Wordsworth says of the sonnet, the car
became a Trumpet whence I blew Soul-animating strains.[3] And

then I came to a place you perhaps haven't seen, Avebury in Wiltshire.

You may have seen or heard of Stonehenge. Well, Stonehenge is modern & pretty-pretty compared to Avebury. Avebury is a vast great ghastly cup, bigger than the Yale Bowl, & in it there is a ghastly ring of grim uncouth gigantic bald rocks, like the devil's decayed teeth.

If you want a religious emotion, you go to Avebury when you come in September.

I hope that you are having a lovely time in Maine. When will you be sailing for England?

Our greetings & thoughts to you from
                                    John.

1. There were two Battles of Newbury: the one J.M. refers to took place on October 27th 1644. The result was indeterminate.
2. *Twelfth Night*, Act II, Scene 3.
3. William Wordsworth, 'Scorn not the sonnet, critic!'

                                    Boar's Hill, Oxford.
                                    [31 Aug 1921]
Dear Florence,

If I had sail-boats to name I would not hesitate. There are 2 good names for ships (the best names possible for ships)
Wanderer.
Pathfinder.
but they are a little heavy for boats. Then there are light & gay names

Kitcat.	Ping Pong.
Gin & ginger.	Pippit.
Pep.	Next Best.
Don't Tell.	Dammit.
Joyboat.	Forward Ho.
Spindrift.	Crojick.
Handy Billy.	Susan Lovewell.
Dear Jemima.	Polly Perkins.
The Bing Boy.	Hurray.
The Spark.	The Pop.
The Limit.	The Pin & Winkle.
The Glad Eye.	The Jim Hickey.

Uncle Tom Cobbleigh.
Peter Gurney.
The Lonesome Mike.
Selah.
The Stand from Under.
Watch your step.
Stand clear.
Crash.
Amen.
I am.
I guess.
It.
Me.
The very Pim.
The Dam my picture.
The Get in and Ride.
Come all ye.
The Trigger.
The Bang.
The Foxy Joe.
The Lee Brace.
The Look at me.
The Bit of Good.
The Hasten softly.
The Wait a bit.
The Hold on.
The Hold all.
The Hop it.
The skip jack.
The Flip Flop.
The Snip Snap.
The Tea & Toast.
Herring Treader.
The Lobster of Love.
The Herring of Heaven Harbour
The Shark of Sky Farm
The Shrimp shatterer
The Prawn Prancer
The Mackerel Mocker
The Whale Wakener.

Harry Hawk.
Dan'l Whiddon.
The Good Hand.
The Glory Hole.
The Mind your Eye.
Look out.
'Helyer coming.
Wallop.

The There and Back.
The Roving Gull.
The Bubble-bruiser.
The streak.
The On. On. On.

The Peter Piper.
The Pepper pot.
The Skeeter.
The Skooter.
The Teeter Bug.
The Dab says Daniel.
The Peach Pie.
The Sea-Hare.
The Wind Hover.
The Sea skimmer.
The glitter goer.
The salt sea shear.
Sea Plough.
Sea new.
Sea soarer.

Lots of these will do for when you tire of prohibition & open up the pubs again. They wd make very nice pub signs.

I hope that Mr. Davison[1] is now out of danger & doing well, & that your anxiety for him is at an end.

Lobsters & whales from us all.

from
John.

1. Henry P. Davison, 1862–1922, partner in J. P. Morgan & Co. and close friend of T.W.L., who wrote his (Davison's) biography.

[Boar's Hill, Oxford.]
[Aug 1921]

Dear Florence,

I am not very sure about your plans for this summer, nor how soon you will be coming over with Tommy[1] for the autumn term, nor how soon you go back to N.Y. to move into the new house. I am sending this to Maine.

You ask me, did I ever see a Baptism by total immersion. No. I never did, except rather far off, near the beastly village of Beer, which nothing seemed to keep you from going to. There I saw the waters of a stream dyked up, or as we say, stanked up (from the Spanish estanca a pond) to make a font, & an old geezer of a man of God standing in it (I think) up to his waist, before a large audience.

There is some account of some such thing in Hardy's Laodicean, which is a jolly book, but there the old geezer was robbed of his prey & got his small clothes wet for nothing.[2]

I don't know that Xtianity is on the wane. I don't think it is. It will flop along as people do, till something knocks it out, & the thing that knocks it out will be only a rediscovery of it as it originally was. I should say that there is more of the early church abroad now than ever in the world; & it is odd, how one sees the point of Diocletian & Nero & these other fellows, whom of old one held to be blackguards. Every half-baked little preacher of crude hysterics who would die for his creed is an early Xtian, and they disconcert the machine of this world like grit in a gear.

Did you ever read *the Century Bible?*[3] It is rather good fun, to see what tricks the corrupt texts have led the world into, & to trace the hands of editors in the making of the books. I've been reading the O.T. historical books, especially Samuel.

Why don't you get an American to film the story of *David* (in the Arizona Desert). Why don't you see to it right Now. Go get your movie king on the phone right now. Right Now. Do it Right now.
Lobsters from us all.

J.

1. Thomas S. Lamont, 1899–1967, eldest son of the Lamonts. He graduated from Harvard College in June 1921 and was a student at Trinity College, Cambridge University, for the academic year, 1921–2.
2. *A Laodicean* by Thomas Hardy, 1881. Few of his critics would describe it so favourably.
3. *New Century Bible* was a series of Bible commentaries edited by H. H. Rowley and M. Black, based on the text of the Revised Standard Version and incorporating the findings of Modern Old Testament studies.

[Boar's Hill, Oxford]
[23 Sep 1921]

Dear Florence,

Thank you for your letter about Gloomy Gus.¹ I'm sorry that we have not sent you someone with more pep. I must write to The Times about it, because, though no-one expects brains from our diplomatists, we do expect social charm. Perhaps however it was his off day; or more likely, he was knocked off his balance by you in your new frock smiling at him. Poor man, he had no chance; you should be more merciful.

You ask me in this letter (á propos of poor Gloomy Gus succumbing to the danger, & going down & out to the new pink) whether I like being in positions of danger. I do not. Whenever I have been in danger I have wished the danger in Jonadge's belly or myself elsewhere. I believe Sir Ian Hamilton enjoys danger, but I never met anyone else who ever did; unless it was a seaman I once knew, who crawled over 100 yards of gassy cargo every night to get at some bottled beer beyond. But he was one of those of whom it cd be said "He hadn't got the sense to be afraid".

I wrote the other day to say, that we had met a very nice young American man here. He has just sent us word that he has married a lady whom we had believed to be his aunt. Is this what people do in your country, & is it a sort of jeu d'esprit or a settled habit?

When do you go to Mexico? You will have a lovely time going to Mexico. It must be the most romantic spot in your hemisphere (next to New York) & I long to hear about it from you. When do you start?

I know nothing about "tinkers", but imagine them to be some abundant kind of fish. We all join in sardines to you.

John.

1. 'Gloomy Gus' – this may refer to Sir Aukland Geddes, British Ambassador to the United States, 1920.

[n.p.]
[9 Nov 1921]

Dear Florence,

Thank you so much for your most thrilling & interesting letters about Mexico.

, It is very strange, that the thing which makes a civilization should destroy it. A northern race goes down into the sun & is stimulated by the sun & does amazing things, as long as it has its faith. Then in some subtle way it is corrupted by the sun & goes to smash, losing faith & achievement & everything else, with sense of decency & style & everything. So I think it has been in Spanish America. The stern men with the superstition were undermined by the climate & now they are only mean men with a superstition, who make one feel, how vile democracy can be, in its degraded forms.

So you went to a bull-fight. I thought you would. And now you must be like the man in Harley's play, who went to France, & was sick going, & hated the cooking when there, & was sick coming back, but wouldn't have missed it. I suppose you wouldn't have missed your bullfight, fainting & all. It must be the nearest thing left to ancient Rome; the last thing left of Caesarism; except perhaps some of the Papal ceremonies. I never saw a bull fight, but have met Wilfred Blunt,[1] the old poet, who was once a matador. He says that the bulls aren't killed, but really commit suicide on the matador's espade. This may be some comfort to you.

You may know Señor Ibañez'[2] book on the toreador's life: Sangre y Arena, or Blood & Sand; it isn't bad.

How many hearts have you killed since you went away, & did they come & serenade you with guitars, & call you O luna mia, O hermosura divina, & these other things that sound so jolly & rich & melancholy, O hermosa rosa dulcissima, & the rest of it, O corazon de miel y de bondad.

Golly, if you were here, & I had a guitar, now that the moon is filling, I could beat them at their own game.

Greetings & thoughts & lobsters.

from
John.

1. Wilfred Scawen Blunt, 1840–1922, English poet and political writer. Author of *Love Sonnets of Proteus* (1880).
2. Vicente Blasco Ibañez, 1867–1928, radical Spanish novelist and politician, also the author of *The Four Horsemen of the Apocalypse* (1916).

Boar's Hill, Oxford.
[10 Dec 1921]

Dear Florence,

I am aiming this letter to reach you just upon Christmas Day, which it should just about do, with my best wishes that the day may be happy to you & yours, & the coming New Year a good year.

You will have received a copy of K.C.[1] from Macmillans, & I hope in a day or two to send you a poem by me, written for a memorial book in honour of good old Mr. Daniel. The book was printed on Daniel's type, & press, in the walls of the Bodleian here: the only book ever printed in the Bodleian & it is *almost* ready now, having been nearly ready for 6 months, & getting on to be ready for 2 years.[2]

I am sending you a copy, because you once sent the Daniels some chewing gum, if you remember, Old C.H.O. was a very fine fellow, a scholar & a Christian & a wit, & I love his memory. I'm afraid the verses are no great shakes.

I have been thinking about the part poets play in keeping people in memory. They do more than you imagine. Someday an American mother will make a nursery rhyme for her little boy; thus

Good old Woodrow Wilson,
Smashed the whisky-still, son.

& that will make W.W. immortal much surer than some darned historian with his "Perhaps Wilson's surest claim to the regard of posterity" etc.

The worst of poets is that a lot depends on the rhymes to the name they immortalise. You know the nursery rhyme about *King Cole*, who was a jolly old *soul*. It all depended on the available rhymes to *Cole* what kind of man the poet said he was. If his name had been Care, instead of Cole, the rhyme wd have been different.

> Old King Care
> Was a darned old bear
> A darned old bear & brute
> He called for his Glooms
> And his hearse with Plumes
> And he called for his funeral mute.

Then if his name had been Cass, the rhyme would have been different again:

> Young King Cass
> Was a silly young ass
> Devoid of sense to-*tally*
> He called for his joker
> And his game of poker
> And he called for his Corps de Ballet.

But if, on the contrary, his name had not been Cass but Cort, the poet would have viewed the subject from yet another angle, & would have said

> Bold King Cort
> Was a rare good sport
> A satyr with a rare good orbit
> He'd have won the Derby
> If he hadn't gone curby
> And he boxed 12 rounds with Corbett.

We are all awfully pleased at the way the Conference is going. It has been priceless, in clearing up situations over here, & your stock is standing very high indeed, & will stand higher yet.

Well, this is a feeble letter, but all I can squeeze out of a feeble brain. You are a jolly good friend, for you write splendid stirring & swinging letters, with great rich sultanas of plums of colour in them, & all you get in return is a thing like this, a sort of seed-cake kind of letter, with a few mouldy little carraways in it, to stick in the teeth & make one cough.

However you always were a jolly good friend & so you put up with it.

Blessings on you & lobsters from us all.

John.

1. J.M.'s poem, *King Cole*.
2. The book J.M. mentions was *A Memoir of C. H. O. Daniel, with a bibliography of the Daniel Press*. Edited by C. H. Wilkinson (Oxford 1921). Charles Henry Oliver Daniel was a pioneer in modern book production and ran his own press. Some of the early poems of Robert Bridges were issued from it. Daniel, who died in 1919, was Provost of Worcester College, Oxford.

[Boar's Hill, Oxford]
[17 Jan 1922]

Dear Florence,

It is a foul cold vile snowy sloppy filthy day so I am writing to you by way of a complete change. Did I tell you of the new Blake poem found in the Ducal attic? It is about just such another day as this.

> I wish to God that the spring were here,
> I wish to God that the winter were old,
> I wish the weather were not so queer,
> For assuredly it is very cold.
> I went to Church on the Christmas day
> To the chapel of Kings where the carols are
> And I came back with a gastric flu
> And I came back with a darned catarrh
> And I came back with a tem per a-
> ture of a hundred and three point five
> And I came back singing "well away
> I am the dreariest soul alive".
> And on my right is a black black germ
> And on my left is my aching head
> And in the midst is me like a worm
> And underneath is my little bed.

It is pretty to turn from such thoughts to the delightful fight, in which Carpentier, the artist, triumphed over the craftsman. It was like a set-to between Shelley and Keats. It pleased us all, because C had been so gallant in his hopeless fight with Dempsey, who is in a class above him: as fine a boxer & twice as strong.[1]

I write in my shack, surrounded by little birds who come in the cold for crumbs. They are finding this a very hard winter & are tamer than I have ever known them. If I had a whiter conscience I should feel a little like St Francis of Assisi. Poor things, we should be put to our trumps, if we woke, as they do, each morning, not knowing where the day's food would be. Someone says we ought to take no thought of the morrow. A nice reckless world we should have if we didn't, without any bother & without any order & without any art and without any life.

I hope that you are really better now.

Greetings & Brit. (Brit is what whales live on. It is billions of little fish.)

John.

1. William Harrison Dempsey (Jack Dempsey), 1895–, American heavyweight boxing champion 1921–26. Defeated Georges Carpentier in 1921.

[Boar's Hill, Oxford]
[1 Feb 1922]

Dear Florence,

I am glad about Tommy, & hope that all will go well with him, & that she is one with whom you will always be intimate & a friend.[1] I expect, being a grandparent isn't as bad as one fears. It is a natural process, like dying or breathing, & it isn't a kind of greatness one achieves: it is thrust upon one. It will be a score for your mother, too, d'être grande grandemère.

An O.M. is an Order of Merit.[2] Old Albert Edward instituted the order & made it very select for the very choice & the very famous & the very old. Barrie[3] is the only member under 70, & generally it is the last order you can receive before you die. It is the only Order here which means anything at all. If you are any of the other orders it may only mean that you have given good dinners enough to the right people, or subscribed enough to charity, but if you are an O.M. it means that you are one of 12 picked souls, of which only about one at any time doesn't quite deserve it, & therefore it is about 11 to 1 that you are a real dog. I don't know quite what the Order is; but it is probably some ugly little star.

Old Bryce,[4] who has just died, was an O.M., & there is wonder, who will have his place. Some suggest Gilberto, but others say he isn't old enough; others Conrad,[5] but he isn't English born; others this that & the other, even Shaw.[6] I suggest Growlio,[7] for the sake of his Quality.

This brings me to the question of Quality. You in your democracy have but one class. We, here, in what is left of a feudalism, have one & the ghost of another; we have the people, and the shadow of what was once called The Quality, in fact is still called so, in country places.

Quite recently, till 1/2 way through the war, the Quality was a reality. You could tell the officer from the man by the face alone. You could tell the lady from the not-quite-quite at a glance. There was here a race of people committed to a way of life & manners by birth and tradition, in which a distinguished quality alone greatly mattered. They were not very wise, perhaps, nor very broad-minded, nor very generous, but they had a high standard of courtesy and breeding and good manners, a fine "tact of exclusion" as Pater calls it, & they had about them a sort of unruffled readiness of fineness which I call "quality" whether it be in a book or a picture of a way of walking across a room. Neville has it, & Geoffroy hasn't; but it can't be explained, only perceived.

Blessings upon your kind head and heart, & many thoughts & thanks to you for the goodness of your friendship. My greetings to your Mother.

John.

---

1. F.C.L.'s eldest son, Thomas S. Lamont, was courting his bride to be, Elinor Branscombe Miner of Rochester, New York.
2. Instituted in 1902, this is an honour personally awarded by the sovereign.
3. Sir James Matthew Barrie, 1860–1937. Scottish dramatist and novelist. Author of *Peter Pan* (1904).
4. 1st Viscount Bryce, 1838–1922. Sometime Regius Professor of Law at the University of Oxford, and also a statesman and educationalist. Author of *The American Commonwealth* (1888).
5. Joseph Conrad, 1857–1924. Polish-born English novelist.
6. George Bernard Shaw, 1856–1950. Irish dramatist and critic.
7. The Masefields' special name for Robert Bridges, O.M., 1844–1930, British Poet Laureate from 1913 to 1930, and author of *The Testament of Beauty* (1928).

[Boar's Hill, Oxford]
[22 Feb 1922]

Dear Florence,

 Thank you ever so much for the lovely fire-lighter.
It came from Cape Cod & now has often lit
Fires at dawn & noon & has made our house the brighter
Partly with thoughts of you, partly with fire from it.
This is a little poem made out of my wit
For I am a witty dog and a pretty writer
And you are a beautiful friend & this is to wish you Brit.

I began this as prose, without a thought of verse, but you see what an inspiration you are. No sooner do I begin to write to Florence than the words go into measure & rhyme, & at once there is a poem.

 The other poem about my having "flu" was mainly a lie. I did have "flu" & felt like nothing on earth for 1 day but didn't go to bed & soon was well. All the rest of the family went to bed with it, but are now cured.

 There is 1 piece of news to tell you. The University of Aberdeen, the one I told you of, that was looking for a Professor of English, & would have taken RN[1] had he been here, has just decided to make me a Doctor of Laws so I have to go north next month to receive the honour. Aberdeen is all built of grey granite & it looks pretty grim, but it is a fine city, & the University is peopled by Highlanders & Hebrideans, & has on its staff some of the picked men of our time: Adam Smith,[2] & J. Thomson,[3] so it is a great honour: would I deserved it: a lot I know about Law, human or divine. I expect I'll have to buy a red gown & a John Knox[4] cap.

A friend is collecting "as" sayings such as "as proud as a dog with 2 tails" or "as helpless as a cat in hell with no claws" or "as blank as the year one". Can you tell me of any American as-es?

Best thoughts & superior herring-roe.

from

John.

1. R.N., i.e. Robert Nichols.

2. Sir George Adam Smith, 1856–1942. Principal of the University since 1909, and a noted Old Testament Scholar. Author of *The Historical Geography of the Holy Land* (1894).

3. J. Arthur Thomson, Professor of Natural History.

4. John Knox, 1514?–1571, Scottish religious reformer and founder of Scottish Presbyterianism. Went into exile on the Continent after accession of Catholic Mary I to English throne.

[Boar's Hill, Oxford]

[Mar 1922]

Dear Florence,

Thank you for your letter about the Nevi dinner. You never let *me* give a dinner in your house. You would have had much more of a show if you had. I would have asked you, & Judge Hand,¹ & Mr. Julian Street,² & an awfully nice man called Russell Loynes,³ & a friend of yours, Mr. Croly,⁴ to act as a chaperon to you, & then Mr. & Mrs. Gavit & Mr. & Mrs. Morrow.⁵ That would have been 10, with 3 ladies, each with 2 & one third men to herself. Of course your husband & Eleanor would have been of the party so that perhaps Mr. H.C. might have been shed, & some young swain substituted for Eleanor's sake. That would have been some feast; & afterwards we would not have played games, of what we would do if we were God, but we would have gone to Henekeys or Flannigans, whichever the place is called, to see the marvellous skaters swinging their wives around their heads & dancing "Goddesses" at 20 miles an hour. It would have been a memorable evening, & the guests would have written it up in their diaries in red.

Did I tell you, that the Vice Chancellor of this University, a conscientious man, with great powers, has been lately enforcing University discipline, & pulling tighter all the strings relaxed by the war & by young men back from the war?⁶ Well, he has been doing that, & has made himself disliked by stopping the young

men going into houses of refreshment, even for coffee, before
1 p.m. & similar rulings.

Lately, in England, there have been two cases of attempted
poisoning by means of arsenic inserted into the creams of choco-
late-creams.

Well, last week, a box of chocolates was sent to the Vice
Chancellor, who opened it, & happened to notice that one or two
of the chocolates had been tampered with. He at once sent for the
leading Chemistry Professor here, who advised him not to touch
the chocolates till they had been analyzed. The V.C. sent the box
to Scotland yard, who at once analyzed the tampered chocolates.
They found what they described as a "subtle Indian drug" in
them. This roused the nation, for it at once seemed likely that one
of the Indian students had tried to poison the V.C.

At this point, the culprit confessed. It was all a rag invented by
a young undergraduate to fool the V.C. The "subtle Indian drug"
turned out to be the substance called ZOG, a kind of metal polish
much used here. I expect you have seen advertisements of Zog.

"Where other preparations fail
    Use Zog.
Zog will get it off.
"Out, out, damned spot." Shakespeare.
    Z O G.
In boxes, of every Chemist."

I hope you'll have a lovely time at Asheville, & wish I were
nearer, so that I could send you a telegram every day to tell you of
the fish.

from
John.

1. Judge Learned Hand, 1872–1961, of the United States Circuit Court in New
York State. A close friend of the Lamonts. Frequently referred to by J.M. as 'the
judge'.
2. Julian Street, American author, 1879–1947. Author of *Abroad at Home*.
3. Russell Loines, 1874–1922, American poet and friend of the Lamonts.
4. Herbert Croly, 1869–1930, American political writer and Editor of *The New
Republic*.
5. Mr and Mrs Dwight W. Morrow.
6. The Vice-Chancellor of Oxford University at this time was Lewis Richard
Farnell (1856–1934), a Classical scholar and Rector of Exeter College. He held
the position between 1920 and 1923.

[Boar's Hill, Oxford]
[13 Jul 1922]

Dear Florence,

I hope that your fevered time in N.Y. is now at an end, & that you are in your beloved Maine,[1] in one of your comfortable cool fogs. Why do you go to Maine? All you have to do is to instal a "cold chamber" or refrigerator in your N Y home, exclude callers, shut yourself in, & read philosophy. That will give you all the cool & all the fog you'll need.

"Yes," you will say, "that is so, but then, I couldn't plant your gorse seeds, & besides Mr Croly would find out I was home & someways he would find a way in & then he would bring in some hot air, the way these journalists do."

My gorse-seeds are coming up. I hope yours will, too. I am sending you a few other seeds to plant in Maine. They are the seeds of an English waterplant called Absent Friends: a very pretty thing, which grows pretty nearly anywhere, in any soil, damp or dry, but mustn't be planted in grass, as grass makes it shoot up & when it shoots up its flowers are dwarfed.

We had a lovely call yesterday from Mr. Owen Wister.[2] This was a great honour & pleasure to us.

But I must put that by now, to say, we went to R N's wedding.

He was married at St. Martins-in-the-Fields, a big, fine church, by Wren, near the National Gallery.[3] Sassoon was best man. Ozzy & Satchy[4] were there & Eddie M[5] & de Glehn[6] & 2 or 3 others of our gang, & of course a whole lot of the bride's friends.

The bells of St. Martins are some of the best in the world. They were cast at Gloucester where most good bells are cast. Note. *Bells* not Belly.

R N was looking very flushed & happy. Miss D looked like a very nice steady & sensible young woman. They were married in the abbreviated form, which takes about 15 minutes, & then they went off together.

Mr. J. J. Chapman[7] (whom I expect you know) said he thought that *the* place for R N was an American College & felt sure that somebody could arrange this for him, seeing that Princeton had already taken A. N.

Young Mr. Chapman is a fine young fellow. He & young Mr. Lewis have been here. Your young American scholars are splendid types: it is a pleasure to see them.

Best assorted algae.

from
John.

1. In 1920 the Lamonts had built a permanent summer home known as Sky Farm on the island of North Haven in Penobscot Bay, Maine.
2. Owen Wister, 1860–1938, American writer and author of *The Virginian* (1902).
3. St Martin in the Fields was not designed by Wren, but by James Gibbs, 1682–1754.
4. Sir Osbert Sitwell, 1892–1969, English novelist and poet, and his brother Sir Sacheverell Sitwell, 1897–, English art critic and poet.
5. Sir Edward Marsh, 1872–1953, civil servant and patron of literature. Editor of *Georgian Poetry*, 1912–22.
6. Wilfred Gabriel de Glehn, 1870–1951. Painter.
7. John Jay Chapman, 1862–1933, essayist and poet. Author of *Memories and Milestones* (1915).

Boar's Hill, Oxford.
[25 Jul 1922]

Dear Florence,

Thank you for your nice letter.

I was for a long time puzzled by what you meant by my having been busy: "interviewing weeping parents & things", but at last I caught your meaning. They have now ceased to weep & begun to growl, & it is all very sad, though it won't be such a complete ruin as we had feared. The parent was misguided when he said that his child "had raked the whole of her inside out for ever". He only spoke the partial truth.

Did I tell you that I went to take the chair at a Penal Reform Dinner in honour of Mr. Mott Osborne?[1] I don't know why they chose me for the job, but I knew Mr. Osborne's books, so I was glad to go. He is a fine fellow & made 2 excellent speeches during the evening, a main speech, & then a reply to criticisms. I don't know what the Americans there can have thought of us, for some of the people who had been asked to speak made sufficient asses of themselves. Among those who shone was Lord Charnwood,[2] whom I had not met before. He spoke well, & sincerely & amusingly. He reminds one strangely of Lord Robert Cecil & just a little of Hami.[3] Did you ever meet Hami? If not you must have heard us talk of Hami.

Lord C is writing a book on Teddy,[4] which ought to be pretty good.

I have been wondering how long it is since any one man here in England had such influence on the young manhood of his country as Teddy had in the U.S. I suppose Baden-Powell[5] has profoundly moved our young men, on rather physical lines, but on ideal lines I can think of no-one who can compare with Teddy for the last 2 or 300 years.

A week after the Penal Reform dinner I went to lecture in the Prison here. I lectured in the chapel to the prisoners, who sat 4 feet from each other (to prevent talking) & had warders on the look-out sitting over them. They were a pleasant looking set of men, with a few old convicts among them & a few young plug-uglies who stood out like the plums among the suet. All the serious crime in this land is now done by boys; everybody else has been changed by the war.

I noticed that whenever I spoke loudly, or made a laugh, a kind of wash of conversation broke out among the audience; so I did my best to give the poor fellows a chance to get as much of this as was possible.

Afterwards, they shewed us the prison. The chief warder looked upon it all as a sort of conservatory of rare human plants. He had everything in that kind of speckless efficiency which I know (from my time in ships) can only be had at the expense of human feeling. The flowers in the garden were not only trim, but polished.

Well my blessings & thoughts to you dear Florence & many abundant little minnows.

from
John.

1. Thomas Mott Osborn, 1859–1926, American prison reformer.
2. Lord Charnwood (Godfrey Rathbone Benson), 1864–1945, biographer of Abraham Lincoln.
3. General Sir Ian Hamilton.
4. President Theodore Roosevelt, 1858–1919, whom J.M. greatly admired. Lord Charnwood's book was published in 1923.
5. Lord Baden-Powell, 1857–1941, founder of the Boy Scout Movement.

[Boar's Hill, Oxford]
[8 Aug 1922]
Dear Florence,

I could not write to you last week, because Lew¹ was ill, with a complaint which proved to be appendicitis. It was diagnosed in what is called the quiet period, & 3 hours after diagnosis, he was operated on, & the thing removed. He has gone on very well ever since, & has been throughout, so far, a model case.

He is down in a big & pleasant room in Oxford, & is having a fairly cheerful time, for an invalid, & should be back here about the time this reaches you.

You ask me about T.H.'s² verse. A man's verse is a part of himself; it is himself. I don't think one ought to say "I admire so & so enormously, but I don't like his kind of soul".

T.H. has not always a smooth way with his trowel, but he builds his things very tight, & that, & not the smoothness, is the main thing. "Now God be thanked for dappled things."³ In verse, one ought always to be thankful for an individual, with a way of his own, & not the other fellow's way. When he likes, T.H. can be as smooth as any of them; & when he does not like, it is because he wants to drive in some nail pretty hard. He has done more exquisite writing than any living English man, & has put in his nails, too.

We expect Edward Reed here in a few weeks' time.⁴

How about that gorse?

We all send greetings & thoughts to you.

from
John.

1. Lewis C. Masefield, the Masefields' son.
2. Thomas Hardy, 1840–1928. English poet and novelist.
3. Gerard Manley Hopkins, 1844–89, 'Pied Beauty'.
4. Edward Bliss Reed, 1872–1940, American teacher of English literature, author and editor.

[Boar's Hill, Oxford]
[29 Aug 1922]

Dear Florence,

Will you tell me, please, when you write, what you (& Americans generally) think of Mark Twain,¹ & especially about his River books, (*Tom*, & *Huck*, & *Life on the Mississippi*?). I have been reading these lately. *Tom* & *Huck* I have known since childhood, but the *Life* I did not see till yesterday, & it has been a great pleasure to come upon it.

The Admiralty here issue huge numbers of *Books of Sailing Directions* for all the seas & oceans of the world, but I don't think they have a *Mississippi Pilot book* on their list, as probably few

British ships ever go above New Orleans. Will you very kindly ask someone if your Admiralty issue such a book; a book of statistics, bearings, sailing marks & buoy-descriptions for the river below St. Louis, Mo? I would be glad to have a book of that sort, & would bless your kindness if you ask about it for me, when you are in N.Y. again, & have time.

Most people like reading books, but a map or a sailing direction is as good as a book to me, especially if it show altitudes by shades of colour.

Nevi surprised us all by turning up suddenly last Sunday afternoon. We hadn't seen him for a year & more. He was in very cheerful fettle, but is now gloomy again, owing to Collins's[2] death.

He is off for Vienna in a few days' time. There is a general rush to Vienna in these days. Five young poets from here (one of them an American) have just gone there in order to walk to Athens. I suppose this would be like walking over the Rockies to the coast from Utah. We had a note from them, to say that they had bought a boat for a million Kronen (ten pounds at present prices). I suppose poets could not resist the opportunity of paying a million anything. It will probably jar their original scheme a good deal. I would hate to carry a boat on a walk over the Balkans.

I was in London last week on business & went to a very bad play. There was one joke in the play. The bailiffs removed a man's bedroom furniture. Presently the man's wife came to call (she & he living apart.) She asked, what had become of the bed. The man said "Mice. You can't think what I suffer from mice here".

That is the kind of play I've been seeing.

The books I've read are Courteline's,[3] *Boubouroche, Le Train de 8.47* & *"Gaites d'Escadron;* & A France's *Petit Pierre & P. Rozière,*[4] & Jammes' *De l'age divin* etc.[5]

Best thoughts & remembrances

John.

---

1. Mark Twain (Samuel Langhorne Clemens), 1835–1910. author of *Tom Sawyer* (1876), *Life on the Mississippi* (1883) and *Huckleberry Finn* (1884).
2. Michael Collins, 1890–1922, Irish revolutionary leader, assassinated by Irish extremists.
3. Georges Courteline (Georges Moineaux), 1887–1915. French writer of humorous plays, tales and novels. *Boubouroche* was published in 1893, *Le Train de 8.47* in 1888, and *Gaités d'Escadron* in 1886.
4. *Petit Pierre & P. Rozière* (1899) by Anatole France.
5. Francis Jammes, 1868–1938. French poet usually grouped with the Symbolists.

[Boar's Hill, Oxford]
[14 Sep 1922]

Dear Florence,

I could not write last week, as I was away in B Nag¹ all the time, down in the south.

First of all we went to Stratford, to see *Hamlet* at the Festival there. It was a good performance, much better than any Shakespeare being done here at the present time, & better than any that was done when I was young. Harley did not live in vain: he killed the old bad tradition, which I suppose had better be called the Tennysonian tradition, of acting W.S.; that is, leaving out all the force & all the manly & godlike, & putting in all the puling & all the wool work & all the sentimental attitudinizing, of the curate, & his mother, & his wife. Now they do almost all the play, with a rush & sweep, & it is marvellous to watch the great texture unfolded.

After the play, we went across the street & had tea with a gang of actors, some of whom had acted for me in the past.

I don't know how you feel about actors. I love them. I like that vagabond artist feeling, which they give, of depending solely on themselves, & of being, all the same, initiate into the mystery. Poets & artists are often cleverer in their minds & talk than actors, yet I never feel about them that they live also in another world, like actors & circus-men.

After Stratford, we went careering down to see T.H. now 82. He was pretty cheerful, but I felt that he was less sure of his memory than a year ago.

We talked of the horrors perpetrated by our ancestors, in the way of whipping & hanging. He told a cheerful tale of a boy of 17 hanged a century ago *for being present* when 2 men set a rick on fire.

It was thought that extra heavy chains might make the boy hang the quicker, so special chains were made for him, & after he had been hanged in them, they were made into paper-weights & other little knick-knacks, which are still preserved in the district as souvenirs of the good old times.

After this we careened along again, up & down hill, with our brakes catching fire whenever we used them much. When we noticed a cloud of smoke we would pull up at a cottage, beg a bucket of water, put the fire out & then sail on. We passed 2 nights in an old haunted house, where the ghost is a priest with a sword, but he didn't bother us at all, & then we passed 2 more nights in a haunted house where the ghost is a headless man, but he didn't

bother us at all. Then we drove home by way of Shaftesbury &
Stonehenge.

Stonehenge is now all spoiled by a great camp almost on top of
it. When it was alone on the down it was awe-ful; now it is not.

Best greetings & rorquals to you.

John.

1. Refers to 'Black Nag', the name Masefield gave to his erratic Overland car.

[Boar's Hill, Oxford]
[22 Oct 1922]

Dear Florence,

I have been gadding about the country, lecturing, for the last 10
days, & seem to have been standing chiefly on my head & talking
through my hat, as lecturers usually do. I went into Shropshire,
where the Masefields had their beginnings, & talked in what was
(if not their native) town at least their market town, & also,
curiously, the market town of the ancestors of Synge. I want now
to rout out some of the older Masefields and look at their family
trees, & find out whether far far back the Masefields & the Synges
intermarried (they were Sings, not Synges in those days). It would
be very interesting to me to find that they did, though I hardly
expect to be able to find it, because I felt curiously akin in mind to
Synge,¹ especially as I came to know him better, right at the end.
Shropshire, that is a good place to start from. You never went
much into Shropshire, that is the one blemish one could in a
critical moment find in your make-up. If you had gone much into
Shropshire you would be too good for earth. A. E. Housman who
wrote the *Shropshire Lad,²* has now written a book of *Last Poems*, to
crown his old achievement with. I am sending it to you. It is, as it
were, distilled essence of Shropshire, and will teach you a little of
what you missed.

It is still curiously like the 18th century in Shropshire: people
drink a lot; & think Squire a mighty man & Parson a deep one, &
on holidays people go out & give a Welshman a black eye. This
they do as the prayer book says "not grudgingly nor of necessity,
for God loveth a cheerful giver".

Mrs. Wheeler has now sailed for America once more. She was
Isabella in *Measure for Measure*.

The Brett Youngs³ were here last week, & hope so much that

they may, when they go to America in January, be allowed to present a letter from me to you, introducing them. I think you will like them. He is a shade like Hugh. She is perhaps liker Violet Bongy than anyone else. He is a delicate man, so please save his life as you saved mine & Nevi's and Robert's.

Bless you, most kind Florence.

John.

1. John Millington Synge, 1871–1909. Irish dramatist, prominent in the Celtic revival and author of *The Playboy of the Western World* (1908).
2. Alfred Edward Housman, 1859–1936. English poet and classical scholar.
3. Francis Brett Young, 1884–1954, English novelist, and his wife Jessica. Many of his novels, including *Portrait of Clare* (1927), were set in the Welsh border country familiar to Masefield from his youth.

[Boar's Hill, Oxford]
[10 Nov 1922]

Dear Florence,

Gilberto looked in today, to say, that he is standing for Parliament, but that he is forbidden to canvass or to speak. I don't think he'll get in, but if he does, there will be 4 or 7 years gone, of a life that is singularly choice.

The temptation to affairs comes to men of thought at the age at which men of affairs feel the temptation to write their memoirs. It is the gout of the soul in both cases.

Here is the election on us, with the toshers yelling each his tosh. "A vote given to ----- is a vote given for UnEmployment." "Your Beer will cost you MORE." "Vote for ----. Peace, Plenty and Retrenchment."

It is such a pleasure to turn from such things to consider you. Hurray for you. Vive Florence.

John.

[Boar's Hill, Oxford]
[15 Nov 1922]

Dear Florence,

It must be a clever doctor to make you take a rest; good for him; & jolly good for you.

I shall be needing a rest cure soon, but in this country rest-cures are taken standing & cost from 3^d to 4^d the pint. A complete rest-cure costs about 2/– but it used to be less before the war.

The election is on still, and again a German Jew comes to ask for my vote. It will be a very odd Parliament, rather reactionary & yet stagnant, & indeed people are weary still, & I daresay politics will not move much for the next 3 or 4 years. A lot of youngish men are standing, but fewer than one expected. The youngish men who were in the war are now finding it hard to live, so that few of them are in affairs.

You might think, from this, that this is a land of disillusion, but it is not that. There is an immense spiritual & social ferment going on, outside all the old machines of politics and arts. If I were younger, I should enjoy it more, but I am still young enough to see its good side. 20 years ago I was one of a company called The Theatre of Beauty, vowed to produce, among other things, Shelley's *Cenci*. We didn't produce the *Cenci*, nor any other play whatever, nor even a prospectus.

Yet now the *Cenci* is being done in London, the ban removed, & the house crowded. It is a bad play, with 5 good moments in it, & it is not well done, the speaking bad, the colour hot, & the action slow; yet the fact that the thing is done at all shows such a change, an inconceivable change. 2500 people yelling hooray for Shelley in a London theatre on a foggy afternoon. "O what a change is there, my countrymen."

You asked me about the Reeds. We have had no cook, as you know, so have not seen them here yet. I have met E.B.R.[1] 3 times however, & his wife once. Now that Lucy is returned, we hope to have them out here. E.B.R. was just behind us at the theatre the other afternoon, not at the *Cenci*, but *Ambrose Apple job*.[2]

What is your frank opinion of London? Gentle shepherd, tell me what.

Best greetings & thoughts to you & a swift recovery from all the germs.

from

John.

I went hunting, last week in Black Nag, or rather went to a meet. It is as lovely a sight as ever. There was an old man of 90 out who had first hunted with the pack 70 years before, to a day. So cheer up about old age.

---

1. Edward Bliss Reed.
2. *Ambrose Applejohn's Adventures: an Arabian Nights Entertainment* (New York 1921) by Walter Hackett, 1876–1944.

Boar's Hill, Oxford
[1 Dec 1922]

Dear Florence,

I was delighted to hear of Mr. Noel's flinging the telephone through the operator's door. It was a poetical act. He did what others only dream; & a grateful country ought to have subscribed his fine. I hope that your gay act in sending the cutting came from a gaiety of mind at being at peace in your hospital.

We did *Macbeth* last week (for 3 nights) & this gave me a feverish week of it, as I was producer & 2nd witch; Judith, Lady Macduff. It was a huge success, & we are urged to repeat it in Oxford, which we hope presently to do. Our Macbeth was a local man, & quite first rate. He carried the play on his shoulders, & by his voice & grace & beauty. Old Nevi came down for the last night, & we all drove home at the end of it, in the bus, sleepy but full of glory. We had a lovely cauldron scene for the witches burning methylated with green & red flares, & then hydrochloric & ammonia fumes for smoke, the witches all men. We had 2 new men as murderers, both very promising, & all our old men showed improvement.

Last week I was away at Kendals, & heard a tale of Wordsworth. W.W. was saying to a friend:— "People say that I have no sense of humour, but I have a sense of humour, & showed it no later than today. I met a man in the road, who said, 'Sir, have you seen my wife anywhere?' 'Why, sir', I said, 'I did not even know that you were married.'"

I hope that this may raise a smile upon your cheek. I expect that you may think it somewhat feeble after a Chaplin film. It amuses me.

Best greetings & thoughts.

from
John.

Last week we had a surprise visit from the Derby's.[1] Teddy's daughter & her husband.

---

1. Dr Richard Derby and his wife, Ethel Roosevelt Derby, daughter of President Theodore Roosevelt.

[Boar's Hill, Oxford]
[2 Dec 1922]

Dear Florence,

Thank you so much for your charming kindness about *the Mississippi(!) Pilot*. It reached me this morning, & gives me huge pleasure. If I were able to spare the time I would study it for a month on end. I know nothing quite so perfect, as a life, as being a pilot on a river like the M or the Amazon, & going up & down, on water, in ever changing landscapes, & having ample leisure for the arts, a sonnet in the dog watch, a sketch in the morning watch before Turn-to, a bit of some handicraft before dinner, and then a book or a play before bed: or perhaps a tie-up at a city & a visit to a theatre or a concert. Sometimes, when I am driving home at night, I fancy myself to be steering along a river, & think to myself, "how perfect a steersman I am: golly I can steer to a $\frac{1}{2}$ inch". Then my lights go out, & I am but a man again. I do think that no-one can have so good & perfect a friend, for you must have had weeks of anxious enquiry rousting out these charts. Thank you so much for your thought & kindness.

Tomorrow, I am posting to you, the large paper R R (a very pretty book it makes).[1] It should go to you on Dec 5 & be in your hands about Dec 15, which day I'll be playing the Ghost in *Esther* in Oxford.[2] I am also going to send you notices of our Macbeth. I should say *your* Macbeth.

Blessings & thoughts
from
John.

1. In 1922 Masefield's poem about a race horse, *Right Royal* (1920), was issued in a large paper edition, with illustrations by Cecil Alden. There was also a limited edition of 350 copies.
2. *Esther* was J.M.'s translation of Racine's *Esther*, with additional matter of his 'own. This includes a scene in which King Ahasuerus is visited by the spirits of the dead in sleep.

Edinburgh.
[1 Mar 1923]

Dear Florence,

I wrote to you last night saying that I was coming here; now here I am, looking out on the Castle.

I believe that you have stayed here & looked out on the castle, & I wish you were staying here now & could come exploring this morning, which would be better fun than judging boys & girls as they repeat Twinkle Twinkle Little Star. As I believe that you once said that you had stayed here, I will not describe what I see. It is Edinburgh as it always is, an everchanging strangeness & solemnity of beauty. Everybody looks very strong. Even the dead look stiffer than elsewhere if I may judge from the graveyard across the way.

Up on yonder rock James the Sixth & First was let down by a basket over the wall, by a lady at least as doubtful as the lady who did the same sort of thing in the Bible. George Borrow[1] was once up there in the barracks. Darnley was blown up just round the corner.[2] Burke & Hare plied their private & profitable morgue within four hundred yards of me, & perhaps "howkit the deid" from this very cemetery.[3]

The sun here emerges from cloud & makes the castle again a totally new thing, of most lovely beauty. Burns[4] was here, & Scott,[5] & Raeburn,[6] & lovely Ramsay;[7] & my good old grandfather a century ago sat near where I sit & painted something of what I still see, in water colours.

To go on with history; David Haggart[8] was hangit, & so was Deacon Brodie,[9] just at the back of the Castle. And near the same place Madeline Smith was tried for murder & acquitted.[10] I met an old lady 2 days ago, whose father had taught M. Smith in English History classes. He said that she was very lovely, very clever & very brave, & that everybody felt at the time that even if she had poisoned the man, he deserved it & that she should go free.

The old lady added that at the time of the murder, the elderly man to whom Madeline was engaged, gave up the engagement. He did not afterwards marry, but lived on, as a bachelor, to a vast age, & died only a year or so ago.

Greetings & remembrances & thoughts to you. I wish you could come to see me judge. "Solemn" as a judge should be changed to "Bored" as a judge.

from
John.

1. George Henry Borrow, 1803–81, English traveller and writer. Author of *The Bible in Spain* (1843) and *The Romany Rye* (1857).

2. Henry Stewart, Earl of Darnley, 1545–67, married to Mary Queen of Scots and father of James VI. Presumed murdered in plot 10 February 1567.
3. William Burke 1792–1829, and his partner William Hare, who jointly kept a lodging house, made a practice of murdering elderly pensioners and selling their bodies to Dr Robert Knox for dissection purposes at his School of Anatomy. Burke was hanged after more than fifteen murders, but his partner got off on a technicality.
4. Robert Burns, 1759–96, Scottish poet.
5. Sir Walter Scott, 1771–1832, Scottish novelist and poet.
6. Sir Henry Raeburn, 1756–1823, eminent Scottish portrait painter.
7. Allan Ramsay, 1685–1758, Scottish poet, best known for his '*The Gentle Shepherd*'.
8. David Haggart, 1801–21, thief and homicide from the age of twelve. Eventually hanged.
9. William Brodie (d.1788), deacon of the incorporation of the Edinburgh Wrights and Masons. Also a burglar leading a double life and finally hanged.
10. Madeleine Smith was on trial for the murder of her lover in 1857.

[Boar's Hill, Oxford]
[3 Apr 1923]

Dear Florence,

Thank you so much for your kind letter about the lecturing chances.

I have felt, that it would be better to put off the tour for at least another year, & perhaps come in 1924, if Mr. Keedick¹ would take me on. Then, I might come in the summer & stay on till December perhaps. I would like to try some recitations, this time; to see how far a modern poet can hold people by speaking verse. I am all for a 3-stringed lyre & speech: the printing press is a mistake: one of the many mistakes that the Renaissance made.

You write in the midst of snow: we are in the midst of summer: fruit blossom out, even on the hill here, & all the hedges green, & at least a month forward. As the poet wrote (in a translation of a German play)

"The little little lammikins
Frolic with their dammikins."

Did I tell you that Geoffroy came over here for an exhibition in Oxford? He did. It was a jolly fine exhibition, with some of his very choicest landscapes & some exquisite drawings of little children's heads; you could not have better. We had lunch together & he said nice things about you. Anybody would do that of course but he said them worthily. Now he has gone back to his home. I wish that either he were not French, or the French were less aggressive on the Ruhr. I worry lest their being on the Ruhr should send the whole of cynical old Germany & enthusiastic new Germany lock stock & barrel to the Left, into Bolshevism & smash.

I am reading a nice book called *A Colorado Tenderfoot*, by an old Oxford don called R. B. Townshend.[2] About 60 years ago the old fellow went out for some years to the far west & had a wild & woolly time, & now at the age of about 85 he writes down what he remembers. He sure was the Bingo. Of course, you probably shrink from the records of crime & disorder, but to English people they are absorbing reading. Look at the success of the *Newgate Calendar* & Capt Johnson's *Lives of the Celebrated Highwaymen*.[3]

I wonder do you ever have the London pleasure of grubbing among old books in frowsty 2nd hand bookshops, & picking up good things cheap, & fine old bits of printing for 2d, & nice old engravings at 1d each, & sometimes an early Voltaire, or a nice little foxy Dryden, with a copper frontispiece.

That is one of the jaunts you must someday make, so as to have a row of dumpy twelves in calf, over your bureau. Thoughts & remembrances.

from
John.

1. Lee Keedick, 1879–1959, American manager of a successful U.S. lecture bureau that for many years scheduled numerous lectures for J.M.
2. *A Tenderfoot in Colorado* (1923) by R. B. Townshend.
3. *The Newgate Calendar; or, Malefactors' Bloody Register*, an immensely popular collection of true-life crime stores first published in or about 1774. Later editions incorporated Captain Johnson's *History of the Celebrated Highwaymen*.

[n.p.]
[7 Apr 1923]

Dear Florence,

I am sorry to hear about the neuritis. It is a devastating thing, but our general feeling is, that it lifts & goes as suddenly as it comes, so I hope that by the time this reaches you it will be completely gone. I feel specially sad always, when I think of you being laid up by anything, because you have such energy & go that the restraint of ill health ought never to be laid on you. You ought to be free as the comet.

And it was so good & kind of you to think of sending a gift to the players while you were ill thus. Thank you so much for this. We re spending 2/3 of it on clothes for *Jezebel*[1] & put the rest of it aside for our Building fund (little improvements in the room, stage etc).

We hope that you will be over in the summer. Do come along. We are going down to Cornwall for the bathing, & shall be able to go to Falmouth to see the ships, & especially to see the most famous of all sailing ships, & the swiftest, the old *Cutty Sark*,[2] now laid up there for a memorial forever (or till she drops to pieces). Lew shall photograph her for you whether you come or not.

I may have seen her masts long ago, unwittingly, because I was once in a port with her. I long to see her wittingly, because one ought to see the rarities of one's time, & this was a real rarity, a thing of wood & steel that could almost fly, the swiftest thing, & the thing nearest to flying before the Wright brothers came along.

You have seen most of the rarities of your time, & now you are having Lord Robert,[3] to add to the collection. I hope he will get up for breakfast for you. It will be the pity of his life if he doesn't. For you, he ought not to go to bed at all.

I have seen some of the rarities of this age but I cannot put my finger on any one as superlative, though at least half a dozen have seemed very big. The fault that one finds in them is the fault that one finds in modern life, that it has no faith, but occasional enthusiasm, & does not burn by flashes.

Greetings & blessings to you, & thanks & ever thanks for your friendship. I hope to hear that the neuritis is gone.

Whitebait & fry

from
John.

1. *Jezebel* refers to J.M.'s play *A King's Daughter* (1923).
2. The *Cutty Sark* has been transferred to the Thames at Greenwich, England, where it is expected she will permanently remain dockside and open to the public for inspection.
3. Lord Robert Cecil 1864–1958, outspoken member of the House of Lords, and a firm supporter of the League of Nations.

Boar's Hill, Oxford.
[7 May 1923]

Dear Florence,

I hope that you have had a smooth pleasant journey to Paris & that you are now enjoying the shops, & what is known and sold as cooking. Of all the frauds on this earth, the bubble reputations, think French shops & French cooking are the chief.

I was away nearly all last week, judging speaking in Glasgow & as usual after listening to a mass of poetry exquisitely spoken am as limp as a rag & cannot sleep. We are starting a speaking contest here in Oxford at the end of July, & we have challenged the best Glasgow (i.e. the best Scottish) speakers, to come to compete. They are coming, & I tremble for the result, for I know none who can compare for a moment with them.

We are sending a Fiery Cross round all the colleges to stir up men & women to defend the English reputation, but I'm afraid these Scots will beat our best. The Glasgow Festival was a most impressive thing (12,000 competitors in music & singing & speaking) & some rough teams of singers, from iron-foundries & ship yards, who sang like quires of nightingales, moved me to the marrow.

But what is a song that is sung beside the fact that you are now in Europe. Cheers & Trumpets.

I hope you will not fail to come here as soon as you can for as long as you can.

Welcome to these shores.

John.

[Boar's Hill, Oxford]
[31 Jul 1923]

Dear Florence,

Last week was something of a nightmare of rush & worry, because of the recitations.[1] We had to jam 4 hard days' work into 2 days, & did just manage to do it & come out alive. Next year we will hope to do it ever so much better. Even as it is, we have done it without provoking any criticism; except, no doubt, the silent criticism of those who did not reach the Finals & felt that they were unjustly kept out of them. We rewarded almost all who really deserved reward, & encouraged others, & those who have written to us since, seem to have been blissfully happy. The English speakers were the best. The English won the things that mattered. The Scots were good, but seemed immature whenever they competed with our best. They were of course far better than our second best.

Some of the speaking was more beautiful than any I have ever heard. The 4 poets judging have been in a kind of trance from it ever since.

Rumour is already saying, that Cambridge is going to start a similar contest next year. If this should be, then we shall have begun to turn the educational machine towards beauty and the arts again.

You ought to have cast aside Maine & everything: family, friends: all things: & come to hear this speaking.

I'm so glad that the gorse has sprouted. It will grow *very very very* slowly for 5 years, & then leap aloft. It burns like paraffin, so be careful not to fling hot cigarette ends into it on windy days.

Bless you.

from

John.

1. For many summers, 1923–9, the Masefields organised and presided over the Oxford Recitations, a competition in which men and women from all over Great Britain came to recite verse. The Recitations were held in the Poetry Room at Oxford University.

[Boar's Hill, Oxford]

[6 Sep 1923]

Dear Florence,

A long search has failed to bring Mr. Alber or Alver or Abracadabra his letter to light: it is gone. Then, by lot or fate it happens, that I have misst Mr. Keedick here, not hearing of his presence till he had started for France.

I quite agree that this writing is perfectly ugly and bad, but it is trying to become better. I want to do some things better than I have been doing them. Writing is one of the things.

I have (like most middle-aged men) very little time for self improvement, and writing is one of the things which I have to do, so I can at least try to do that with a grace. At present, I have not attained to the grace, nor to any other power over it, but the effort is well worth the while, and the study of noble forms of writing has been a pleasure to me.

And when I take up a thing, I generally get some power at it before I lay it down. Look at my chauffeuring, my carpentering, my sewing-on-of-buttons-ing. Julia says I sew on buttons tighter than anybody. That shows you the kind of man I am when I'm determined.

I am distresst about your news of R.N. & G.C.

It seems to us that, if the Tokyo University be destroyed, R.N. will not return thither. I cannot see him finding peace in the Movey business but one never knows. I don't think he quite reckons with the types of brains with which *his* brains will have to work in the Movey trade. He is not very tolerant of his fellows, nor old enough yet to see what allowances have to be made for people. I think he would do it better than teaching; & it would be streets better for him than this accursed dog's job of reviewing, to which our clever lads are turned till their skulls are sick.

A dramatic duologue about the Earthquake.

Ille. Five hundred thousand yield the ghost.
Illa. How shocking. Will you pass the toast?

Best shrimps & prawns & Cornish pilchards.
John.

By the way, you will like M. Gaston Leroux' new book *Les Avantures de Cheri Bibi*, the first 2 vols of which have been publisht.[1]

Cheri Bibi is a bandit of good heart; rather like me, tho' less good at buttons.

1. Gaston Leroux, 1868–1927, French novelist.

[Boar's Hill, Oxford]
[25 Nov 1923]

Dear Florence,

The ink is freezing in my pen as I write, indeed, if I were writing to anyone casual, to whom I felt just ordinary & cool, it would surely freeze, but as it is to you that I write it keeps fluent.

The poor little birds hop at my feet for crumbs, & it is just freezing cold. The ink is frozen in all my ink pots, which I have only known twice before.

What would you not give to be in a nice cool English house at such a time?

I am off to Scotland tomorrow to speak for a week again, in the town of Glasgow, etc. I will write a proper letter from there, if I ever get there in this cold & fog.

I must fly or I shall freeze.
Blessings on you.
John.

[Boar's Hill, Oxford]
[1923?]

Dear Florence,

Once again I have to thank you for your generous kindness to these players. Your gift shall go entirely to fitting out my new play of *Jezebel*, which I hope will be done here at the end of May.

The Chatauqua[1] people have not bothered any further about me, so that I suppose they do not really want me, & therefore do not look for me this summer; but do not say alas; say, rather, "3 cheers, now I can come to France and England". When may we look to see you?

A year ago, we started "intensive playing" with a mixed company about 2/3rds of whom had never acted, nor heard, nor read a line of verse. In the 11 months since we started we have performed:

King Lear. 2 performances.
Iphigenia in Tauris. 1 performance.
The Alchemist. 2 " s.
Esther. 5 " s.
Measure for Measure. 2 " s.
Macbeth 5 " s.
The Winters Tale 1 "
Two Molière farces 1 "

In all 19 nights playing, and 9 plays, or a play a month, for we do not play in the summer. All this is largely made possible by your gifts, (for we mount the plays beautifully now), and although the quality of our productions is still poor, it is improving. You cannot make a trained artist in 11 months out of anybody that comes along.

We have just finished *The Winter's Tale*, which the men were very happy in, & the women (I think) rather harassed. It is a very beautiful play, ripe & rich, & of the texture of *12th Night*, but maturer; that is most noble romance. Hay was most feeling as Leontes. If he would speak verse liker a poet he would be a fine actor. I watched his face from the wings in the statue scene, & saw how intensely he was stirred. J was Perdita; most charming. I was old father Time & felt it in every pore. The men don't care much about coming to rehearsal, but they deeply love "the night", & the ragging in the dressing rooms & above all things the dresses, and the "make-ups" on their faces. Ladies are not vain when compared with men; perhaps because the desire to look nice is habitual with them. The looking glass is always thronged by men 6 deep.

You ask about artists having their skill prolonged beyond an instant. That is true of the best ones, but only of the very best: growth is the rare thing: improvement with age; it is genius itself; and rare as genius; so rare that nothing is rarer.

Your old friend Pieface came up yesterday to tea, together with 4 Americans. I was beginning to fear that your country was wearying of me, but these 4 Rhodes scholars came yesterday to reassure me.

I like to see young Americans, for in them I look on the future of this civilized world.

Now greetings & thanks & blessings to you my most awfully good thoughtful kind helpful never failing friend.

from

John.

1. The Chautauqua Institution, dating from 1874, organises combined educational, recreational and religious activities, and has annual meetings at Lake Chautauqua in New York State.

[Boar's Hill, Oxford]

[8 Jan 1924]

Dear Florence,

I am plunged in doleful dumps, because it is now 2 weeks since I had a letter from you, & I fear one of three things:—

a. The influenza.

b. New York.

c. the children.

has been too much for you during the holidays.

I hope that this is not so, but that the silence is simply Christmas business pressing on one so truly kind that she makes Christmas seem like Spring to all.

This is New Year season; all good resolves & tidying up. I am tidying up my shack, & have already carted out and burned 2½ bushels of miscellaneous junk, including many pounds' weight of bad poetry. It is like in a sense dying & being born again. One comes upon all sorts of oddments, which one had forgotten. The most frequent find is a dirty unused envelope which has stuck fast n the damp: the next frequent is a piece of old candle. So far I have only found one mouse. He was rather like Polonius. "I nosed him as I went up the stair."

I am taming the birds this year. 3 or 4 of them come into my shack to eat; 2 chaffinches, 2 robins. They wait for me: know my hours; and are glad when I appear; about 15 come regularly to near my door & 4 come in. Two little rare fire-crests come, too, & are exquisite to watch. I preach to them sometimes, like St. Francis, but don't see much spiritual change in them; though as Carlyle said of Tennyson, they seem to say of me "I like to hear the body talk".

Greetings & thoughts
from
John.

[Boar's Hill, Oxford]
[14 Jan 1924]

Dear Florence,

Thank you so much for your very jolly letters, & for the lovely tale of your President. You have now told me lovely tales of three Presidents & made me feel that I understand American politics.

Your letter about Wytter B¹ made me very envious. Two years with the Pueblo Indians. That is indeed a thing to do, & to dip a spoon into a platter of strangeness. Are not you envious? Would not you give, say, one back tooth to have done it? Even to live for two years in the pueblo country would be much forever. I don't doubt that it has changed Mr. B. profoundly. I would rather have done that than gone to 50 Mexicos with 100 English novelists, or 1000 for that matter, with Fielding at their head.

I daresay I told you about La Chartreuse de Parme & Le Rouge et Le Noir. I read them all, some years before the war: but have no wish to read any of them again; nor indeed any novel, except Don Quixote, & Moll Flanders & parts of Jonathan Wild.

The Chartreuse was one of the test books of my particular gang, when I was beginning. If people liked it, we thought there was hope for them, if they did not like it, we reckoned them as damned. It is quite good. But it is not one of the books I would have been glad to have written myself. There is always something about a prose book which seems to a verse writer just as dull as gas light after sunlight. It is not a good enough kind of light. Put the whole

big Chartreuse beside one fine stanza of any fine poet, & it is just
nowhere at all. The novel exists because life is not exciting
enough: the poem exists because life has excited the poet. This is
not quite just, but near enough to go on with. Blessings on you &
thoughts

from

John.

You may be puzzled at my fondness of the Pueblos. I saw them
in N.M. & they moved me to the marrow. I have a picture of one
always fronting me in this shack, & whenever I see it, I think, that
is what wide-wayed Troy was like, & out of that came nearly all
the poetry that is truly living & stirring & forever lovely & lovely.

1. Witter Bynner.

[Boar's Hill, Oxford]
[21 Jan 1924]

Dear Florence,

I am grieved that you should have had the sorrow and shock of
the near presence of death.

Without a religion, death is hardly to be borne. With a religion,
it is a shattering thing. The affections are all we have, and there is
nothing left when those are taken, with no answer of where nor
why. The dumb unanswered anguish of this world is the only solid
earth under our feet. That is the certain thing: the rest is so
seemingly and relatively unreal: the earth, in the rain, with
thorns, is our background & stage.

Hope is the only solace. It is True (as the Bible says) that
"Upon them that Hope is his Mercy".[1] Hope makes mercy: it
makes whatever it hopes: eternal life or any other thing. That is
the only thing we have in the anguish. "Hope as an anchor of the
soul" in the very rotten holding-ground of this life and death.
Hope will pull you through. "Hope shone in him like a beacon",
someone who knew him said of Cromwell, "long after it had gone
out in all the rest". Think how splendid that sentence sounds &
how it makes life shine. How can death really touch anything like
that?

Still, as Adam Smith very feelingly says somewhere: "no child
ever died without breaking someone's heart". There is no herb in
the garden to medicine that.

I have written to Lee Keedick, to say, that I don't think we can manage America this year. The decisive thing is Lewis's going to Rugby. The fall will be his second term in Rugby & the second term, always a forlorn time, will be the cold & dismal autumn term, with no jolly cricket or bathing, but muddy Rugger on the clay. We just feel that Lew would feel frightfully forlorn & dismal if we were to be right out of England then. In 1925 he should be fairly on his feet; but this year he will still be a fag & a beginner.

I thank you most heartily for your very kind helpful thoughtful friendship in going to L.K. for me. I never thank you one tenth enough for all the many many things you do for me.

Bless you for them all.

With many thoughts,
John.

The Labour Govt begins today with another insane strike planned by a man with about as much brain as an angry hen.

1. Psalm 33. v. 18.

[Boar's Hill, Oxford]
[28 Jan 1924]

Dear Florence,

We are now in the throes of building or of being about to build. On Tuesday, the 22nd, the men turned up to begin. I, with a saw, cleared the first gorse-bush from the site; then they turned-to with a fagging-hook & a hatchet; & now the old jungle is gone; & they are trenching for foundations, on a site all pegged out with white wood markers. They say that they will be done in late June. We shall see.

The architect has made a very nice plan, & I think that you will like the looks of the place when built.

We went over to Rugby last week, to see what may be Lew's home for the greater part of the next five years. I daresay that you have been to Rugby, to see the places mentioned in Tom Brown;¹ but it was new to me; & it impressed me more favourably than any of the other big schools which I have seen. Marlborough perhaps runs it a close second.

We saw the room where Tom was roasted. It was the room in which Tom fought Slogger as it happens. It is a smallish room now used as a dining hall: the fireplace used for the roasting is now covered up.

In the chapel, they have a plaque of Rupert,[2] done from the sentimental photograph, and missing his chief beauties, his marvellous mouth & the weight of the upper head, & making him all pretty-pretty. They have a very beautiful memorial chapel, which has a more religious feel to it than any modern chapel I have seen. It made me feel again, that in this country, the memory of our 750,000 killed in the war will in time become a sort of religion of ancestor-worship.

It was a lovely day at Rugby, which, after months of cold & rain, was much; but, apart from that, I liked being in a place which had, in one century of time, produced or helped to form, Landor,[3] Clough,[4] M. Arnold, & Rupert as well as the game of football known as Rugby. Landor, as it happens, was expelled, but he was there for a while, first. As the Master said "He warmed both hands before the fire of life" too much.

We went yesterday to White Horse Hill again, by way of Hanney & Goosey and Kingston Lisle, which are villages you haven't seen. You would have loved to have seen the place on fire. They were burning off the grass, & a strong wind was driving the flame up the hill. We went up to the Roman camp, behind the fire: it is truly a noble hill. I thought of you there, & wished that you could have been there with us to have seen it in winter. It is lovelier even than in summer, & lovelier with you than without you.

I don't know why they were burning the grass, whether from sense of beauty or from a thought of bettering the sheep pasture. Men do odd things in this land because they have been done in the far past. Here in Oxford, about the year 1260, a man called Simon killed an undergraduate. Until about 1830, every graduate of Oxford, when receiving his degree, had to swear a Latin oath "that he would never be reconciled to the said Simon". However, since 1830, they have buried the hatchet & the ill feeling against Simon has died.

I daresay the burning of the grass is a part of some old religion, which that strange hill created & cannot let die. There is something holy and uncanny about all that strip of Down.

Now all good thoughts & blessings to you.

from
John.

1. *Tom Brown's Schooldays. By An Old Boy* (1857) was a novel about the famous nineteenth century English public school at Rugby, and a celebration of the ideals of its founder Thomas Arnold, 1795–1842, father of the poet and critic Matthew Arnold. The author was Thomas Hughes, 1822–96.

2. Rupert Brooke.

3. Walter Savage Landor, 1775–1864. Poet and prose writer, and author of the well-known lines,

> I strove with none, for none was worth my strife.
> Nature I loved and, next to nature, Art:
> I warm'd both hands before the fire of life;
> It sinks, and I am ready to depart.

4. Arthur Hugh Clough, 1819–61. English poet and close friend of Matthew Arnold.

[Boar's Hill, Oxford]
[29 Feb 1924]

Dear Florence,

We laid the foundation stone[1] today with many tender thoughts of you.

Under the stone, we put some American coins, some English coins, an address to St. Hugh, the saint of English builders, & a little poem by me & an inscription with it, thus:— "February 29th, Friday, being Leap Year Day, 1924, a violently westerly and north westerly gale blowing with squalls of rain.

> We lay this stone & hope this house[2] may be
> A home of friendship, mirth & poetry
> And may it be the home for many days
> Of many splendid, many merry, plays,
> And may we all enjoy it and get good
> From its companionship and brotherhood."

This, being copied out, with my mark of the cock, went under the stone which has your & our initials thus:—

C.M.[3]	F.C.L.
J.M.	T.W.L.

Con laid the stone, in a burst of sunshine (the only warmth for 3 weeks) & then we gave the 13 builders tea. The Architect and David Rice were the only guests, but with our household, it came to a party of 21. Lucy made a cake, a piece of which will go to you tomorrow. It was about 18 inches high & the same across, & we ate it all I think.

Special greetings & thoughts go to you on this occasion, & a feeling of the beauty and the depth of our friendship.

God bless you, dear Florence.

                                          John.

1. This was for a small building that later became known as The Music Room. In it J.M. staged many plays and concerts as long as he lived at Boar's Hill, and formed a small company 'The Hill Players' to be in charge. The construction of the building was mainly financed by the Lamonts.

2. The Music Room.

3. Constance Masefield, wife of J.M.

                              [Boar's Hill, Oxford]
                              [17 Apr? 1924]

Dear Florence,

I have been much interested by your stories of Gasparillo, but I wish to add a little criticism to them.

Pirate Gold.

The belief everywhere is for it: the evidence everywhere is against it, as Dr. Johnson said of the ghost.

What was the pirate's gold? Where did they get it?

The belief is that they took it from merchant ships.

I don't believe that they ever took any big merchant ships, & that their take of gold was very small. The big merchant ships which carried trading stocks as well as rich passengers, were well armed and manned, & able to beat off attacks by even the smaller ships of war. The pirates attacked small vessels in unimportant trades. They took very little gold: a few pounds in trading-cash and ship's money: perhaps a little could be made in the sale of the stolen cargoes.

The Lives of the Pirates show, that very few made more than a bare living at the game.

But granted that they made gold, why should they bury it?

"A long-boat full of gold" would weigh something like three tons. It would take some burying. A pirate-chief would do well, who could do the burying single handed in a hot climate. And to bury two Mexicans at the same time, so as to round off the plantation: it shows a sense of style.

An expedition went from here 18 years ago to dig for pirate gold (they had a chart drawn in blood on a white cambric shirt to guide them) but they didn't find any. They didn't find anything, except an iron ringbolt let into a boulder. That was a strange thing to find in a lonely isle in the Pacific, but it paid them no dividend, and they never learned why it was there. Why was it there? There was a rock on a hill in an islet 500 miles from anywhere, & in this rock there was an iron ringbolt, leaded into the rock.

Somebody sometime came and put it there for some pretty strong reason. He must have wanted to heave something heavy up the hill.

Long afterwards I met a sailor, who had searched for treasure on that island with all his ship's company, and had not found a cent. He was there a month with 300 men, & dug it all upside down, & got nothing but the exercise. But Gasparillo, I will hope, did bury some treasure some time, & perhaps presently lifted it & lived in style on some of it, with candy for all his twelve wives, so that a charming friend might some day write of it to me, to my great delight.

Long boats,
John.

Boar's Hill, Oxford.
[May? 1924]

Dear Florence,

What fun to think you must now be half way across the beastly sea. Hurray for your coming.

I've been to the Zoo aquarium, to get some new names so

Golden Cyclids
Lungfish
Garfish
Cyprodonons,
Miniature pike
Butterfly fish
& Chelodones
to you.
John.

[Boar's Hill, Oxford]
[16 Oct 1924]

Dear Florence,

Thank you for letting us know about the grandchild.[1] We were so glad to hear that all is well, & that you like the sensation d'être grandmère that I sent you a cable straight away. I hope that the cable people haven't made any hash in the cable, but sent it as it was. I'm sure that this excitement will have quite cured the neuritis.

Poor Nevi has neuritis, too, & is wandering England, electioneering with the P.M.: no grandchild for him to soothe his cares; nothing but the Tory egg & the Liberal cabbage on platform after platform.

Corliss[2] came up the other night & I hope will often come: he is a young man of whom you may well be proud. We are going to try to persuade him into being one of the crowd in *The Young King*.[3] We are rehearsing 3 times a week at present: & are in the doleful dumps stage which always comes just before the actors begin to know their lines. The work is ease itself compared with the exhausting struggle each rehearsal was at Wootton. Then the toil of a rehearsal laid one low the next day.

The actors sit on the stage under a radiator at the wing. They are in warmth, light & comfort & can see the whole show, such as it is, of me on tip toe in the hall telling them to put some pep into it. At the end of each rehearsal, we brew cocoa & tea & bring out buns, & each mouth that has been chewing blank verse is fed & refreshed with these carnal pleasures.

I think (& hope) that they like it. I wish you could see them at it, as it would make you so happy to see their happiness, which is so largely due to you.

Bless you. I hope the neuritis is gone, & the grandchild growing hourly.

John.

---

1. Thomas W. Lamont II, born in New York City 1 Oct. 1924, to Thomas S. and Elinor Lamont. He died in April 1945, when his submarine was lost in action in the Pacific Ocean in the war against Japan.
2. Corliss Lamont spent the academic year of 1924–5 as a student at New College, Oxford. He saw the Masefields frequently, bicycling up to their house at Boar's Hill for tea or supper.
3. By Laurence Binyon, 1869–1943, English poet and playwright.

[Boar's Hill, Oxford]
[29 Oct 1924]

Dear Florence,

I must say that I was amazed at the speed with which your letter came as an answer to mine. It was just like the old pre-war days, when sometimes an answer came from the U.S. in 12 days.

We are just back from a visit to a biggish public school: one of the important ones: the 4th of the really big ones that I have seen. I had to dine in hall, with the head, under 400 pairs of eyes.

It is not an old school, having been going only a century: but an old man there knew or had known the first head master, & had also known a man who fought at Trafalgar in 1805, so we were linked with the past sufficiently.

I thought the school nothing compared with Rugby, but it had a good feeling about it, & some beauty. I was allowed to read the first head master's diary, a sufficiently sickening record of Christian principle and mediaeval practice. There were entries like "disregarding his appeals for mercy I flogged him soundly and noticed with satisfaction later that he was still crying at tea time." "To our amazement —— stood up in hall & had the impudence to say that he did so because he had not enough butter."

I am ever so glad that you're better.

Corliss was here last night. He is much enjoying Oxford, I think. Blessings

from
John.

[Boar's Hill, Oxford]
[17 Nov 1924]

Dear Florence,

We opened the room[1] on Thursday with a very fair performance of *The Young King*. Thank you so much for your most kind cable of good wishes.

Corliss, I'm glad to say, was able to be present, & was photographed on the stage afterwards with us. We had 5 photographers blazing away at us with more or less result, & some of the results I hope to have for you during the week. The men played up in a way that did my heart good. The Maniac was superb & Knipe very fine & moving. The two Hays & young May were different beings & acted with real beauty, helped by their very great personal beauty, being all 3 fine lads to look at. I forget if you saw them. Hay was John in K.D. & May Ahaziah.

The author had a good call. Lillah spoke the prologue, & I made a little speech, & Rayson the architect played the dance music & God save the King. All went with good feeling and friendliness from first to last. I wish you could have been there on Saturday, when the room was packt to congestion. I thought of you as I stood in my corner prompting and wisht that you could have been in front, so that I could have called you onto the stage for a cheer at the end.

Poppa Pappa held out, all thro, God bless his heart.

Greetings, & thanks & thoughts.

John.

1. The Music Room at Boar's Hill.

[Boar's Hill, Oxford]
[1 Dec 1924]

Dear Florence,

We have today taken Corliss to his first hunt.

The meeting was at a house beyond Faringdon, in a lane near which you have several times been, but in a place that you cannot quite have seen. It is at the back of Faringdon Clump.

It was a sodden sort of morning with gleams of sun, quite perfect for beauty, but very muddy under foot. There were about 55 horses out, quite a jolly show, including some most noble hunters able for anything.

After the meet, we saw them run thro a spinney or two, finding nothing, & then we watched them into a covert once owned by the poet Pye,[1] whose works you will know by heart probably. Here, of course, were foxes. One come out our way, but alas another came out the other way & the hounds went after him, so we were thrown out & missed the run. Still we shall take Corliss out again before long to show him the matter fully.

Your letter came at this point. Many thanks for it. It is splendid of you to be speaking for the League. I wish I could hear you. I expect you persuade all you address. I don't suppose this Egyptian trouble will pass without being submitted to the League. Perhaps this will help things a good deal.

Always many whales,
John.

1. Henry James Pye, 1745–1813. Long forgotten English poet who was Poet Laureate from 1790 till his death. Masefield was to accept the same post in six years' time.

[Boar's Hill, Oxford]
[25 Jan 1925]

Dear Florence,

It is jolly to think that we may be with you part of the time in Italy. Viva Italia, if it is possible to fit it in with the holidays of you & Lew. I think we shall be starting from England on about 7th or 8th April, but cannot say for sure till we hear from Lew.

Geoffroi is here for a couple of nights, & is coming with us tomorrow to some of our old haunts in W Berkshire. We went yesterday over to Loll, where I think I will not again go.

On the way back, it became quite strangely dusky in mid-afternoon, which puzzled me very much, but it turned out to be an eclipse which had not been properly announced in the press & had stolen in as it were by the back door. I thought for a moment that God was signifying displeasure with the times.

Geoffroi has been doing some divine drawings of houses here, & is also at work on a lifesize painting of his family, which (from a photograph) should be a most heavenly group of intelligent & lovely people.

I hope ever so much that it will be possible for you to see a play here in May or June. We long to have your presence at one.

Blessings and thoughts surround & attend you.

John.

[Boar's Hill, Oxford]
[17 Feb 1925]

Dear Florence,

I am sitting for my portrait at the moment & can only write in a certain skew-eyed way which does not make for neatness. Unlike God, I cannot see that it is good.

On Saturday, we had a great day of adventure. We set off betimes to fetch Corliss from his studies to see & hear the Handel opera in Cambridge. It was a greasy, wet sort of a day, but forth we went, out of Oxford to Thame, then on to Aylesbury, then on to Dunstable, where we get out of the pastures into rolling chalk downland, very nice indeed. Then we went on to a place, wh I will

not name, wh is a horrid place, but useful, in that it makes 9/10ths of all the straw hats in the world.[1] When you are in Paris, & see
                [Drawing of hats]
                Lawn Tennis. 25 fr 50
                Première Communion 37.35

You may safely bet that both were made in this nameless Gomorra of a town at 4 fr 13c.

At this point, I took a wrong turn & drove the party some miles astray into a very lovely land which I'd never seen. However, we were in Cambridge for lunch with S.C.C., whom I think you know. To our great joy, Neville & his wife were there. I hadn't seen him for 2 years I think.

They gave us a bobby-dazzler of a lunch; which pen & ink cannot hope to describe.

After gorging to repletion, we (I don't mean that Corliss gorged, only we) went to the opera, which Handel wrote 210 years ago & which is now being done for the first time.[2] The opera had a sort of delayed-action fuse I suppose; or perhaps the British felt that it would be rash to let so much new thought into the world at once, & that it would be better to let the edge wear off it first.

The opera was done entirely by undergraduates, fellows & townspeople in Cambridge, & it was perfectly beautiful, music, colours, dancing & singing. I am green with envy of it. It is infinitely finer than anything I have done: it has me whipt to a frazzle.

So send me no more lovely valentines till I have deserved them.
                Greetings & thoughts
                        from
                        John.

1. The unnamed town is Luton in Bedfordshire.
2. The opera by Handel was *Semele*. It was the only one of Handel's operas to have a libretto in English.

                                        Boar's Hill, Oxford.
                                        [1 Mar 1925]
Dear Florence,
    We did Gammer Gurton,[1] oaths & all, for the three nights; & it was generally voted one of our great successes. Corliss was an

absolute trump of a right-hand man throughout: both in his belief in the play and in his help at the door. We heard of him from another last night, "that Mr. Huxley[2] says, that he has never known any Oxford man work anything like so hard as Corliss works".

We are fixing May 9 for our play of *Trial of Jesus*.[3] Please arrange to be at it. If you can come for the play you will be just about there with the bluebells as well.

Gammer & the Trial play between them have suckt the life clean out of me. I would like to be a dormouse with a secret room all snug with chewed up leaves & moss & wool & down, go into it & curl up & sleep for a week & only wake up now & then to hear the wind howl & say Well you can howl, vaunt couriers of oak-splitting thunderbolts, but for me I stay in bed & take my ease at my inn.

Mind: May 9

Greetings & thoughts
from
John.

1. *Gammer Gurton's Needle*, second extant English comedy first produced about 1552 and first published in 1575. The author was 'Mr. S.', whose identity is unknown.
2. Julian Huxley, 1887–1975, author and biologist, teacher of zoology at New College, Oxford, 1919–25. Knighted in 1958.
3. *The Trial of Jesus*, a prose play by J.M., first produced at the Music Room, 9 May 1925.

[Boar's Hill, Oxford]
[Jun 1925]

Dear Florence,

We see that the *Homeric* has reached N.Y. safely, but we are not yet assured of the Captain's inner peace. I expect he will be thinking. "Well, I have carried over, one way or the other, some 3 or 4 hundred thousand passengers, & only one of the lot had the sense to ask me about rigging. Well, some day I hope she'll come back again. I'll have a model fixed up for her, & then she can set up some for herself."

We have not been again to Banbury nor Segsbury nor any of these other places: but Corliss has been to supper two or three times, including last night, & is very full just now of the Stratford

Shakespeare company which came here for a week. I believe he went to every performance: he being a first-rate heeler like his mother. We only could go to *Macbeth*, which was well done: only just a shade too much on the lines of the butcher's apprentice from the beginning. This is all very well for the 2nd half but one wants a poet in the 1st half.

It filled us all with desire to be doing M once more *properly*: with you & Tom to see.

We shall miss Corliss so much when he goes, he is so keen & eager & such a jolly good fellow in every way.

I hope the heat wave isn't too much of a burden after cool England.

Blessings & thoughts to you
                    from
                    John.

                              Boar's Hill, Oxford.
                              [Jul 1925]
Dear Florence,
    I think the text runs:—

            "There once was a Rector of Speen
            Whose musical taste was not keen
            He said "It is odd,
            But I cannot tell God
            Save the weasel from Pop goes the Queen."

I'm doubtful about the first line but the rest is certainly near enough to serve.

I hope so much that time is making the thought of Eleanor's going easier for you.

Why don't you buckle to and read some Dante? He would be a change after this pop goes the Queen verse.
                    Best botargoes.
                    John.

                              [Boar's Hill, Oxford]
                              [1 Aug 1925]
Dear Florence,
    By this time, you will be all together for the summer, and the question which has been worrying us ever since June will have

been settled. May we know the worst, fairly soon? Has the new sailing-boat an auxiliary engine or not?

The other day, two of the Cumnor men came over, to ask me to judge costumes at their fête. So we went over to the village pub, where about 20 costumes and a band were assembling. When duly primed (I suppose) the band struck up, and the costumes marched thro the village, headed by a quite good but plump Britannia with her trident (now somewhat obsolete, I fear). We went to the field of the fête, where they were to march past us.

It is a biggish, rough pasture just below where the Hall used to be. We at once made out that it had been a part of the pleasance of the Hall in the days when Amy Robsart lived there.[1] There was the wreck of a sort of terrace on it and close to where we stood was the wreck of a long artificial pond now all overgrown which in Amy's time was probably stockt with fish. With a small expense of trouble it could be made into a divine bathing pond still. Poor Amy probably did not bathe, but no doubt she came to be melancholy there, like Ophelia.

The costumes weren't at all bad: the people had taken a lot of trouble over them. We gave 1st prizes to a sort of bustle dress of 1885, a Neapolitan dress, a gloriously handsome boy in a Tudor costume (I think he was a farmer's son, but he looked like a young god & was as nice & merry as a boy can be) and a little girl dressed as Puck & another little girl dressed as an old woman. The strange thing to me was that the fête looked exactly like all the village fêtes I've seen for the last 40 odd years: except that the drunken-ness was gone, and there was no fighting-booth, where Sam Pop, the Lambeth Peach, would undertake to knock anybody out in 2 minutes.

If we could have stayed, we could, instead of being knockt out, have bowled for a pig (gents) or smiled thro a horse-collar (ladies) and won a table ornament even if we failed to win the pig.

These things show the real abiding England, that was, 20 centuries ago, before the Romans came, & will be 20 centuries hence. I wish you could have seen it. However here is the account of it with all sorts of flounders and dabs.

John.

1. Amy Robsart, 1532–60, first wife of Robert Dudley, Earl of Leicester, a favourite of Queen Elizabeth I of England. She died in mysterious circumstances: the incident features prominently in Scott's novel *Kenilworth* (1821).

Boar's Hill, Oxford.
[12 Sep 1925]

Dear Florence,

In my last letter I began to tell you of the time in France: but did not get very much further than a sketch of the landlord & the household.

The sea was about 1/4 mile from the house, across a couple of pastures. The beach was nearly all small shingle and facing north. The shingle made the sea noisy at high tides; with a northern wind it made a roar which used to waken me. All the left-hand half of the bay was like the left-hand half of Cushendun bay: the right was flatter & rockier, & the rocks all harsh with seaweed.

I'm afraid that bathing and meals were the things we thought of most there. They gave us enormous tubs of a sort of Irish stew, which they called Soupe Normande, & when we had each swallowed three of these they brought in omelettes, as whets, & soon after that the real meal would begin.

We ate for 5 hours each day.
    "   bathed (for) 1 hour some days.
    "   slept (for) 12)
               13)
               14) hours most days
    "   read (for) 1 hour (most days)
    "   played P.P. all the rest of the time.

Of course, not all the time was holiday. We went on excursions to places which I expect you will have seen. One expedition was to Coutances, to see the cathedral, 1 to Mont St. Michel, to see the Mont, 1 to Valognes (a dud) to see some old houses which don't exist, but we saw a falcon coming home, 1 to Bayeux & Caen, to see the tapestry & the Abbayes, & 1 to a place called Vauville to see some cromlech or Kits Coty House, like Wayland Smith's Cave, up on the top of a moor there.

On the whole I liked the last jaunt the best. The stones were vaster & ruder than WS's cave, & therefore less out of the original design. Probably the smallest stone in the work weighed 2 or 3 tons. But the beauty of the jaunt was the moor, which was vast, wild & windy, smelling of billy goat & honey, from goats, heather & gorse, & looking over the vast stretch of Vauville sand, with the sea, & the Channel islands & similar wildness. You would have enjoyed it best too, I think; though the other jaunts were good fun, for the churches were very noble, in spite of all the green mould in the chancels. Bayeux was the best of them. Bayeux nave & Caen transepts & chancels. Mont St. Michel seemed to me a pale imitation of Malta, in the town part, & to be a desecrated shrine in the church. To see the filthy tourists pawing it over with their hoofs & to be one of the beasts oneself was too much. I was glad to get away from it to the restaurant where one could be complete tourist, even to the guide book, as one gorged.

When people in M St. Michel didn't like visitors in the old days they hove them over the parapet at low tide, 230 feet to soft mud: a short way with your tourist. Now the tourist is the boss of the place: the place exists for him: & I felt the need of an ounce of civet.

> Best greetings from
> John.

[Boar's Hill, Oxford]
[25 Dec 1925]

Dear Florence,

Your letters & your magnificent tool chest were opened this morning, Christmas Day, and I now write my first Christmas letter to thank you so very much for your kind thoughts and wishes, and for the beauty of your gift. The tool chest at once swells me with pride and deflates me with misgiving, because although I can use half the tools with tolerable skill, at least half I have never used and am doubtful of: but as soon as ever the evenings lengthen a little I shall launch out on a big work & see if I cannot get the hang of them, & so become master of my chest. A carpenter once said to me: "there is only one tool really: the edge: and only one way of carpentering; patience". I long to get to work on some thing at once: such as a spear or two for *Boadicea*. You could not have given me anything more delightful, nor anything that will be used so often, with so many pleasant thoughts of you.

Christmas has been a very jolly time this year, except for the weather, which has been very severe, with a lot of frost and snow (for us) & hardly any hunting possible anywhere. I had to drive into Glos the other day, & coming back we came upon the famous pack, the Heythrop, returning from exercise on a road like ice, the horses skating to & fro, & the hounds as sick as the huntsmen: but the Heythrop people wear green instead of the usual "pink" (i.e. most lovely scarlet) so it was a novelty.

There has been skating, but the snow spoiled it. Lew has learned to skate. I have not skated myself this time being so busy with my story & then the rehearsals of *Boadicea*, which are being perfectly devilish, with people away for Christmas or down with flu. This is the sort of thing:

Me.	2nd Briton. Is 2nd Briton there? Not come yet? Mr. M will you read 2nd Briton?
Mr. M	I can't. I'm reading 1st Roman, & then I'm the Druid besides.
Me.	Mr. N, will you read 2nd Briton, then?
Mr. N.	You asked me to be the corpse in this scene.
Me.	Miss O, will you read 2nd Briton?
Miss O.	I have to quarrel with 2nd Briton at the end of this scene.
Me.	O dash: so you have. Mr. P, you don't come on till later. You read 2nd Briton, will you?

Then we fling ourselves into it with Mr. P, and do the scene 3 times, till it goes with a certain swing. Then, when we are ready for the next scene, a voice comes from the dressing room. "Do you want 2nd Briton? He's here." Then 2nd Briton appears, red and shiny, & says, "I'm sorry if I'm a bit late; can we go through my scene a couple of times?"

It is slowly teaching me a kind of patience, which I sadly need. How much better these plays could be, if I had about 50 better qualities. There can be no quality, physical or spiritual, not needed to the height in the arts.

All sorts of thanks & thoughts to you, & wishes for your happiness in the New Year.

John.

[Boar's Hill, Oxford]
[20 Jun 1926]

Dear Florence,

Your steamer letter arrived yesterday the 19th; it was certainly, as you say, a whale of a letter, but a puzzle to me; because it was written on *Mauretania* paper, whereas you sailed on the *Aquitania*, & then it was post-marked Plymouth, 18th June, or just 1 week after you reacht N.Y. Still, so nice & big a letter is very welcome, however mysteriously it came; & to think that you gave up all these cardinals & men of God to write it all to unworthy me, makes me very proud. I have no friend like you; & never deserved one like you. Thank you.

In all my life, I have only met 1 cardinal, & 1 cardinal's chaplain, 3 bishops, 1 Archbish, 2 Deans & a colonial. You have me beat in church dignitaries, & to have had them on an ocean voyage, when they couldn't fly into any sacred vestry or other holy dodging place gave you a great advantage. You ought to have pumpt them dry of all the secrets of the confessional & the inquisition.

> If you talkt with the B of Toledo,
> Say what his Eminence said O
> About all his merry tricks
> Burning the heretics
> Who wouldn't join in when he prayed O.

I have certain mental pictures of Chicago, which make that city, seen as I saw it, in all the filth of a big thaw, the blackest & foulest I have seen. Now I shall think of it as a place to which men come from all over the world to be grateful for the holy ghost.

We went y'day with Lew to the Arden at Strat,[1] to have tea as we did with you: only as it is strawberry & Devonshire cream time, we had a juicier meal than we were able to give you. Coming back, we went over Edgehill battle field, where Englishmen 1st killd each other in the Civil War:[2] a confused and bloody fight, which fill'd all the little churches near with the bodies of men. Charles had a shade the better of it; but retired after it. The place is quiet enough now.

Afterwards we got onto a Roman Road, which runs pretty well straight for 100 miles, & is now hardly even a lane between great hedges of every coloured & white dog rose, now in full blossom & smelling like heaven.

Greetings & blessings & thoughts to you.

from

John.

1. The Arden Hotel, Stratford-on-Avon.
2. The Battle of Edgehill took place in 1642.

[Boar's Hill, Oxford]
[24 Jul 1926]
Dear Florence,

The Time Table & other devilries combined have made me miss a mail. I am so sorry. I hate to let a week pass without writing to you, but this week I fear I've done it.

I have heard nothing more about the T of J[1] & New York; & hardly expect to hear again: but may have news in early autumn.

You ask: does T.H. enjoy life? I should say, that he enjoys it more than he ever did; far more; & really does now enjoy it, horrors and all. He gives me the impression of growing within however much he may be declining without. This is the main test of greatness anywhere (as I may have said 1000 times.)

The Recitations will begin three days hence; but I must say that I am not looking forward to them as in the past, because Gilberto has thrown us over again, & we are not having Nevi, this year, as we wanted to change the judges. G's having to go to Geneva has made it necessary for me to judge, wh I don't wish to do, as I have now at different times judged 3/4 of all the people who have entered. Still, it is now too late to get any other judge, & I must do it again. Colonel Buchan[2] & W.J. Turner[3] will be the new judges.

Nevi was here for a week-end about a week ago: getting ready for Syria: & showing signs of not being totally at variance with H.M. Government, which must either be a sign of prosperity or old age; for even Reds have seemed "not quite" with him hitherto, & Tories liberticides. Time has its revenges thus. I suppose I shall become a golfer someday. But then, I suppose, deep down, my loathings are only envies; golf may be the sugar-cake in the shop, & I the little boy with his nose upon the pane outside.

My robin has just hopt in for a currant or two; but he now eats off the floor.

We may begin our next season with the First Quarto *Hamlet*, in Novr, but we've not yet found a Hamlet, as tall Mr. Martin, our Pilate, has now gone to be a professional actor, & will not be able to act here again.

Did I ever tell you of Krause, a remarkable man who has just died? He was coming home from the Pacific in a small sailing ship off the Horn. One morning, the captain said "Some devil has been pricking off a course on the chart in my room: prickt it off with pins while I was asleep". Everybody denied the charge, because one would as soon enter the captain's room at sea, to play with his charts, as one would enter hell to roast chestnuts.

"Well, someone's done it," the captain said, "There are the pin marks" (and there were.)

"And now", the captain said, "You may think me mad, but I'm going to sail that pin-prickt course." And he did.

During the forenoon, they rose an iceberg, & took off from it 4 survivors of a ship wh had wrecked on it that night.

This sort of story is common: but Krause was an uncommon man and voucht for it.

Your wireless continues to give great pleasure & delight. I wish that I could think that I did, to anybody: to be a sort of nice digestible cake that would delight & feed everybody & cause no indigestion: & be in continual demand & a blessing to people.

Blessings on you. I hope that Maine is continuing to be lovely.

John.

1. J.M.'s *Trial of Jesus.*
2. John Buchan, 1875–1940, 1st Baron Tweedsmuir. English novelist, historian and statesman.
3. W. J. Turner, 1889–1946. English poet.

[Falmouth]
[9 Aug 1926]

Dear Florence,

I am writing this in the sort of rectory where we hope to be throughout August. It is a big, old, comfortable, insanitary and ramshackle place, about 700 yards from divine bathing, wh is the only thing to do here: except hide & seek, which we are becoming skilled at, & shall be expert in when the children's friends arrive later on.

We motored here (270 miles) in a 2 day trip, by way of Dartmoor, & shall motor back, I hope, 3 weeks hence, in a one-day trip, starting soon after midnight.

I was glad to leave home this time, for the Recitns make one very faggd. The Rs are very good fun, but, like a play, they drop into a kind of well as soon as they are done, & leave one empty flat & stale. The day before they fill one's life, the day after they do not exist, they are gone, they are nothing: and this year they seem to have died more utterly than ever before. This year, I was very happy, because some people who had entered every year, & had been duds for 3 contests, came into their own, & one was 2nd, the other 3rd. This sort of thing fills me with joy for months, quite as much as it will fill them.

The *Cutty Sark* has been re-rigged, almost as of old, & there she lies in the harbour & moves me almost to tears to see her. Only 20 years ago, when I first came here, this harbour was full of divine lovely sailing ships: now there is only the *Cutty Sark* & she is a museum not a ship now. Well, these d———d transitory things show one the value of enduring things like friendship, & bring me grateful thoughts of you.

Blessings on you.
John.

[Falmouth, England]
[13 Aug 1926]

Dear Florence,

The Liverpool photographs of ships, which I promised to get for Eleanor, have never come, because the man has died, & his successors have not sent them: but here in Falmouth, where there should be the best of such things, I have found a few that may amuse her; chiefly of lame ducks that came in with broken wings & were lucky to get in at all.

I did just meet once the very clever able man who (with a partner) was responsible for her, who passed the draughts & had her built; little thinking, I expect, that she would be the wonder of the seas for years, & that an old sailor would in the end spend his life's savings to buy her back for the nation.

I was on board her 3 years ago; but I've not yet been on board her this time, tho I must go. You will think me a great ass to maunder on about ships thus: but they were the only youth I had, & the only beauty I knew in my youth, & now that I am old not many greater beauties seem to be in the world. I was probably the worst sailor the sea ever wetted:—

> "But many a man that cannot stand a pull
> Yet liketh at the wrestling for to be."

It is strange to stand on the Cutty Sark's deck and to know that she has gone romping and roaring past so many ships I knew, & been hailed by so many voices I knew, & has had men killed in her, & carried overboard, & inspired one of Conrad's stories,[1] & has now outlived her builders & most of her crews, & all the ships of her time & is now alone in Falmouth,[2] where she must often have been with a hundred of her kind.

Please tell Eleanor, that I hope to get her some more of these ships here, before I leave the west.

Always best greetings & thoughts.

from
John.

1. The Cutty Sark inspired Conrad's story 'The Secret Sharer', included in *'Twixt Land and Sea* (1912). See 'Author's Note' of 1920.
2. See p. 127.

[Falmouth, England]
[21 Aug 1926]

Dear Florence,

I envy you being able to teach your children useful things like tennis. I know no useful thing & have taught no-one anything, except you, perhaps, to make bread tops: a wasted life is mine. When I look into my mind I see an abysm of ignorance, ladlefuls of which I dispense whenever I talk: alas, alas.

I am writing this from Cornwall where I hope to be for yet another week. Mr. Connely[1] will probably be here tomorrow & will stay for some days. We shall use him hard in hide & seek, which is a popular game here, some hours each day, as we have 2 young ones staying with us.

We hope to come here again next year in August, & we have the wise thought: why should not Florence come to the Recitns in July & come to Cornwall in Augt? This is something for you to ponder. It is a soft mild climate; the bathing is good; the landskip is romantic; the food fresh fish & fresh cream (eaten separately) & Oxford seems a distant nightmare & Maine a distant dream.

I am not reading Plato: but the Iliad. I've never read much Plato: but I respect him; because he is the only philosopher whom great artists make beautiful. There is none of the Knotty & shaggy & clench-the-browy, & look-at-me-thinking-y, in the portraits of Plato. I think he was a sort of Christ without the character. I ought to have been reading Dante: for for about 18 months now I've read a page or 2 of D every day, & have read him all once & was 2/3rds through the second time; but have switcht on to the

Iliad, which is a marvel & a despair. I wd have been glad to have been able to write the Commedia, but would not if I could have: but the Iliad, O Golly, Florence.

On this note of O golly I must end this note, with my thoughts and greetings & remembrances

John.

1. Willard Connely, 1888–1967, American author, educational director, and teacher of English at Harvard College who was carrying on studies for a M.A. at New College, Oxford.

[Boar's Hill, Oxford]
[30 Sept 1926]

Dear Florence,

We have been perplexed by an announcement in *The Times* that Tom was en route for England in the *Olympic*. Con wrote to him, c/o of the ship, & we had hoped to see him or hear of him.

We passed the days in wondering whose iniquity it was that brought him over again, Germany's, France's or England's.

Mystery deepened over the matter when letters came from you & Corliss saying nothing at all about Tom's coming. Our hearts sank at this: We thought that something very secret & dark & ominous was happening, & that the coming was not to be mentioned, but had leakt out by some Bolshie in the press. We wondered whether it was our Labour crisis, or the Moroccan War, or some new unsuspected devilry.

Yesterday the telephone called for Con, & we thought, here is the enlightenment. She went to the telephone, where a man's voice was calling, thinking that it was surely Tom: but it turned out to be the Lockinge butler, saying

"Lord & Lady Ernle present their compliments, & will have much pleasure in accepting Mrs. M's kind invitation to lunch." So there the matter rests: & we are perplexed: but suppose that he has not come & is not coming.

I'm so sorry to think of your grief at losing Eleanor.[1]

I'm afraid that these things have to be: *as things are at present*: but I am myself convinced that boarding schools are wrong, & that the world will gradually learn that they are.

No nation of antiquity had them: no nation has them much

today except England: & England had them as a forcing ground
for men who were to pass their lives away from home: in India or
with the devil in some other beastly hole. Now we no longer send
our lads to India or colonies, & the need for these beastly schools
has passed: but I'm afraid, they'll go on for some generations yet:
because our filthy towns are so foul that the children have to be
sent out of them to have any chance of growth. Thus one vile thing
makes another necessary.

In America, I think the schools are probably all to the good,
because Americans are so much fonder of community life than we
are & are so much happier together. By this time you will
probably be reconciled to Eleanor's going by watching her happiness in the new life.

Best greetings
from
John.

1. F.C.L.'s daughter, Eleanor, 16 years old, went away to school at Milton
Academy, Milton, Mass., in the fall of 1926.

[Boar's Hill, Oxford]
[28 Oct 1926]

Dear Florence,

Thank you for your letter posted just a week ago. Really you
might almost be on the (English) telephone when words from you
come so quickly. It is very jolly that the mails between us are
speeding up again. I'm afraid I never write one hundredth part of
the letters so good & dear a friend deserves, but all the same I do
jolly well enjoy getting the excellent answers with which you
outpay me 1000 fold, every time.

If I never told you about Shivering Jimmy: I must do so now.
He is a ghost, I think, though of an odd & capricious kind, more
like what is usually called a poltergeist than a spectre proper: that
is, his appearances are associated with tricks done to those who
see him. He himself is (I think) supposed to be the ghost of a monk
of an abbey in Derbyshire. He lives in an old house, inhabited by
old friends of mine, & he comes in a shivering condition to the
bedsides of those who sleep in his room; then they hear him shiver,
and while they also shiver, he yanks the bedclothes from them,

chatters his teeth at them, induces horrid cold in them, and slaps and pinches them. Many people are scared half out of their wits by him, and run screaming in their night attire out of the room & from the house. He will sometimes bedevil people's clothes, so that they cannot dress or undress. I have slept in his room: but he tried no tricks on me: which was weak in him, because I should have been sufficiently thrilled. Lately, he has been less tricky than of old: poltergeists are usually not very lasting: they are supposed, generally, to manifest when a youth is in the house & to cease when the youth grows a little older: but there was no youth there when Jimmy was at his best.

I had another midnight drive two nights ago: from Birmingham to here, 70 miles. There was no fog this time, but a lovely half-full moon, a clear road, no one about, & the car moving like a sylph. All the big night was mine: not even a burglar stirring. I was here at about 2 in the morning: but the cocks heard me & began to crow, & for miles round other cocks replied, so I was for a while a sort of Dawn god. Last time I was in B'h'm I thought it was Hell, but this time, talking to a church of puritans (Wesleyans) I found my mistake. I never had an audience which gave me such a sense of goodness and Christian feeling: it was a very happy evening.

Now all sorts of blessings & thoughts & greetings to you, from
John.

[Boar's Hill, Oxford]
[13 Nov 1926]

Dear Florence,

Thank you for your nice letter from Asheville. I hope the rain lifted for you before you left, so that you could get some jolly rides into the mountains & show off the red coat in the only way red coats ought ever to be shown: i.e.:— riding cockhorse in it, as though you were going a-hunting. I hope you will now be back in N.Y.: all the better for the holiday. If one has to live in a city, I suppose N.Y. or Paris is the choice one has to make: but I don't know how one would make it.

Paris, one would say: ah, Paris, La grande ville, such sanity, such calm.

Then one would say: moi, je n'aime pas ces Parisiens: ils sont si malicieux, ah, à bas cette ville.

Then one would say: New York: ah, what a burg: the free lunch
f one's youth: the town with pep: the city with a present & a
future.

Then one would say: It cannot be. NY spins the wheel clean off
its hub: none but the comet can keep pace with N.Y.: so I suppose
one would choose Paris & then regret it ever after. Then the press
at one's decease would have this head line.

Deceased Sage moped for Mannahatta,
Said N.Y. was written on his heart.

I am rehearsing 5 nights a week now, which is a hard job with a
long play but easy with 2 short ones, as one can switch from one to
he other & so keep fresh. Both *Gruach*[1] & *Evil*[2] are shaping well: &
we are doing both with none but local talent: our own people: so I
wish you could see them. Miss B as *Gruach* will (I think & hope)
get a professional engagement as a result of the performance: but
this is a hope better kept secret.

I have never thankt you & Tom for your very generous &
never-failing help to these plays. I don't know how bad our work
is, & I suppose never shall know, but I know that to do them is
spiritual good: it wedges open a crack: & others will come & burst
the crack to a chasm, & the light will come thro: not better light
than our crack gives: the same light: but suns of it not chinks. Here
in this land are perhaps 100 theatres doing comedy & foolery &
plays of problem & opinion: no-one doing poetry or religion, or
going to the depths of men.

> Greetings & greetings
> John.

---

1. Play by Gordon Bottomley, 1874–1948, English poet and dramatist.
2. Play by Sir Rowland Ross, 1925.

> [Boar's Hill, Oxford]
> [2 Dec 1926]

Dear Florence,

I hope that the patient, & you, the chief nurse, are both doing
most wonderfully well. The very best of good wishes to you both,
from all of us, for a happy recovery. We await the next bulletin
anxiously. Lucky G to be so nurst.

When you write, could you tell me anything of the *New York* (or *American*) *Academy*, whether it is a literary body, or an artistic & literary & scientific body, or only a newspaper? I feel that I ough to know this without bothering you, but the question arose & could not answer it. We have 2 or 3 Academies here, one of each kind there is probably, so I expect you have several, too.

When you come to England, we want you to come to an old house here, to see a girl portrait by Sir Thomas Lawrence;[1] that is if you should still be looking for a painting to go in your dining room.

I expect I have told you of a famous miser who lived here 15c years ago (or so) with great wealth & in awful squalor. He cut up a dead sheep, warmed the carrion by sitting on it, to save firing, & then ate it. His only extravagance was a pack of hounds, but I expect he ate those when they died & ate the foxes they killed perhaps, as well.

Well, this Lawrence portrait is a picture of his daughter, who couldn't stand the life at home, so eloped with a neighbouring squire, & was married by the blacksmith at Gretna Green. "And came, as most men think, to little good, But came to father & raw sheep no more."

We send you all sorts of thoughts & remembrances. It is such fun to think that now we know the house you live in, & can picture you living in it 27 hours to the day.

Blessings from

John.

---

1. Sir Thomas Lawrence, 1769–1830, English portrait painter.

[Boar's Hill, Oxford?]

[1926?]

Dear Florence,

Your very kind generous letter about the plays here gave me great pleasure. Thank you so much.

We had small, but wildly enthusiastic audiences for *Peter Pat* (snow & honour mods & toggers made them very small) and Mrs. D, whom you have met several times but won't remember (she is a local lady who is always giving motor rides to consumptives, paralytics, female imbeciles and cases of dementia praecox) said that she laught so much in Act I that she was too weak to laugh in Act II. This is the sort of audience we like to get to fling our pearls at. The cast was a brilliant one, all stars, our pick: & even the lowest of the jokes made the Bishop smile, so delicately was it put. *Gammer Gurton*, our triumph of last year, was voted funny, but vulgar. I don't think anyone found *PP* vulgar.

The day your letter came, I had to go to the Censor of Plays, to hear that the *Trial of Jesus* could not be permitted in public here. I expected so much: but wonder at the way people's brains work.

It means that the play may be done privately anywhere, the acting of the play is not stopped, only the public acting. Any one may act it but actors, in fact.

I asked, if this were not rather foolish? I was told that it was the rule.

I asked, if it were not a bad rule? I was told that it was the rule: Our Lord must not be publicly represented: and that if one tampered with the rule, why then ...

I asked, what then?

I was told, that the rule had been made, to be a rule, & that if it ceased to be a rule, why then it would not be a rule, and that I could imagine for myself, what would happen if the rule were relaxed; there would be no rule, and if there were no rule, it would be open to anyone to break the rule, and then if the rule were broken anyone else would feel that he could break the rule, and though the rule might be foolish, still, it was a rule, you couldn't get away from that.

But cheers & thoughts & greetings,
from
John.

Since I wrote & had your letter, I have met Mr. Chubb, the poet & engraver, & I now send you his other poem, which is scarce & will be very scarce. He is a very remarkable man, of the Blake, Saml Palmer, Calvert school, & likely to do memorable things.

---

1. *Peter Pat* by Enid Rudd, a two-act play for one man and one woman, was first published in 1964.

[Boar's Hill, Oxford]
[1926]

Dear Florence,

I have 6 letters & a lot of stories & photographs to thank you for, & hardly know how to begin, as I am still dizzy from driving home from Cornwall. The old proverb says "business first, pleasure afterwards", but I say show your thanks to the Lord for your friend first, & that I do, my dear Florence, & then my thanks to you, the friend, for so much thought & care for me. I have loved all the tales especially the Arizona Jim & John Smith tales (you were in the vein that day) & I am so glad to have the photographs & see how all your trees & shrubs have thriven in these last few years. You will soon have to be cutting them back.

And now, before business, I would like to thank you & the New School for thinking of asking me to lecture. Thank you all very much for the compliment.

The trouble is, that I am not much of a lecturer, having little or no exact knowledge, small critical capacity, & little pleasure (as a rule) in lecturing. I am a story teller, & all my knowledge, criticism & pleasure I put into stories.

It would take me 6 months to prepare 6 lectures, & only 1 of the 6 would be worth hearing.

I suppose that they would not care to hear me read from my writings, or tell tales? That is the kind of *lecture* that Dickens used to give; & the lecturers of his time, too, I think, such as Artemus Ward;[1] but people have the feeling now that that kind of lecture isn't improving. Alas, I am not an improving person. I have never improved any body, not even the man I once lent 6 dollars to & he didn't pay, for he spent it all on drink & died soon afterwards. You & the school wouldn't get any improvement from me: you would only have me, which I suppose is all I have, & anyway its an attraction or blot wh this planet will not very much longer carry; not more than another 50 years anyway.

Then, the question of time when. We have been planning *Hamlet* for mid November (First Quarto) but that could be postponed. I could do *Deirdre*[2] instead: a short play easily prepared.

But another point is, I do want to finish my T & I[3] play before I do anything or go anywhere. It may be that I'll be able to finish this in Septr. I shall try hard to do so, & if so I could probably come for Oct. or part Nov. but I must get it finisht, *must*.

You *must* come to Cornwall next year. We've taken the house again. Beds like rocks, garden a wilderness, the only food cream & ish, but the bathing divine.

Here are some ships for Eleanor.

Many many thanks & thoughts

John.

I'd love to come to read, *love to*, & Con wd love to come too; only I long to end *T & I.*

1. Artemus Ward was the pen-name of Charles Farrar Browne, 1834–67. He was an American humourist, journalist and lecturer.
2. *Deirdre* (1907), a short verse play by W. B. Yeats.
3. *Tristan and Isolt* by J.M., a play in verse first produced and published in 1927.

[Boar's Hill, Oxford]

[1926?]

Dear Florence,

I think I told you of our successful opening of the season with *Evil & Gruach*. All went well, for a wonder: no-one fell out ill, though Sir R.R. & our Macbeth between them infected us all with poisonous colds & coughs, which were a torment all through rehearsal & linger on us still. I am sending the only notice & photographs which have appeared: but there should be more photographs later. On the whole, these 2 plays were better acted than any we have done. They were done by ourselves alone, with no imported talent; which was a sign of grace and growth. They were well done. The shaggy J.B. expresst himself well pleasd. Miss B was given a bouquet, & Macbeth was well applauded.

One lady swooned & had a fit in the love scene, which some attributed to the beauty of the acting: others to the gloom of the play: others to the cold of the room. Lucy filled her up with brandy on all 3 counts, & one of the audience drove her home: so that was that.

Yesterday we drove to Coventry,¹ which is a city probably well known to you, tho it was new to me. It has a cathedral, of the Perpendicular style, vast & in one key & marvellous: an English thing, not much toucht with any foreign Gothic. You may know the Coventry plays, wh the monks of Coventry made for the Corpus Christi festivals: they are very beautiful. Well, these monks, probably the very same, built this vast church for the citizens, in order that they might use the church & leave the church of the abbey entirely to the monks. The church of the abbey was dingd down later: even the bones of it are dingd: but this fine building is in good trim still, & ripe for another 4 centuries.

Greetings & thoughts
from
John.

1. Coventry is a large English city of which the entire central section, including the beautiful Cathedral of St. Michael, was destroyed in the Second World War in a bombing raid by the German Air Force in 1940. The Cathedral was rebuilt in 1962.

[Boar's Hill, Oxford]
[15 Jan 1927]

Dear Florence,

We were both saddened to hear of William's¹ sudden death, & to think of the sorrow of all of you, to whom it was such a personal grief and loss. All your people are members of the clan, if not of the family, & the death of one must be dreadful pain to all. We, too, are sad, because so recently William was driving us about from one merry adventure to another, & not being 1/2 thankt by us for the trouble he took for us.

And I am sad for your sake, because I know how death smites at you, as Dürer said, "terrible blows over the heart".

Contra vim Mortis
Non est medicamen in hortis.

A near death cannot be anything but a terrible blow over the heart, a wrenching and a breaking, & a tearing up of foundations. Whatever one says it must be that; though before, & long after, one may, and does believe, that the living soul lives and must live, more happily and fully than here, far more; & influences this life & people as much as ever. I know that affection, & hope, & courage, & acuteness of perception, & skill, in a soul, cannot really die. They are goods achieved into the world & abide. They are permanent fire whatever temporary smoke may be. This is all

aith & hope & charity: don't look to prove it: accept it like sun
moon & stars & the rolling of the earth. Whatever is a kindling
thought is a living thought & the food of life.

Now about the Corsair. Hurray for the Spanish Main.

I long to hear about the Main and buried gold and albacores,
sombreroed gentlemen of Spain & ships with silver in the hold &
salted flying fish for stores & topsails sodden with the rain &
golden visions in the brain of Lima as it was of old, St. John before
the conquerors, Port Royal builded up again, and buccaneers,
long since in mould, alive & uttering loud Hoorors.

Tell me all about your voyage's itinerary, please, please,
please.... Hurray for 1927 if it sends you to the lovely W Indies.

Greetings

John.

[Drawing] Alive & uttering loud Hoorors.

1. Chauffeur to the Lamonts, who died of pneumonia in January 1927.

[Boar's Hill, Oxford]

[2 Apr 1927]

Dear Florence,

Your jolly letter (posted on March 25th to go by the Olympic)
was a great delight. Thank you for it.

T & I was so long ago, that I think the news of it must have been
written to the Indies.

In a way, it was a success; but the people who did it, of whom I
think I spoke to you, only do their plays for one week in their
theatre, and then do them for two weeks in the halls near London,

one night at each hall: doing no play for more than the three weeks.

I think they did it well, but too slowly. If we do it in the autumn we will do it in 2 hours 20 mins, including waits. Passion isn't a funeral service. The man who played K Marc was very good: so was Kai.

The poetical theatre cannot be run on the lines of the commercial theatre. It needs a technique of its own, which we, who only play verse, begin to know now.

More & more, I shrink from any contact with the professional commercial stage. With all its skill, it fills me with horror. I would rather have my little gang of fumbling heroes than the whole profession. One little group trying to give the art a sanctity behind home-made masks seems to me to be worth it all.

Don't think though that I grumble at the company who did *T & I*. They did it well, & were nice to work with, & fac't the musick for me & I daresay lost money by me. I did not see any of the photographs, tho' of course I was taken with the players.

They were gallant good souls to do it all, for my plays. . . .

It was very well produc't, by Mrs. Norman, & *beautifully* dresst: it looked lovely.

I've been much considering things in these last weeks; especially "the deceitfulness of riches", & how true Christ's eyes were, & how courteous & wise he was from basing all his thought on the fact that God loves all equally, & that in God's eyes we are brothers. This has distresst me very much, for latterly I've been impatient; & am now learning how wrongfully; & proud, & now know with what slight cause.

I want to do the agony in the garden scene again, with Christ thinking himself a failure & blaming himself, & cut by every one of his friends as a leper; really outcast. I do wish we knew some more about him; & had not this fear of inventing.

I was at a banquet the other night of *Master Mariners*, among whom were 4 old friends, 3 of whom were vital to me at 3 critical times in my life: but perhaps they did not guess it. It was a glorious evening, & we drank out of gold loving-cups, the only time I have ever drunken from gold or a loving cup, & I didn't really drink either, being all for temperance.

Greetings & blessings to one more most dear friend.

                              John.

[Boar's Hill, Oxford]

[19 Apr 1927]

Dear Florence,

We were all much concerned to read of your illness. I do hope that the famous doctor, who did me so good, will do the like by you, & fit you out for the Spring, in good time to have your portrait finisht.

Before you finally renounce philosophy, perhaps you will resolve me these two problems:

A. When you *face the music,* what music do you face?

B. When you *go the whole hog,* why might you not go the 1/2 or 1/4 hog?

What wd happen if you did?

Anyway, how do these 2 expressions come into speech!

I suppose A is theatrical slang for being on the stage, facing the orchestra & the audience. B I suppose is pig stealer's or bacon lifter's slang for taking a carcass rather than a leg of pork; but give your lofty mind to it, will you, & let me know what you think, if you can without making yourself weary, or going against Dr. C's orders.

It is today just one year since we had the wonderful drive to Ávila, through Villacastin, & lunched beside the Roman bridge, & saw Santa Teresa's finger. That was indeed a day. Indeed the Spanish journey throughout was full of beauty & strangeness: and the anniversaries of it, & the fact that V. Hugo,[1] who was there as a child, & whose work was much influenced by it, mentions it so often, have brought it all back very vividly.

I suppose you will not like about 1/3 of V. Hugo, as not the kind of thing that is tolerable to English-reading people. I suppose another 1/3 you will laugh at as too absuyid for woyds (as people say in New York), but what do you say to the other thuyid, when he goes all white-hot and withering?

I do hope your next letter will say that you are really better & enjoying the Spring. Mind you tell me all about Long Island & whether you see the Roosevelt House from your window & can wave signals to Mrs. Derby.[2]

Always best greetings

John.

1. Victor Hugo, 1802–85, French poet, novelist and playwright.
2. Mrs Richard Derby, daughter of President Theodore Roosevelt.

Boar's Hill, Oxford.
[30 May 1927]

Dear Florence,

I was interested in what you say about your theatre managers. They are beginning to learn the truth, that the theatre is not a way of making money, but a place for the display of art, and that in a sane community, such as Athens, the community builds the theatre in the honour of the gods, and patrons with a sense of style pay for the plays, to which the whole community goes. With us a gang of speculators builds or buys the theatres, & people with no sense of style accept the kind of stuff they produce; but the thinkers & workers of the community avoid the theatre all the year round.

Oxford has 2 theatres, seating, (between them) 700 people at a time or 11,000 people a week. The thing has become almost as daily as a newspaper or a lending library, & as little to the soul; whereas one big thumping worth-while week of it, that brought the soul into touch with the Destinies she is linkt to, would be worth 10,000 such, & would bring in the wise i.e. the poor & the great. The theatre should be a feast: this time has made it a digestive, or after dinner nap.

It is jolly to turn from such thoughts to the fact that we shall hear you in about 5 weeks (we hope) and see you in 6. Hurray.

Go on with V. Hugo: he is the greatest man France has produced, in the writing line, since she had the madness of revolution. I suppose all poets since then have had something of the unease of the prophets in them: but V.H. has the beauty that came to the best prophets in the heart of the storm. He is a little like a circus performing lion who sometimes gets back into the desert and sees John the B eating his locusts and wild honey. Of course, we won't accept rhetoric, wh suits the French genius so well. Hurray for your soon being here.

John.

[Falmouth, England]
[24 Aug 1927]

Dear Florence,

I am thrilled by your charming account of Mr. Ringling:[1] it was quite beautifully written and gave me a great deal of pleasure. I admire circus people deeply and love their art a lot better than the frowsty stuff called such in cities. So many thanks for telling me of him.

I am grieved that I spoilt the Fowey day: I was feeling very unwell & ought not to have come.

Now I weigh 173 lbs, & have a beard wh curls, so that French visitors near the Ernest Louise say "Quel type de Boxeur: O heureuse Angleterre(!)" whenever they see me.

Greetings
John.

1. John Ringling, 1866–1936, proprietor with his four brothers of the Ringling Bros. Barnum and Bailey Circus. This circus was widely patronised throughout the United States and in 1930 was the largest circus organisation in the world.

[Boar's Hill, Oxford]
[Sep 1927]

Dear Florence,

Alas, the farmers say that Maine is too far for cream to travel to in the summer: but they want to try in the winter: so sometime in the winter some cream shall go to you in New York.

It tastes very good when slightly sour, I think, but then most of my tastes are depraved.

I am going to beyond Severn tomorrow, to see the Roman remains, just as good King Arthur left them 1400 years ago.

Always best greetings and thoughts
from John.

[Boar's Hill, Oxford]
[16 Sept 1927]

Dear Florence,

Alas, I cannot picture Maine any the better for the poet's mot. It means nothing to me, though I can understand how it jarred upon the girl. If he had said "Now I know why sailors call joy *splicing the Maine brace*" I wd have understood him: but then I have had only a specialized education.

We went yesterday 180 miles to the Roman ruins, rising at dawn & continuing until dusk, when we reacht home. We went by way of Tewkesbury, where we once went with you, & where I have had many jolly days of old. Tewkesbury is I believe rightly

called Theoc's or Theoca's byrig, which means the byrig of Theoc
or Theoca, and a pretty good byrig, too, once famous for mustard,
& now not much noted except for the fact that WOAD grows
there. Formerly Britons with style (like me) stained their skins
blue with woad. If you come across a man called Wadster you can
be fairly sure that his ancestors were woadsters and dealt in blue
dye.

I tried to get you some blue British make-up, but there was
none in any of the ceappings in all the byrig.

Passing on, we crosst Severn, and so on by where poor Nan[1] was
drowned till we reacht the ruins, wh I had not seen for 20 years.[2]
They are now less ruinous than they were, having been cleaned up
as well as excavated. Where there is now a tiny village, with
probably no drain anywhere, nor any public water supply, was
once a little neat walled city, with 2 temples, a big and splendid
basilica, 2 theatres, a market hall, public baths (hot & cold) and a
fine memorial to a soldier commanding a legion. Alas, it has fallen
like Tyras in Ezekiel & its drains chokt and its baths gone out of
use.

Coming back I had a good view of Buttington, which I believe
to be the Mons Badonicus of Arthur's victory.

Greetings
John.

1. 'Poor Nan' refers to J.M.'s play *The Tragedy of Nan* (1909), a study in poetic
naturalism.
2. The Roman ruins of Uriconium are near Wroxeter in Shropshire.

[Boar's Hill, Oxford]
[7 Nov 1927]

Dear Florence,

The Huxleys[1] came for the week-end, and Austin[2] came to
lunch to meet them and also to meet the Miss Silcox by whom you
sat at the play one night. J.H. had a long talk with Austin about
his work. I could not hear what they said of course, but it was a
real good collogue of about an hour. After that we had tea while
the Hs went out to see the Ms. Austin was looking very well &
handsome, and his two friends, Norie & Birbeck, who came to tea,
were both exceedingly nice.

After supper I beat all comers at PP [ping pong], which is so unusual that I brag of it.

The weather has suddenly stricken us with a bleak cold easterly wind wh makes your lovely foot-warmer the joy of ones toes.

I hope that you have found all your people well & hearty.

Greetings & thoughts
John.

1. Julian Huxley and his wife Juliette.
2. Austin Lamont, 1905–69, third son of F.C.L. and T.W.L., who was a student at New College, Oxford.

Boar's Hill, Oxford.
[15 Nov 1927]

My dear Florence,

Austin came up to sup with us last night, looking both well and smart. He played a few hands of bridge with us and then rode back to his work. I think he is enjoying his time here.

The theologians are suddenly aghast at the play,[1] and I expect to hear tomorrow that it has been cancelled. I wish they would buck up and decide as I hate to keep you waiting thus for news of our movements. You would not believe the poor little play could shelter so many indefensible theological positions. I may have led you into theological errors which will be your undoing if you don't look out. It is rotten with Arianism, toucht with the worst kind of Pelagianism, a bit Socinian, and just reeking with Monophysitism, so do burn it before you're done for.

Bless you
John.

1. J.M.'s *Trial of Jesus*.

Boar's Hill, Oxford.
[13 May 1928]

Dear Florence,

I am off betimes tomorrow to rehearse the play at Canterbury, & I'm afraid this will be a paltry scrap of a note. As usual, when it comes to a rehearsal, I wish it were some other play, but there will be a certain rest in having abundant actors, who will all know their lines, and who will be sackt and miraculously replaced if they cut rehearsals. This will probably halve the woes of rehearsal at the very least. To think of being able to sack an actor instead of having to woo him all the time & comfort him with flagons: golly.

I shall go by the road we went in October.

It is extraordinary to be working in an institution. I suppose it is a sign of old age that I am. Hitherto, I have always been outside all the institutions; now comes old age. I was bald long ago, now I am fat, soon I shall be respectable.

Well, cheer up, we have had some jolly times.

Nevi is in Oxford as I write, but hasn't been up to see us, alas.

Austin is coming to the Canterbury play on one of the two days, so he will be able to tell you what it seems like from in front, which I shan't be able to. I shall only be able to say "the actors forgot themselves at such a point, & the audience cought at such another".

Best greetings & thoughts from
John.

Boar's Hill, Oxford.
[9 Aug 1928]

Dear Florence,

Thank you for letting me know that Austin arrived safely at his port. I expect you fired the guns when his ship was signalled off the Heads.

I fear I have missed the mail with this, which is very wrong of me, but anyhow this is to say *Hurray for the Dartmoor Jaunt.*

We are just back from the Highlands, where we have been staying for a week. I suppose that this July has been the hottest recorded in Britain, yet the Grampians still had patches of snow on them from the awful winter. We only passt the Gs however, & had a most warm & happy time in Skye. I expect you have been in Skye & know all about it. It is a great place for trout & salmon fishing, & has some lofty & evil crags & rocky pinnacles which are as hard to climb as any rocks in the world, so that many mountaineers go there, & many are killed. Some of the crags have never been scaled yet, but a lot of bold sprigs are there now wrestling with them.

I was not drawn to the crags, but felt that I would like to climb one great naked conical rock, almost destitute of life, about as steep as this [drawing]. The spike at the top is a cairn wh marks the grave of a Viking's princess who was buried there some 12 or 1300 years ago.

Imagine the funeral procession & the piling of the cairn in such a place.

The people talk Gaelic there.

Coming back, we went over Culloden, where Bonnie Prince C lost his chance; & thro' Killie Crankie,[1] where bluidy Clavers got his paiks, & so on by a sleeper to Euston.

Hurray for Dartmoor.

Seatrout & starfish

John.

1. A wooded pass in Central Scotland where Jacobite Highlanders defeated government forces in 1689.

Boar's Hill, Oxford.

[8 Dec 1928]

Dear Florence,

In the rush of the *2 Angry Women*,[1] which was one of the most troublesome of all our plays, I sent you but skinny scraps of notes, for which I am sad & ashamed. The rehearsals spread into all my afternoons & sapped my writing times.

However, we got thro the play, & have had a good deal of praise for it, as a jolly old comedy very well worth reviving.

Since then, we have been to Canterbury again, to see the new Archbish enthroned. We had planned to motor there & back in one day, but fog stopped that plan, so we went by a special train from London, with most of the Bishops & a multitude of clergy, priests, ministers, monks, padres, pères, pastors, Moravians, Greeks, elders, Rechabites, etc, etc, Christians of all sorts, & nuns & abbesses, sisters of Mercy, Jesuits, & English rectors, the holiest company I ever was in: the oaths froze upon my lips as I sat among them.

The fog cleared as we entered the good part of Kent, & gave way to a day of divinest beauty, in wh the Cathedral was lovelier than ever.

I put on my Yale & Harvard robe, wh is rather the worse for having been often acted in, & took my place in the seat reserved for me among the poets, actors & musicians; at least I should have taken my place, had not some child of Baal, who looked like a bad politician, up to all kinds of graft, been already in it, so I sat next to the Great Archimandrite of the Greek Church, who had a most lovely embroidered cope (perhaps it was a scapular) & looked exceedingly distinguisht & noble. The whole vast place was crammed with people in robes, uniforms & distinctive dresses; & after the enthronement, we all marched down out of the Quire, down the steps of the play, & thro the crammed nave into the crammed precincts. All the time I longed to be trying things on that vast attentive, moved & weeping crowd, to be getting them to sing or something of the sort. I have never seen anything so beautiful: if they had only all been singing it would have been overwhelming.

Greetings,
John.

1. *The Two Angry Women of Abington* by H. Porter (Repertory of English comedies, Vol I. Ed. Gayley).

[Boar's Hill, Oxford]
[14 — 1928]

Dear Florence,

Many thanks for your nice letter from the Olympic. I was rather afraid, from what I saw of the weather, that you would find cause to prefer the Homeric before you reacht home. However, you could not have found her worse than the Italian ship, whereas we, going the same day to Calais, found one infinitely worse, and had such a gruelling as falls to few. However, it is a complaint soon cured by the dry land, and by the time we were quit of Italy we were well enough. We had a very jolly time in G, & saw a good deal, & kept very well, & had most full days each day, & went dog-tired to bed & rose eager next morning.

One of the things I likt best was the port of Athens, which is perhaps the only "forest of masts" now in the world. There must have been 100 or 125 ships of about 100–150 tons, schooners, brigantines, speronases, etc, & one big barquentine, all lying side to side, & working sensible cargoes of fish, bread, tiles, wood, wine, fruit, vegetables, wood, macaroni, currants, stone, pots, etc, all the things you would rather have than not, & suffer if you don't. There they were, all lovely, all different, some a bit old & battered, but some beauties among them, heavily sparred & with first-rate gear. They were all little, but it was a scene now gone from the world, & such a scene as once made a walk in Liverpool a joy forever, only then of course the ships were ten times the size, and glories of their kind.

It was the only port I have seen for years that had real life to it. I have rarely seen so much animation anywhere, nor so much varied colour & beauty. The port was that in which the fleets of the ancient city moored, I believe.

I hope you have found all your chickens & chameleons in 1st rate trim.

Greetings & thoughts,
John.

[Boar's Hill, Oxford]
[14 Jan? 1929]

Dear Florence,

We hope to see Austin here again in 3 or 4 more days, when term begins. We have not heard from him since he went, but Mr. C sent us cheery word a few days ago, that all was well. Oxford is beginning to receive its youth: there must be already 500 sprigs in flower there.

One notices a great increase in the danger of driving when term begins. 5000 push-bikes suddenly come onto the roads from all angles & all entrances making the heart to stand still. One never hears of one of them coming to harm. "The dog it was that died". The people who die are the middle-aged & old who jam on all the brakes suddenly to avoid them & collapse from heart failure over the wheel.

We read here that Americans take much interest in the K's illness.[1] It has been very severe & wd no doubt have killed anyone less well cared for. He seems to have had some form of blood poisoning, with pockets of infection in the pleura. He must have been nearly dead for days together, & tho he is mending, he must be very very weak, and cannot be well for many days to come. I'm afraid that it has been a specially uncomfortable and miserable kind of illness, most of it passed in what doctors call "a typhoid state" of low muttering, etc.

I feel that he will now recover, & be able to attend the Derby, though not the Grand National.

By the way, if you are here in June, won't you come to the Mersey, to see my ship row for my cup, & shout "Come on, now; put your weights on"? [Drawing of crew in shell] The cup is really rather jolly [Drawing of cup] with verses by me on the sides.

Greetings & thoughts from
John.

---

1. Towards the end of 1928 King George V had undergone an operation for pleurisy.

[n.p.]
[17 Jan 1929]

Dear Florence,

I grieve that you should have had such a shocking end to your charade, & that Judge Hand should have had such misery.[1] It must have been an hour of dismal wretchedness to you both. As for the lady's nose I do not remember it in its glory, & am inclined to think that such a hand & such a surgeon probably improved it. This, coupled with the importance of the occasion & the distinction of the unusualness, & the satisfaction of being an interesting invalid, with hosts of callers longing to see the broken organ & invitations from Hollywood to come & act it for the world, will probably amply repay the sufferer. It is the Judge & his hostess for whom I feel. Artificial noses may be had at every general store, but no such hostess & Judge are in this universe.

I say about the nose what Ezekiel said about a vine, "when it was whole, it was whole, it was meet for no work, how much less shall it be meet for any work, when the fire hath devoured it?"[2] I thus dismiss the lady's nose from my mind, & concentrate on you & the Judge. My sympathy to you both.

I once had to strangle a chap in a play. I was only a ghost, & practically didn't touch the throat at all, but the silly ass who had the throat was in such a gurgle that he jolly nearly choked himself.

Grassi,[3] in his big parts used to bite large pieces out of his cast and eat them. They however were Italians & knew that it was for the cause of Art, & felt each tooth as a jewel in the crown of martyrdom. You might tell the lady this, if she should seem cold towards the Judge, whose cause I have much at heart.

Best greetings'& thoughts, from John.

1. Judge Learned Hand broke the nose of Faye (Mrs Walter) Lippmann in an after-dinner parlour game of 'Murder' at the Lamonts' house in New York City. In this case Judge Hand as the 'murderer' accidentally used more force than necessary.
2. Ezekiel, Chapter 15, v. 5.
3. Giovanni Grasso, 1875–1930, Italian actor.

> [Boar's Hill, Oxford]
> [6 Sep 1929]

Dear Florence,

Your steamer letter made a rapid cross, & was here yesterday, 13 days from your sailing from England. Many thanks for it.

We, too, are in the throes of a heat-wave, hard to bear after cool Cornwall. We think of the lovely rocks & green sea & long to be back there, & you to be there, too, to see how heavenly it can be in really fine, hot weather. However, being here is good fun, for grapes are ripe

    plums (are ripe)
    peaches ,,   ,,
    greengages (are ripe)
    apples (are ripe)
    figs (are ripe) (nearly)

and blackberries squirt juice as one passes, & drip sweetness as one walks. The only drawback is a want of pears: ours do not ripen till much later.

I am hard at work again, & am also preparing a brief address on W. Blake, to come in a Blake Concert at Edinburgh, before the S.A.S.V. in October. W.B. is all very well; but to deal with a mind of that sort in 20 minutes is a bit of a problem. I am again stuck in the Prophetic Books where so many flounder. However, I am resolved to get at the heart of W.B. & so I am beginning on them with system. Soon I hope to know why "Bowlahoola is the Stomach in every individual man" and why "Theotormon and Sotha stand in the Gate of Luban anxious".[1] Perhaps you have already mastered these points, & find the system simple.

Do you ever see a paper called *Antiquity*?[2] There is rather a good article in the current number about K Arthur's twelve battles; & placing them in Sussex and Hampshire & Western Kent. It is all perplexing, because the places are mentioned by their British names, & we now know the places by their English names. He makes no shot at the whereabouts of Badon; so my two sites, especially the better of them, still hold the field with me.

Greetings & thoughts & thanks,

John.

1. These are not misquotations. See Blake's *Milton*, Book I, Stanzas 26 and 30.
2. *Antiquity: a Quarterly Review of Archaeology.* Edited by O. G. S. Crawford. The article in question was by the historian and novelist W. G. Collingwood (1854–1932), for many years secretary and friend to John Ruskin. His contention that Sussex and Hampshire were the scene of Arthur's battles rests on the contention that at the time assigned to them there were no Saxons in the North or Celtic west.

[Boar's Hill, Oxford]

[9 Sep 1929]

Dear Florence,

Are you in Maine or where? You have vanisht into an unknown part, and I know not where to think of you.

When we reacht home from Cornwall the other afternoon, we found a Javanese Love Bird (a little green & blue parrot thing) on the lawn, to welcome us. Lord knows where it came from. It flew about resisting capture & refusing any food that we could offer; & in the night a cat ate it, & strewed lovely tropical colours about the lawn.

Once before (about five years ago) we found a locust in the garden. I suppose it had rashly mistaken me for John the Baptist & had come to be lunch with my wild honey.

I went to see Growly[1] yesterday, to take him some grapes, of wh he is very fond. The grapes & the fine weather had wrought him to a very good mood; & he talked about the Jesuits, one of whom had been consulting him on a literary point. "I can't make out", he said, "whether these fellows (the Jesuits) are only pretending to be fools, or whether they really are fools."

We go to Paris on Thursday, until Monday. We plan to go to Chartres on Friday, Vezelay on Sat, & Beauvais on Sunday. This should be a triple feast of some of the best things in the world.

Nothing but the power & the beauty of the mind of God can explain such miracles. And such & stranger miracles are in that mind always, waiting to be given, from the inexhaustible abundant well.

Greetings & thoughts from
John.

1. Robert Bridges.

[Boar's Hill, Oxford]
[30 Sep 1929]

Dear Florence,

I am so grieved at your distress & the Reed's anguish about poor Bill,[1] who was a dear lad & fine. Alas, alas, who can recover from the death of a child & the quenching of youth.

I hope that this will reach you in New York, for I hope that you will now be away from Maine, now that this shadow is upon it. I am writing to Mrs. Reed. Alas, alas.

And yet, not alas, for one knows that death is not all-killing: something it cannot touch in any of us; tho this is no consolation: the death of any one dear is the end of a kind of life often pitifully dear: and we have to be born again.

My thoughts to you.
John.

1. William Thompson Reed, only son of Mr and Mrs Edward Bliss Reed.

[Boar's Hill, Oxford]
[Sep 1929]

Dear Florence,

In about 23 days I have to stand up in Edinburgh & address the company on the subject of Wm Blake. This wd probably be but a trifle to you, but it is filling my days with perturbation & my nights with perplexity; for what the devil W.B. meant in nine tenths of his poetry is more than I can fathom: whether it is the Harrow of the Almighty or the Delusion of Ulro, Dante is child's play to him.

I think I told you of our going to the Geoffrois. On our way back from Chartres, we stoppt at Pontoise to see G's painting of *St. Martin & the leper*, now in place at the end of the aisle, & a fine distinguisht thing: only I wd have been glad if St. M had been a bit peppier in his giving. The leper had only a little bit of linen, & St. M had a rather superior gown, & St. M was only giving the poor chap a kiss, wh I expect is a doubtful benefit from a saint anyway: & no benefit at all from a sinner. However, perhaps he was only beginning with a kiss & was going to go on from there.

I don't think it has rained for 10 minutes since you left England: things are dying of drought: our field looks like a plaque of burnt toast.

Where are you now? I suppose back in N.Y., bossing the new house & beginning to get things into it.

[John.]

[Boar's Hill, Oxford]
[19 Nov 1929]

Dear Florence,

I have just had your letter about the crisis in Wall Street[1] & am wondering & sorrowful at the wide-spread misery, & poor Josephine. Alas, alas, this ruin that falls on people, this Fortune whom Necessity compels to be swift: it is one of the mysteries of life; & nothing that one can think or say will avail with it.

(You might let your friends know just how completely ruined you are, & if we can help at all.)

I like the name of your new house & long to hear all about it, & am jealous of H.W.N. having so good an innings: but you have never told me the full postal address of the new house, & I am not able to write to you there. Please do not forget to send me this, so that I may write to you there.

I am filthy within & without (I don't mean morally more than usual) as I have been cleaning up the mess of *Meleager*[2] on the stage & rehanging the curtains for the little Blake play, the day after tomorrow. All the paint on the *Meleager* scenes has come off on me.

Austin was here on Sunday & was very well & cheery. He playd a little bridge after supper: he is pretty happy here I think.

We are having a fine gale at the moment, with a roaring westerly wind & torrents of rain, bringing down the last of the leaves.

Greetings & thoughts from John.

1. The great financial 'crash' that led to the decade-long Depression in America.
2. A play about Meleager, a hero in Greek mythology who killed a wild boar that was ravaging his native land of Calydon. The author was the poet and classicist R. C. Trevelyan, 1872–1951.

[Boar's Hill, Oxford]
[1929?]

Dear Florence,

Many many thanks for your nice letter about RN's play.[1] I am so very glad that it all went so happily. I know how much of the making it go so happily was done by you & Tom, who never rest in the doing of kind things. Anyhow, RN wrote me a most joyous happy letter about it: & I always feel that happiness is the only thing that keeps him going. It is much, necessarily, to all, but to him it is life itself; and it is his friends' duty to give him that. I think that all his friends feel that: for I never knew anyone draw down love upon himself so: not even Rupert, (not near).

I fear I didn't tell you the half of the glory of that Canterbury day.[2] I had never before taken part in a thing of the sort, & though in a feudal land like this such pageants aren't infrequent, with royal weddings, crownings & funerals, etc, etc, I had always dodged all, except Lord Mayor's Shows in London City, and trooping of the guards colours at Jimmys: both which shows I have often seen.

It was therefore strange to be *in* such a show, as one of the 1000 performers; but I cannot tell you how strange it was to be *there*. The vast cathedral was crammed: I can't tell you the effect of it: all the clerestories & triforium openings were black with peoples' heads: as all were looking down one saw the darkness of the hair. It was as though the great ship had suddenly got her crew & were about to navigate heaven.

But to pass out through the Quire Arch onto the Quire steps, above the vast singing mass of 5 or 6000 people was staggering; and yet not so staggering as to come into the light in the Precincts into the vast crowd there, with other vast crowds in windows, on walls & on roofs wherever men could climb.

Poor Con is laid up with a chill, but is now fast mending: & will be up tomorrow I trust.

Greetings & thoughts,
John.

1. Robert Nichols' play was probably *Under The Yew; or The Gambler Transformed* (1928)
2. The enthronement of Cosmo Gordon Lang, 1864–1945, as Archbishop of Canterbury took place on December 4th 1928. J.M.'s play *The Coming of Christ* had been performed in Canterbury Cathedral on Whit Monday and Tuesday 1928. He could have been referring to either of these occasions, though the former seems more likely.

[Boar's Hill, Oxford]
[17 Jan 1930]

Dear Florence,

I am sitting in my shed, full of affection for you, but using awful language, because your lovely & heavenly letters show me that all my Christmas gifts have arrived a week late, when I thought I had timed them to a nicety. Alas, alas for wo: or, as others might say, ————.

I am glad you are liking Gen Smuts.¹ I met him once here & shook hands with him, one of 20 or so, but only to say goodbye. He was one of the few imaginations in the War, perhaps the best of them, & I shall never forget the "Hope that shone from him like a Beacon" when I saw him in the mud & smash of the battlefield in 1917, in the midst of a party of generals who had faces of putty, raw beef & pipeclay, & the souls of drunken boys of a depraved Vth form at St. Dominics.² He burned among them like an angel of God.

Thank you so very much for sending me the address. I am hoping to see Austin in 2 days & shall then hear full details, I hope.

About Greece. I hope to go there for a few days early in April; a very few days; to see a few lovely places & then away, as before: it is too lovely a land to stay in long: too much ecstasy.

The Italian paintings in London are divine. Do be prudent. Dash over to see them, as the Bible says, *while it is calld to day.* Many will never be on view again, & words cannot describe the joy of seeing so much beauty that one did not know was in the world. And on the 9th Feb my *Masque of Liverpool may* be done in Liverpool Cathedral, which is our best modern building, whatever the masque may be. But the Italian paintings are the real spur to effort. Do think of it. Come here, stay with us, & we'll go up every day for a week for 2 hours each day.

John.

1. General, later Field Marshal, Jan Christiaan Smuts, 1870–1950. Celebrated South African soldier and statesman.
2. *The Fifth Form at St Dominics* (1881) was a famous novel of school life by the writer for boys, Talbot Baines Reed, 1852–93.

[Boar's Hill, Oxford]
[Jan 1930]

Dear Florence,

I have now finally settled the account of the *Wanderer*,[1] and sent the script to be typt. It is jolly to be quit of a job that was hard work to little purpose. You take on the job of writing the history of a New York street car, yard number 3007, 1891–1907, and you will realise what sort of a job it was: most of those who knew the car well, quite illiterate, and failing in memory; those who can write about her, just a shade too anxious to make her seem romantic. However, it is done, all but the horoscope promist by an astrologer.

I hope so much that the New Year has begun well & pleasantly for you. Here, all has begun pleasantly, with nice mild wet weather & all things sprouting. My birds have come back all about me, as usual in the winter, & my robin passes most of the day in my shed, but it is not cold enough yet for him to eat from my hand.

The Italian pictures are most wonderful but really too many for peace. They have the divine big Naples Bellini, and other exquisite works, which lay one in humble ruins. *What a pity that you don't DASH over to see them.* Now is your Chance. They won't be here again. Come to see them. Unique, and for a few weeks only. What fun to have you here & go up to see them time after time.

John.

Be bold, I say, & come & see them.

1. J.M.'s *The Wanderer of Liverpool*, partly in prose and partly in verse, 1930.

[Boar's Hill, Oxford]
[Feb 1930]

Dear Florence,

Thank you for your delightful letter.

Would it suit you, do you think, if we joined you at Paris on Monday, 7th April, & left you on, say, Wednesday, 23rd, or Tuesday, 22nd, April? We shall have to be here on the 24th.

Ruskin says somewhere, "if you do not like a picture, do not spend much time on it: spend a quarter of an hour". I would love, this time, to spend time on the marvels I have hurried over hitherto, for on the whole I never cease to regret that I am not a painter; & care for painting more than for any of the arts; & the Italian wave of painting seems to one more marvellous as one grows older.

Perhaps you will live to see the American nation caring for painting, and demanding it in churches, houses, & everywhere else, and starting a new Renaissance more wonderful than the old.

Greetings & thoughts,
from
John.

Mawnan.
[12 Aug 1930]

Dear Florence,

We have been in this old house for nearly a week, of arctic weather, having cold & uncomfortable windy swims, which would remind you of Maine & remind us of tales of the search for the Northwest Passage.

The great storm, of last year, which slew so many thousands of trees in England, was very savage here & played old harry with the garden, which is now much clearer & brighter, tho less good for Work. It is said that some of our roof was blown off, but this seems to be poetical invention.

I try to read from 50 to 100 lines of the Iliad every day, & also do a lot of serious reading in the library here, mainly Biblical criticism & neat points in theology & dangers besetting the Church.

One of the main beauties is, that at odd times throughout the day, many times a day, one hears the cry of curlews, which are more frequent this year than formerly, & come from high in heaven, from some strange thought in a strange souled bird, with whom I would fain fly: but not just yet.

Some people eat curlews, & put them on lists in dining rooms. "Curlew à la haute Cocotte." "Curlew Maryland". "Curlew Imperatrice de Russie" etc, etc. This shews you to what depths man can sink when he doesn't have to get his food for himself.

Blessings & thoughts to you.
from
John.

[Boar's Hill, Oxford]
[19 Sep 1930]

Dear Florence,

Thank you for your very welcome nice letter saying that you will be here for the weekend of Oct 11th. Cheers. You shall be most welcome.

Thank you, too, for the poem about Spring. I am sending you a much better one about the weather.

> O, Hel; the rain.
> The wind that brought it brings it back again.
> It wets me. Ah. Right through
> Sole, upper, laces, of the second shoe
> Where does it go? It should go down the drain.
>
> O hel: the gutter has been clogg'd again.
> Has the rain ceast?
> See on the ground a $\frac{1}{2}$ drownd furry beast.
> Poor little squirrel, or
> Rabbit or puppy to be sorry for
> Or pretty weasel or familiar cat.
> Lord, it's my Sunday hat
> The one I paid 3 pounds for at a gulp,
> Blown out of window, soddened to a pulp.

You needn't expect to beat that, even if you have me as a subject.

You gave me Murray's *Rise of the Epic*. I think you will find that I wrote you a letter once on the cover or wrapper or flyleaf of it; being short of writing paper. You should get Leaf's book *Troy*.[1] I think you'd enjoy it very much.

I am sending you a letter which came yesterday. I send it to you, as in spite of the Wall Street crises, you are probably more of a millionaire than I am. But don't pay heed to his request. We have several Rhyming Dictionaries in this tongue, & need no more.

Hurray for your coming so soon.

John.

---

1. Walter Leaf, 1852–1927, British banker and classicist. Author of *Troy, A Study in Homeric Geography* (1912).

Boar's Hill, Oxford.
[Sep 1930]

Dear Florence,

Did you ever have to set up a bowsprit?

I don't suppose you ever had to; even I never had to, & now I have to, on a small scale, & I can't see how to make my bobstays neat, & a bowsprit with untidy bobstays looks just like Sodom & Gomorrah. Now perhaps you, a loyal friend, & a rakish craft with a very neat figurehead, (as they say in marine romance about the heroine), may be able to tell me whether to shackle clean through, or pudden over, & so save your desolated friend from shivering his timbers in Breaking Up Reach.

Dorades et Delphines.

John.

Boar's Hill, Oxford.
[Sep 1930]

Dear Florence,

I believe this may still find you in Maine, enjoying the delights of grandmotherhood & *Murder*.

Murder has had a great success here in the last year or two, but it needs a large party, & we have not yet tried to play it. We were not many at Mawnan this year. Thank you for the vivid letter in which you described it; & congratulations on the success of Corliss's baby.[1] I hope that she may grow up to every beauty & every grace. I hope, too, that she may be immortal as well, if that won't be too painful to her Father & Mother.

I am now very busy rigging a brig, & have many fathoms of rigging cord stretching across my study from wall to wall, & I am continually working at Hare's Seamanship, to try to find out how to fit things which are now no longer fitted. It would be a pleasant life to be a rigger in some small community like Phaeakia, where people took great pride in ships, & where the rigger was always dealing with gear & spars that a couple of men could shift.

Your letter raisd some doubts of your coming here this autumn, but surely there is no doubt? Surely you would not let your tender Daughter, apple of your Eye, come motherless to a strange land, to a town of male ogres, where every other person is a don? You must think twice before you do a thing of that sort.

Blessings & thoughts
from
John.

1. Margaret Lamont Heap, born to Mr and Mrs Corliss Lamont September 1930, in New York City. Mr and Mrs Masefield sent a small silver drinking cup to baby Margaret for Christmas 1930.

[Boar's Hill, Oxford]
[6 Nov 1930]

Dear Florence,

Thank you so much for your gracious kind letters, which fall like live coals upon this repentant sinner's head; for I have written little or nothing to you for so long, owing to whirl upon whirl of work, in what has been the busiest month I have so far had on earth.

Today, I have been over to the grave of Morris, & have gone from there 1/4 of a mile, & have seen the bed he was born in, & the bed he slept in, & the room he workt in, & much of his work. It is 50 minutes from here by car. On the way, I stopt at Gt Coxwell Barn, that he so lov'd; & tonight I shall read some of his poetry again. It makes one wonder: what would my life have been without him? Supposing I had never had that influence, nor had those particular thrills, & special lurings into special ways?

Coming back, we passt thro' the hounds, & had the pride of being recognized by the huntsman. H.W.N. will someday explain to you that this is near to what canonisation is in religious lands & times, only rather more important.

After 14 consecutive weeks of hellish weather, hardly unbroken, it was a heavenly cold day of sunlight, & the land at its best, in deep colours & beauty.

Our 2 new little plays went off quite well yesterday, & pleas'd the authors hugely, & gave them some useful help I hope. I wish that you could also have heard the Yeats' poems, wh came in between the plays. They rous'd all my old enthusiasm, & were quite beautifully spoken.

Blessings & greetings,
John.

Boar's Hill, Oxford.
[25 Nov 1930]

Dear Florence,

Thank you for your letter. I hope that by this time some of your guests are gone & some of your perturbations, about possible marriage bells, allay'd. We long to hear what is decided.

As I get my knowledge of racketeers & gangsters from the

highly coloured novels & plays of my prose contemporaries, I am wondering whether you & Tom are living in more actual danger than usual. Perhaps you will write to me about this, & tell me if you carry a gat & are becoming nippy on the draw, & can plug a guy full of holes, it would do the heart good to see.

I hope that you will have all the toughs shepherded in before they get too fresh.

Did I tell you of my visit into Shropshire, & how coming home we passt a superb great wooden chariot draggd by three great dray horses, the noblest of their kind, & atttended by three splendid Shropshiremen, who are always rather finer than other men, (as I feel sure you will have notict).

"And what do you think was in the ship?" A marvellous great roaring Hereford Bull, the Wrekin's Astounder, going to or returning from the goodly herd.

Who wd live in a city, where such sights are never to be seen?

Greetings & thoughts from

John.

Boar's Hill, Oxford.
[5 Dec 1930]

Dear Florence,

Thank you for your letter.

There is no herb in the garden against Death, nor any philosophy. Only religion gives such certainty of life that it can bear thinking of.

I am sad for your sorrow for your friend.

I'm afraid I cannot care for any religion bas'd on reason; & could not turn to reason for the mending of a broken heart. Splendour & ecstasy & power & order seem more of the nature of the universe than reason: & we are parts of the Universe, and not very small parts perhaps. We know how small we are. Who knows how big?

I sometimes feel that we are motes in sunbeam, but parts of the sunbeam, & can become sunbeam sometimes, & sometimes sun, but that in this life we are mainly motes: & yet who can have a spiritual experience once & ever again feel that the mortal part is an important part? It isn't, but it can't be reason'd about, & no word from another ever heald the grief for a death. Against Death there is no herb in the garden: nor word in the dictionary.

Bless you,

John.

[Boar's Hill, Oxford]

[9 Dec 1930]

Dear Florence,

Some time a'go, you bought, at Falmouth, a little model of a ship, the *Lena*. I think you still have her, & I have often try'd to find out about her for you. I have now met a man who knew her, & saw her dismasted in a cyclone at Hugli Mouth.

She was one of a few fast little lofty old clippers employed in carrying coolies from Calcutta to Fiji or West Indies. The coolies went in large numbers for 7 years at a time, & always sailed in one of these clippers, because they were slower than steamers, & gave the coolies a chance to become accustom'd to change of climate & life. At the end of the 7 years they came back to Bengal, often as rich men (by their standards.)

When the cyclone struck the *Lena* she was just returning to Bengal with coolies. The captain battend the coolies down below: the storm put the Lena on her side: & blew out her fore-mast & then passt. When it calmd, the captain opend the hatches, expecting to find over 300 coolies in fragments: but there they all were complete. In his joy, he gave them all a special breakfast, which they ate. They then brought their beds on deck & went to sleep in the sun, & there 20 of them died, apparently not from the breakfast, but the shock.

I thought that you wd like to know this tale of your *Lena*'s original.

She was one of the last of the clippers, & was very fast: could go like fun, if things favourd her.

> Blessings & greetings.
> from
> John.

Boar's Hill, Oxford.

[3 Feb 1931]

Dear Florence,

Many thanks for your kind & charming letter, wh smote my unworthy heart, lest you should be hurt or disappointed at our not coming with you to Greece. Alas, if we have given you pain.

Perhaps we may be able to meet on our way back to England from Greece, or in England certainly after we have all returned.

You are I believe at this moment on board the Erie 700 going to the South & West for Arizona, where I suppose you will count as a Pale Face, & will have a big 7 shooter in each pocket, & a chew of tobacco in each cheek. Mind you send me a letter from there beginning "Dear Pard", & ending "Yours till the Mustang laps". I don't think you Americans can realise how extraordinarily romantic & thrilling the Western World seemed to us over here: the frontier world, of Reid,[1] & Buffalo Bill[2] & Bret Harte[3] etc: nor how we would read *Hiawatha*[4] for hours & pore over the illustrations of Catlin,[5] & long to see those same expanses, & same strange figures.

I write with a crick in my neck, & a sort of sideways slue to my body & an aching arm because I am being painted (portrait, not personal decoration or cure for a rash) & have to keep in this odd position for beauty's sake. Il faut suffrir pour être belle. The portrait is to be one of a series: Writers of the Day:— & I must say I wish it were done. Bless you.

I hope you'll have a lovely holiday in Arizona.

John.

1. Thomas Mayne Reid (Mayne Reid), 1818–83, British author who wrote popular novels about the American West and the American Indian.
2. Buffalo Bill, i.e. William F. Cody, 1846–1917. He was a celebrated American showman, popularised by the best selling dime novels of Ned Buntline (E. Z. C. Judson, 1823–86).
3. Bret Harte, 1836–1902. American poet and short story writer.
4. *Hiawatha* (1855) celebrated long poem by Henry Wadsworth Longfellow, 1807–82.
5. George Catlin, 1796–1872, American traveller and artist who published books on and illustrations of the American Indian.

[Boar's Hill, Oxford]

[Jun 1931]

Dear Florence,

I am sending this to Paris, as I know not where you are, but suppose you to be on your way to Europe.

We go to Geneva on the 3rd, & shall be away on the 13th, & go to a place called Zinal, in the Swiss mountains, till the 16th, when we start for home. We hope to be here again on the 17th.

Betty Bartholomew[1] came here for our short Festival[2] last week, spoke her poems, dasht into a car, dasht into a train, sped North, was promptly married, leapt into a car, flung herself into a tug, boarded a liner at sea, & is now with her husband, going to New York, where she should arrive this week. She should find NY restful after these recent adventures.

The Festival was a great success, & got better as it went along.
t was one of the best things we have done here: all the speakers
very good; the best being H. Langley, as Wolsey: Mrs. Wheeler,
as Katherine; Miss Heriz-Smith, as Rosamond; Miss Rean as
Anne; & Judith as a story teller: the Love Gift. We had pretty
good weather, & some extraordinary cakes made by Lucy, & a
tent with coloured lights; & only about 4 gate-crashers. I send the
programme of it. I wish that you could have heard the superb
Wolsey.

We have been looking at lovely houses, & have now taken a flat
in London, in an old part of the town, not very far from the B^r
Museum, where in the old days I used to see Swinburne & Lenin.
We have old pannelled walls, & a view of London thro wh I often
walkt with Synge; & shall, I hope, walk with you.

Greetings & thoughts
from
John.

I hope that the Harvard ceremony was great fun.

---

1. Elizabeth Bartholomew, 1895–1975, talented Scottish reader of poetry and
frequent prize-winner at Masefield Poetry Festivals. She became a close friend of
J.M. and carried on lively correspondence with him. She married Henry P. Van
Dusen, President of Union Theological Seminary.
2. The Poetry Recitations.

[Geneva]
[6 July 1931]

Dear Florence,

I am writing this in a room of the Secretariat while waiting for
the session to recommence, when wisdom will again be flowing.

It is a good deal cooler than it has been: the first cool day since
we left England: & this is a great blessing: for the lake makes the
heat humid & hard to bear. Torrents of rain have been pouring
down, & every cataract in the land must be spouting into the lake,
full force.

In the evenings we wander in the very respectable streets &
look at the bold night life: one small brasserie without a band, &
one big café with a band: & here we take the desperate step of
ordering a chocolat, & sip it on the pavé, & feel really tough.

In the building here there is a neat collection of opium, heroin
& cocaine found thro the League in pots & shoes & pans & balls of

lard & even cemented into mill stones for export into differen
lands. I wonder wd things buck up a bit if the Committee were tc
take these drugs before beginning a session. It would be worth the
trial.

I hope that the Italian Art studies are prospering, & that you
are having a glorious time.

Please give my greetings to Eleanor & her young man, & tc
Neville & his wife: & if you see them, to the Berensons, & the
Podesta di Firenze & the Lubbocks[1] in the Villa up above.

Greetings & thoughts

John.

---

1. Percy Lubbock, 1879–1965, English critic and biographer, and his wife,
formerly Lady Sybil Scott and mother of the biographer Iris Origo.

[Boar's Hill, Oxford]
[28 Aug 1931]

Dear Florence,

I hope that you are now gaily dancing on an unplastered foot, &
singing

A fig for Dr. Smith.
A bas les medecins Anglais.
Vive la poésies. etc.

I hope so much that the Atlantic kept quiet while you were
crossing, so that you had a not so bad time. The weather here
cheered up a little, tho, of course not the political weather, wh is
somewhat dark, & may be darker. There is general relief at the
changes in the cabinet; & the usual wonder: why was not all this
done months ago? However, one feels a little like the ancient Skald
in the poem, who reckon'd up all the evils that had happen'd to
him, something like this:

1. Being Bloodaxe kill'd my Father.
2. Stein Wolfgrim killd my Mother.
3. Digmar Skullbones burnd all my other relatives.
4. I lost both my legs under a buzz-saw.
5. And had all my teeth out
6. But it wasn't the teeth after all.
7. It was the jaw bone.
8. The thing I eat with now is a wooden jaw
9. But it doesn't work always

10. And I have indigestion after eating meat
11. And I live in a graveyard with ghosts
12. And one of them is a blue one, & swollen, & it will come to my bed at night & clack its teeth.
13. Still, it isn't so bad, these things passt or are passing, & will soon be passt: it is a noble world, & with poetry & the Sun, one could ask nothing better.

Good luck to the mending bone.

John.

[Boar's Hill, Oxford]
[4 Sept 1931]

Dear Florence,

Of all the wet & sodden days of a cold & sodden summer, this is the soddenest & the likest gloom; but by good fortune, I have your letter, & can think of you in the sun, waving an unplastered foot to the mosquitos.

Can you dance yet?

We are sad to think of you in the *Olympic* in a heaving sea.

We drove over to Stratford 2 days ago, to see Henry IV, part 1, & also had a look at the new theatre, which is certainly a lot higher than it was in June, & gave me some hopes of its being ready before I die. If they wd put their backs into it, they would have it ready. It is only the Will that lacks in human affairs. Only the Will shuts us from Paradise.

It is odd that the Stratford Theatre should mean so much to me, but I hated its being burned more than I can tell you. I went to see it burning & it was like poetry dying.[1] And all this delay in rebuilding is the devil to me. And you & Tom turning to & rousing up all those sums of money for it has been most beautiful to me; & I long to see the theatre open, & Stratford again a place, or a remade place, doing better plays than ever & stirring people's hearts as never before.

If they would buck up, or hire some brisk young bucko mate to boss the workers for awhile, or to give them a sense of the glory of God, then, they would be ready by Easter, & *you would have to come to the opening* on WS's birthday.

Greetings
John.

1. The first Stratford Theatre burned down in 1926. T.W.L. and F.C.L. helped to raise the money for its rebuilding in 1932.

[n.p.]
Oct 7 1931

Dear Florence,

I am grieved that the Milton poem should have been shelved, but nowadays pain affects people in ways unknown to ancestors. Our tough forebears never could pass an exam unless they had at least the gout to give them leisure to study for it; & your real scholar was then, therefore, usually a sot, who became so by arguing,

a.   If I do not drink, I shall not get gout.
b.   If I do not get gout, I shall not study.
c.   If I do not study, I shall not pass.

Argal: come port, come gout, come knowledge.

As a result we had a famous 18th century of scholarship & solitary & sodden scholars: never was such a time.

I am sending this to Sky Farm, for I think it may just reach you there, just about the day when you fling off your crutch & the last bandage & sing begone, dull care. I wish that I could see you cast them away; & go dancing.

The burglars who were here (2 of the 3) are now in gaol, awaiting trial on many counts. One is called Dirky & the other Soopy. Both have many surnames, being real old hands at it, & the police think they will get 5 years. The only things recovered so far are a few old gramophone records. But what good will the 5 years do to the two poor men? None; but great harm. What will they do after the 5 years? Burgle again. What will come to them, then? Another 5, or 7, or 10 years. What good will that do? None, but great harm. And so forth.

It has set me thinking about all this beastly problem, which we shelve & never tackle, century after century. Good luck to the No more Crutched,

John.

[n.p.]

23 October 1931

Dear Florence,

Some weeks ago, I had the honour of being offered the honorary Freedom of the Shipwright's Company, an ancient body, with a certain history of 800 years, & a less certain history of some 300 years further back. So, on the strength of having built, or cut, some small models, I agreed to be a Shipwright; & so on Wed last I was made one, & took the oath, to obey the Master's lawful orders & to keep the Company's secrets. As I shall never receive any orders, nor hear any secrets, this oath might safely be pledged.

The ceremony took place in the Hall of the Barber-Surgeons, in London; an ancient room, of very great beauty; & after I had taken the oath we all adjourned to another room to taste a famous wine. I did not taste it, but only smelled it, & whatever its taste may have been, its perfume was like Araby the Blest: a sweet heavy fragrance: the sort of smell of really good verse. A good bit of Milton wd smell so when uncorkt.

After this, we went back to the Hall, wh was now spread for a simple, but very good dinner, with most exquisite porcelain & silver, all old, some very old.

The table was old, too, being the Dissecting Table of the old, extinct Barber Surgeons.

Formerly, the Barber Surgeons had a perquisite of all the bodies (some were hanged in chains) of felons hangd at Tyburn; & would dissect these, on this table.

But the old way of hanging only strangled people. So that in dissection lots of felons came to life & asked what in Blazes, etc etc. Then the surgeons used to smuggle them out to the Indies, & start them in life afresh.

And at the end of the table was a very noble old Oriental screen of great size & splendour.

One of their resuscitated felons went to the East & became very wealthy; & then, in gratitude, he sent this Screen to the Barber Surgeons, & they have had it ever since.

Now that I am a Master Shipwright please bear me in mind if you want some little neat yacht or cruiser or anything of that sort. I would love to build you something with more style to her than the *Jane & Sarah*.

I am so rejoict at your Foot being well. What a joy to you.
"O joy it is to her & joy to me".
Blessings from
John.

[n.p.]
October 1931

Dear Florence,

Alas, I have missed a mail, by an increase in work of different sorts: I am so very sorry.

And I have to thank you for so many letters, & to congratulate you on the healing of the foot, & now to condole with you on the death of Mr. Morrow,[1] whose loss all the world feels with you: & I, too, who admired him for a quick, clear, interested & interesting mind, joined to a singular capacity for friendship & friendly dealing. He was one of the very great Americans of this time, in whom we all here hoped we saw a great President soon to be. And he wd have been a very great one, for in addition to his practical grasp of things there was a mental range & power & beauty very rare in practical men: & an extraordinary loss at this time, when there is a mess, & an audience for every noisy fool. All thinking people here know that a very great American has died; & there is real feeling about it. And I (& we all) are truly sad to think of the sorrow of you & Tom who knew him so well, & were associated with him so often, so closely, & in things of moment which make all links so strong & close. For Death: I think of Dante's lines about Hope. "Isaiah says that each one shall have double garment made in his own land: & his own land is this sweet life." (i.e. in Paradise.)[2] I want you, please, to forgive my writing on this paper. It is so easy to write on; & I have had so much writing this week that an easy paper is a rest to the hand.

The Lecture was well-liked (I thought) but I know I didn't do it well. There must have been about 2000 people there; & if there hadn't been an Election, with meetings in every room & hall in London, England, Scotland & Wales, & free fights in some of them, the place wd have been full. It brought me a lot of letters of thanks (& this is very rare) so that it may have pleased people. But my part of it was not well done. However, I feel that I must have another try at some later time.

It is puzzling: what to do for poetry. One tries to write it: And to interest people in it: And to get it acted: And to get it spoken: And to get it read & understood as a part of the fun of life.

It is best not to try to do more than to enjoy a thing hugely & share the enjoyment somehow with others. If you sow poetry, you have to sow prose with it, & prose is the crop that comes up: violent prose, leading to bad acts & folly.

Now I must stop this, with my thanks & blessings to you for letters & cable.

Greetings from
John.

1. Dwight W. Morrow, who died 3 Oct. 1931. American banker and diplomat.
2. Dante Alighieri, *Paradiso*, Canto 25.

Westminster.
Nov 16 1931.

Dear Florence,

Many thanks & blessings to you for all your letters & thoughts & cables during this wearing time.

Now that the crisis is past, & recovery quickly going on, I can tell you something of what it has been.

At first, the diagnosis was biliousness. Then uraemia was feared, but disproved. Then the suggestion was made, that it was watery pressure on the brain. Then the symptoms were called just toxaemia (a convenient term). Then a very great doctor thought that the confusing symptoms pointed rather to sleepy sickness: Encephalitis lethargica.

But after some days of really careful thought he decided that it might be a growth in the brain, in one particular place, & in this view a famous surgeon concurred. They advised a speedy operation in London. So, in all haste, C[1] was transferred to London & operated on next day, on the imagination of a great man, who had very little positive to go upon.

The tumor was in the exact spot indicated by him, & by blessed fortune was not rooted, but could be easily removed.

It was not in itself a malign growth but was pressing heavily & would speedily have killed.

I am wondering now what chances of such salvation come to poor men & women so attacked.

I hope that they have some chance of a great imagination considering their cases & getting at the truth of them. I wonder if they have.

At odd moments, I consider my great man (a little like my big brother in some ways) & compare him with the ruffian Connemara vet who dealt such havoc to you.

I believe that the case attracted a good deal of interest, & that it will be written of (under some judicious veil) in the chief medical papers, as a masterpiece of diagnosis on a few & very confusing symptoms. If it make my great man to be raised to the peerage I shall be happier still.

The K & Q[2] sent me a telegram of extraordinary charm.

The PM[3] sent me a letter.

But you sent me cable after cable & had the lovely kind thought to ring me up & cheer me by word of mouth, for which I will ever bless your name & the thought of you.

Bless you for this & for so much more.

Always devotedly your friend
John.

1. Constance Masefield.
2. King George V and Queen Mary. J.M. had been appointed Poet Laureate in 1930.
3. Prime Minister Ramsay MacDonald.

[n.p.]
Jan 9 1932

Dear Florence,

We had a quaint little gale here 2 days ago, not much compared with the great gale of three years ago, but still a brisk young thing.

It took Judith's pony shed, (the pony being in another field), blew it over the fence, & left it upside down in the next field, where it lies, forlorn, "a mighty one mightily fallen", a sight for gods & (I'm afraid) little devils of boys. To you, this is nothing, for you come from a land where (as a man told me he had seen) a two-horse buggy with men in it is/are swept by the summer zephyrs right over the railroad & set down by the drugstore. To us quiet folk however it is a stirring opening to a new year. Symbolically, it means that the old order must go. En avant. Tambours au front.

For a few minutes in the gusts, I thought that the chimneys would give, but they stood it like little men.

Constance is doing well & getting along. Next week we shall hope to have her downstairs; & I hope that the week after that we may even get her out of doors, if the winter holds off.

I've not read anything for months, save Ronsard,[1] a little Homer, & some Crabbe,[2] whose Centenary will be on Feb 3rd, & I have to speak about him.

> Friend, Did you ever read George Crabbe?
> His verse comes slab on chilly slab
> Cold slab, that doesn't always fit
> And strikes but doesn't always hit
> With gloom about the village poor.

Dear Florence I can write no moor.
                    Bless you.
                        John.

But good old GC loved women & opium & sometimes burst out into splendour.

1. Pierre de Ronsard, 1524?–85, French poet of romantic love.
2. George Crabbe, 1754–1832. English poet whose realistic verse narratives anticipate, without resembling, J.M.'s own *The Everlasting Mercy.*

Boar's Hill, Oxford.
19 Jan. 1932

Dear Florence,

We have now had C downstairs for a few days, & out of doors yesterday & today, in a very mild patch of weather that comes luckily just when wanted. So you will judge that she is progressing well & getting every kind of strength again.

In the intervals, I am reading the Lincoln books which you gave me years ago: & these, & Lockhart's Scott[1] & some light fiction beguile the time.

In only 2 more weeks, I have to speak about George Crabbe:—

> Linkt as the flounder to the dab
> My spirit will be linkt to Crabbe
> And I shall have to say how this,

> That & the other thing he is
> And all the whichness & the whatness
> Of all his coldness & his hotness
> And all the howness & the whyness
> Of all his wetness & his dryness
> And all the cowness & the bullness
> Of his placidity & dulness.

But I have now read $7\frac{1}{2}$ of his 8 vols, $6\frac{1}{2}$ being poetry, & I think that he is a much under-rated poet, & has 3 or 4 things, of which I had never heard, which are really very fine indeed: so I will hope to up, & say good things of him.

Bless you. I hope that the U.S. is not in great distress this winter, but, like us, managing a little football in spite of it.

John.

---

1. *The Life of Sir Walter Scott* (1837–8) by the novelist's son-in-law, the journalist and novelist John Gibson Lockhart, 1794–1854.

[Boar's Hill, Oxford]
[24 Mar 1932]

Dear Florence,

I thank you for your letter about the deplorable plays.

But you excite all my worst curiosities about these plays. Tell me more. What were they all about? "Of Thee I Sing",[1] seems to be a prelude to romance if not to poetry; but of course if it were not of thee, but of a pert hussey unknown, then no doubt it was not much of a song & you did well to be vexed.

I do not see that you can do anything to prevent the playing of vulgarity. If vulgarity be pushed to the extreme limit of vulgarity, it becomes poetical by reason of its excess: & the outrageously low is in its place in the satyr play & the wildest farce. You do not want these things & are shocked by them: but the comic theatre really lives by them, if it be in a lively state. And I think that New York is creating a new kind of play that comes out of the life of the streets & has a curious zest to it, the zest of the New York underworld, which is unlike anything else: & I suppose is pretty awful in some ways, but it is life, & it has zest.

George Ade[2] said a wise thing: "In lifting, get underneath".

But to blazes with morality: a fig for sermons. You are sailing on the 6th and will be here in about three weeks. Joy and cheers. Hurray. I am so glad.

Bless you.
John.

1. The popular new Broadway musical of the era. *Of Thee I Sing* was written by George S. Kaufman and Morrie Ryskind, with music by George Gershwin, and was a satire on the American presidency.
2. George Ade, 1866–1944, American author and humorist, whose best-known work was *Fables in Slang*.

Boar's Hill, Oxford
March 1932

Dear Florence,

Many thanks for your letter about the poor Lindberghs.[1]

They are probably the most felt-for people in this country at present. Being a sinner myself I have a great love of forgiveness, but I must say I have felt that the people who can deal such pain to fine characters & let a little tiny boy run such risk of life-long shock, would be better put out of the world, if they could ever be certainly met with.

We go over the crime with all manner of suppositions. The thing that is so shocking is, that some dreadful crimes are done with an apparent easy smoothness like the lick of a quick wave that takes a man overboard in a lurch, & buries as it takes.

We just hope that the good in the world will rise up & strangle the bad here, & bring the little boy back.

I suppose that nothing has so stirred this people since about ten years ago, when some policemen bullied a girl, & roused the nation to fury.

I hope that you have found your Mother better, & that soon there will be good news of the child.

C is really very nearly well now, & is starting going to see people for brief visits.

Thoughts from
John.

1. Charles A. and Anne Morrow Lindbergh, close friends of the Lamonts. Their first child, Charles Lindbergh, Jr was kidnapped and murdered in March 1932.

Boar's Hill, Oxford.
[June 1932]

Dear Florence,

Many thanks for your letter & the accounts of the Columbia degree-giving. I admire the tact with which these men of learning disguise gin cocktail as orangeade. Here, in Oxford, on similar occasions, the learned gather to drink a preparation of champagne & to eat strawberries & clotted cream. They call it "partaking of Lord Crew's Benefaction" which sounds as though it were a kind of communion service.

I hope that you will have lovely weather for Eleanor's wedding: & that all will go off most happily. I shall write to her next week & send her a book & a blessing: it won't be the Life of Cavour, which she probably expects from me, but something more personal.

I was in Liverpool this week, following the boat race in the tender *Bison*, with young Mr. Muncaster,[1] the painter. Our crew was the best we have had for four years, & at first I thought we might do it, but it was not so fated by the gods. In the evening we all met at dinner, about 120 of us, and had rather a jolly time, but for some speeches wh were too long, including about 5 by me as President. After dinner, I got aboard a sleeper & was at home to breakfast.

Mr. Muncaster has just been sailing round Ireland in a 3-tonner, & round the Horn in a 3000-tonner, & has done some fine paintings. I think that he will be much the best of living marine painters in this country.

Wishing you all sorts of happy & fortunate circumstances for the Wedding, & with many thoughts & blessings
John.

---

1. Claude Muncaster, 1903–, English painter represented in the Tate and other British galleries.

[n.p.]
June 28, 1932.

Dear Florence,

I hope that the wedding[1] has gone off with every beauty & happiness; & that now you are to have a little peace. I am sure that Eleanor looked lovely, & that she will now be happy. I thought of her & of you all day long, & so feel sure that my good wishes reached you both at the most critical time.

Bless you.

John.

I look forward to hearing all about it, when you can find the time.

We are now planning to leave this place about March next.

1. Eleanor Lamont married Charles C. Cunningham 27 June 1932.

[Boar's Hill, Oxford]
[16 Sep 1932]

Dear Florence,

I'm afraid I am always asking you for one thing or another. This time I am going to ask you about the case of 9 negroes, who, it seems, are all condemned to death, for having ravished 2 girls, white, in a freight train near a place called Scottsborough,[1] in Alabama. The case is being re-tried by the U.S. Supreme Court in October, & I have been asked to help in the raising of funds here to fee counsel for the defence of the 9. I don't know much about the case, except that there are undoubted, good reasons for the re-trial, ably set out by the U.S. lawyers who caused the re-trial to be granted.

But before I help in the raising of funds, or join any Committee, I would like to have a Transcript of the Original Trials of the 9 men, in Jackson County, Alabama, April, 1931. Do you think that you could have this sent to me.

It does exist, & is pretty certain to be printed, & obtainable: because the lawyers allude to it in their Brief continually. It seems to us likely that Corliss will have filled your house with copies of it for the last year or more, so if you have one & could spare one, I would be grateful.

It is not a question of interfering at all, or meddling. The 9 men are destitute, & subscriptions are being opened in their behalf in all the European countries.

Do you remember motoring us once from Devon, & stopping at a pre-historic Earthwork, of great beauty, in Wiltshire, & getting some mushrooms there? We were there yesterday, looking at some manor-houses (which were either too small or too big) & they have been excavating there, & found a fine big skeleton of an

Early Iron Age man (say 200 B.C.) who was wearing leather boots with iron hob-nails and bronze decorations.

Lew is off for Russia.

Greetings

John.

1. This refers to the Scottsboro case, in which nine young blacks were accused of raping two white girls. Their conviction was set aside twice by the U.S. Supreme Court and by 1940, after long legal battles, all but one were freed. He later escaped from jail.

Edinburgh.

Oct 13, 1932

Dear Florence,

Whenever I come to this place, as I do once in every year or so, I make it a rule to sit at this table, looking out at the graveyard (& the castle, & the passing Scottish beauties) & write to you.

It is always raining when I do this, & therefore you must not be jealous of the Scottish beauties, for from this upper window, they all look like this [Drawing of three girls carrying large umbrellas which hide their heads completely]. I have come up here to read in aid of the S.A.S.V., of which Betty van Dusen was once the famous Secretary; also, I have to see some portraits & things, of various beauties and blackguards, whose sins figure in something I am trying to write.

Just before I set off, Neville came to lunch, which was very delightful: he seemed fairly cheery about things.

Lew has not yet recovered from the poisonous water & food of Russia, but is slowly getting better. We get from him a feeling of an utterly incompetent people living feverishly, with something rather generous & noble not quite killed by the incompetence & the fever. To us, probably, the results would not seem worth the price they are paying & will pay: & yet, wherever the effort & the energy is, sympathy should & does go. I would hate it: but they are trying to stop some evil things which make the heart bleed in all lands. And yet: it must be hellish. So often, a nation, like a man in love, thinks itself heroic, whereas it may be merely blind: & I think Russia is swoln with her own excitement & quite blind. However, not to recognize the effort & the energy is to be old, if not dead. We are making a greater effort & showing greater energy, but we make less noise about it.

Young Mr Robert Byron is writing in *Country Life* about it; & Y.B. in the *Spectator*. People are now beginning to see Russia for what it is: a great in-competence under a considerable bluff.

Even this land of John Knox has changed since the war. A young male Scot has just gone by in the rain under a very skittish green & white parasol, wh John Knox wd have said was "a bonny love gift from the hussie of Babylon to gar a man gang the way to Hell."

Bless you.
John.

Edinburgh.
Oct 14, 1932.

Dear Florence,

Today, for a wonder, the sun shines unspeakably, & I can look out on a bright graveyard, & on a castle that is like mist with a sharp edge, & on Scottish beauties [drawing] each more beautiful than the one in front.

I have seen a lot of historical things here, portraits of the Stuarts, Craigmillar castle, etc & go to Glasgow this afternoon. I saw at Craigmillar the little room where Mary Stuart had her private chapel. The young Scot who showed me the place knew all his land's history as tho a poet had taught him, he having learned it from the country folk's memory, that never forgets, here, what happened at the place & which clans did it. He had no romantic feeling about M whatsoever, & none about her enemies, he was as accurate as man can be & as dispassionate as God. He interested me very much. He lived at C, which is a lone swell, hardly a hill till you're on top of it, & then you see what a marvellous survey the rise gives. You see Edina, & miles & miles of moor, & hill & river & sea, divine in beauty, & every bit he knew the story of, where the castle got its water, & who did what, & where Cromwell put his guns, & their range & almost what each shot did.

Coming back, I went to sleep, & then read to my audience & so to bed. There was an old man at my reading, who had been one of the Volunteer Artillerists here 60 years ago; & the memory of the bangs he then occasioned still cheered his old heart. "I mind the time we firrred the RRRoyal salute."

Bless you.
John.

[Boar's Hill, Oxford]
[18 Nov 1932]

Dear Florence,

I expect that your life is being made a burden to you by the Election:[1] however, that will be at an end in a few hours, & then you will have some peace. I hope that the rest at the Palisades will set you up & fit you for the strain of Christmas & the following Masefields.

We have been preparing a little scene of the killing of Mary Stuart, a sort of cheery little Xmas tableau; & in order to get the hang of it, we went to Fotheringhay, which is about 84 miles from here. You have probably been there, & I therefore won't describe it, but I am sending you a sketch of a part of the site. The only bit left of the castle is a mass of masonry inside some rails on the R of the sketch. The river is the River Nen or Nene, a famous river: it served as castle-moat on this side. The mound in the sketch is artificial. The first Norman Keep stood on it. The main Elizabethan building stood below the keep, behind the big thorn-tree. Mary was killed about 20 yards from the tree in what was then the castle hall. The window of the hall, which gave light to that "acte si barbare" is now in an old inn at Oundle, where we afterwards lunched.

The castle was demolished, & the site is now all nettled and kexed: & the moat is now a mass of reed rush & rubbish, with a little water at the bottom. The outer moat is a rather damp field.

For some months, this quiet scene was thronged with all the peers of England, & their followers; & where they put up, & how they got themselves fed, is a problem. During M's so called trial, the press of people made something like a local famine: the district was eaten out of bread & drunken out of beer (not out of water: few parts of the globe can be damper).

I send a card for the play, *in case.*

I do hope that you are now rested.

Greetings & blessings, from
John.

1. Of Franklin Delano Roosevelt, the new Democratic President who was to launch the New Deal and initiate legislation that many in the U.S. financial community found burdensome.

Boar's Hill, Oxford.
[1932]

Dear Florence,

I have two letters to thank you for. Many thanks for both.

In the one, you send an S.O.S. about a poem by Mr. Eliot: about a Mrs. Porter and her daughter, who washed their feet in soda-water.[1]

Well, you must not think that Mr. E wrote that: it is as it were a ghost floating into the poem from outside, or someone singing it in the street. The poem is about London, & Mrs. Porter was a popular song in London just before the war. It has a rather good tune; & the tune is as it were the soul of the London of that time, & therefore when it comes into the poem it is supposed to suggest or evoke the image of that London.

I don't think that Mrs. P & her daughter ever did what the poem says, because it is poetry not history, & poetry deals in excessive statement. At the most, they may have said "there's too much soda in our glasses, no room left for the whiskey", & so poured some of it out onto the floor; & to their neighbours in the bar this may have seemed like washing the feet etc.

Eleanor came with Charlie & Mr. Hallowell to lunch on Sunday: all 3 very well & cheery & it was so jolly to see E & C & to find them so glad to see us: & to give us news of you.

Lew is slowly recovering from the internal poisons picked up in Russia.

When I am 72, I shall be in my ashes, my dear Florence, but I hope that what of me is not ashes will think grateful & beautiful thoughts of you.

Bless you.
John.

1. The lines occur in section III of *The Waste Land* (1922).

On one of his brief lecture trips to the United States, Masefield comforted a recuperating F.C.L.

New York.

[14 Jan 1933]

Dear Florence,

You were ever a giver of light & help. Many grateful thoughts of light & help must be flowing to you now on the living love of many, to be both screen and rest to you.

I hope that these will be as lovely presences near you all the time, by night and day. I hope that you will have a quiet happy night of rest tonight, & a peaceful day on waking. With many tender & grateful thoughts of a great & long friendship.

John.

Buffalo, N.Y.

[14 Feb 1933]

Dear Florence,

Greetings for the new day.

I hope that it will be a good day, both for you & Tom, with steady progress for both of you.

I am going now to Troy, & I do wish that it might prove to be the real Troy, so that I might be lecturing to Andromache (not to mention Helen) & be introduced by Hektor, & have a look round the walls with Priam, by moonlight, before my train goes.

Greetings,

John.

Boar's Hill, Oxford.

[14 Mar 1933]

Dear Florence,

Since we landed here, the Fates seem to have dealt grim blows at your country: & I'm afraid that each blow has meant more work & anxiety for you & Tom, & still no clear sky to windward.

The only consolation I can offer, is, that the world has gone through worse, & emerged.

I used to be much cheered in dark days by a remark of Don Quixote's to Sancho (when he complained of some disaster, all but final),

"What wouldst thou say if thou wert on the Riphaean Mountains?"

And similarly I ask myself "What would I say if I were dipped in oil & set fire to, by some modern Nero, for my religion's sake?

Or baked in an oven by a Turk, for sheer joie de vivre?

Or set to a post for the tide to cover, like the coastguard in the story?

Or beggared, & reduced to making toys or singing in the streets for a living?"

One must think of people sacked & harrowed & led into captivity, eyeless in Gaza, at mills with slaves & utterly hopeless & knowing it is all their own fault, in order to realize how very much better off one is.

This damned time will pass, if not for us for others, & the world will go not so ill, & there'll be love & fun enough for us; so cheer up, my lads, 'tis to fortune we steer: this iron time is passing.

Bless you,
John.

Seeking new if not greener pastures, Masefield and his wife Constance decided to move from Boar's Hill, Oxford, and make their new home in Pinbury Park, Gloucestershire.

Pinbury Park.
Cirencester.
[2 May 1933]

Dear Florence,

The first Lamont to enter these doors was Eleanor, who came for a night at the end of last week, & seemed exceedingly well & happy, though perhaps a bit homesick: & who can wonder? Lew, who was here, played to us, but it was too wet for bowls, which is now the household game here.

We hope so much that all the worries that have been assailing Tom & you are now dying down. In your next letter I shall hope to hear of you at home, well, & already packing for Pinbury. "Josephine:[1] put in my pale green silk, to match the Pinbury Lawn. Josephine: put in my dark green satin, for when I walk in the Pinbury Ghost walk. Josephine: I must have my mud-boots, for when I ford Pinbury River etc."

This is certainly a heavenly place, & time slips away fast, there

are so many things to do, & so little time. The range is today
disembowelled & scrapped, & a new one inserted. Please God
they won't have to change the boiler, too.

Blessings & thoughts to you, & many invitations to come here
soon.

John.

1. Mrs Lamont's personal maid.

Pin.
[18 May 1933]

Dear Florence,

Of course we will not book up July, but keep it clear for you.

I think you will like this place although the garden is not yet
ready for you. We are slowly learning its old & romantic history,
& are enchanted to learn that it was once Anne Boleyn's, &
probably sent dues of some sort to her, though she may never have
seen it.

The ghost has not yet been seen, but a friendly seer says that her
influence is good: "so do not fear, beloved dear, but come and join
the party."

I am so happy, that I have just seen here a wild dormouse, a
rather rare & charming little beast that few see out of cages: there
are also wild duck, such as I wrote the verses about; & so it only
needs you to be perfect.

Greetings & thoughts
from
John.

[Pinbury]
[20 Jul 1933]

Dear Florence,

Many thanks for your nice letter.

I ought to have told you that the S of Devon is very relaxing, &
will, in days of low barometer, make even a New Yorker inclined
to a siesta. It is probably just the very place for you all & will send
you to sleep as by enchantment. But I never knew that T wrote
Xing the Bar¹ there. That is something worth having about the
place; the knowledge that a thing so much loved should have been
made there.

You must go to the Moor, & also to Tor Cross, to see the lagoon near the sea. From Tor Cross, you can strike inland on foot up a little valley along a little river, the Gara, which is a place of great beauty, (or used to be); & not far from it is a little beach where, after storms, old Spanish gold & silver coins used to be found (never by me); a little beach just to the east of Strete.

This place misses you much, & hopes soon to see you again.

Please give my loves to all the household, & get yourself thoroughly rested, & sunburned & red-Indian-looking.

                    Greetings & thoughts
                        from John.

Geoffroi has done a charming drawing of Pin.

1. Tennyson's poem, 'Crossing the Bar'.

                        Pinbury Park.
                        [31 Jul 1933]

Dear Florence,

Thank you for your thrilling poem, wh, alas, confirms the world in its belief, that everybody is really a jolly good poet, but that only a few fools go in for it as a business. I am glad that the cheeses arrived in a cool & edible condition.

The novel has gone off to the press: & there is a chance that Mr. Muncaster may do a few pictures for a special edition of it. I hope to see Mr. M about this tomorrow. Few men know how to draw sailing ships now: & I suppose very few have seen studdingsails set; & yet now & then I hear someone with prominent ears hailed as "Stunsails", as tho' some memory of them were still in the popular mind.

If you go to Tor Cross, to see the lagoon, go up the Gara Valley. It was once open to the sea for some miles, & men digging there used to find anchors & remains of vessels. There is a pool in the valley, reputed to be bottomless, but a friend of mine probed it & found it to be 3 feet 6″. So does criticism dispose of a poet's reputation.

It was there that I saw the bird, the water ousel, running along the bottom of the clear brook at least a foot below the surface, wh wd be a lovely faculty to have.

May the bathing & the cheeses restore you to perfect health.

                    Greetings from
                        John.

[Pinbury Park?]
Oct 16 1933[?]

Dear Florence,

Thank you for your letter from Atlantic City.

Although you wring my heart, in suggesting that I ought to have the lunatic to live with me, I am not going to do it.

Lunatic to me: Come poet, let me live with you,
      You as the rose with me as dew
      You as the bread, with me as butter,
      You as the dove cot, me the coo
      Of quiet doves that flutter.

Me to Lunatic: Keep out, and tend whatever cot
      Your frenzy happens to have got;
      And if you haven't, go to dwell
      Within some sanitary cell.
      If none will have you, take a rope
      And fix it round your neck in hope
      And hitch the other end to rafter
      And leap, & watch what happens after.

I have been wondering much what sort of a state the U.S. is now in. Is it improving & tending towards prosperity, or not yet bettering? Things here are better than they were, a little, but are still pretty bad. However, they are better.

Do you hear anything of a Company called the Book of the Month Society in your land? They made a suggestion the other day that they should distribute fifty thousand copies of my books gratis to their subscribers, & pay me three cents on each copy given. I thought that this was just about the limit: & refused with more oaths than I wd be justified in writing here: real good Georgian oaths, like ──── & X X X & uuuuu & nnnnn. How would you like to have your children chopped up small & given to the hens as chick food, & only 3 cents per child allowed to you? My blood boils whenever I think of it.

      Bless you
      John.

Pinbury Park.
[29 Nov 1933]

Dear Florence,

It seems a long time since I heard from you, and hope that this means, that you are having a royal time at the Palisades[1] with philosophy & contemplation, a sort of heavenly twins, one on each knee, much more restful than the grandchildren you mostly affect.

Do not get so robustly hearty that you will try for the North or South Pole next summer instead of coming to Pinbury, for that would be indeed jolly for you but a cruel pang here.

The place is as lovely as ever, now that the leaves are off. The jasmine & the violets are out: the berries are scarlet on shrubs & trees, & the storm-cock loudly sings, & marvels that no American beauty tries to catch his notes on the piano.

I have been trying to write about a ship called the *Gry*, but not with much success. She was like this; & you will see at a glance that she was a wicked kind of filibuster, up to no good at any time. [Drawing] I have written her thrice & must still do her twice more: she will not come. This is not due to old age but cussedness.

Bless you. Write soon & tell us all the stirring news: what gangs are out in the Bronx & who shoots who.

Greetings & thoughts.
John.

1. In 1929 the Lamonts had moved from Englewood, N.J., to a new house they had built atop the Palisades of the Hudson River at Palisades, N.Y.

Pinbury Park.
[27 Jan 1934]

Dear Florence,

The dark two months of the year are now over, & we can have tea by day-light & know that very soon, now, the snowdrops will be in a great mass all over the garden & Spring visibly here. Who wd not be a Briton? Think what your ancestors so rashly flung away at Boston harbour.

We have had some gay weekend parties with Lew & others. We play bridge & other games & Lew plays to us; then in the mid week we read modern French novels (none very good, but all now dreadfully proper, about young women who die of grief etc, the real mid-Victorian touch.)

We have even played some games of bowls, but must stop for a while while we dress the grass with lawn-sand and lime.

Your note & letter came this morning, for both of which I send my grateful thanks.

Good luck to your B.C. clinic.[1] Here, in these parts, rabbit-warren nature is not improved upon by these aids. There is rather a spawn of younglings, and the neat little devices invented by the thoughtful are passed by unbought and unused.

All good wishes to you all. I feel sure that Ellie must now be secure in health. I am so very glad & thankful for all your sakes.

Bless you.

John.

1. Birth Control Clinic. F.C.L. had a lively interest in Planned Parenthood and making birth control accessible in general.

Pinbury Park.

[26 Mar 1934]

Dear Florence,

Thank you for your comforting cable, which helped to reassure your wretched and devoted friends. I am glad indeed to think that things are a little better.

We are filled with rage at the dirty trickeries of the politicians, & wish that they may sink in their iniquities, & be cast out upon their fitting muckheaps; as they will be.

I could not write in these last days, as I had to go down to Devon, to speak, & then had somehow to finish my Wm Morris speech in time for the centenary; yesterday.

We drove over to Exeter College,[1] & ate & drank in his memory, & then I gave the speech in the College Hall, & I hope it was better than it seemed to me at the time. Miss M was there, but not Miss Lobb.

I had never been in the hall before. I suppose Morris has gone on now to new activities, but I had the feeling that he was conscious of our thought of him & perhaps saw the bright side of our intentions.

Bless you.

John.

1. Exeter College, Oxford, founded in 1314. Morris was an undergraduate there 1853–5.

Pinbury Park.
May 1934.

Dear Florence,

By all means come to us for the first week in July (or any other week or month) & bring Austin's baby,[1] too, for she looks a perfect charmer. What fun to have you here; & what fun to think of you a grandmother over & over again; have you taken to wearing a nice cap, with purple ribbons in it?

I am so thankful that those damned skunks have withdrawn their damned devilries. Men are none too good as individuals, but collections of men, state departments & the like, are infinitely worse than rabbles of men, or mobs; they have the blind power of a mob & the cold devilry of an institution; & men have given them the reins once held by princes.

It is bitter cold here: 17 May: ice in the open air & snow yesterday. We go to Exeter Coll tonight to see an open air performance of *Everyman*.[2] We shall go in furs and cower under eiderdowns.

Greetings,
John.

1. Lavinia Lloyd Lamont, born to Mr and Mrs Austin Lamont, 23 March 1934. Married Alan Rosenthal.
2. *Everyman*. English morality play, c.1500.

London
[12 Jun 1934]

Dear Florence,

This is a note from London to say that we are now off for Pin. Hurrah, my lads, as they say in marine romance.

I hope that Eleanor will come happily through the ordeal & bring you a grandchild as lovely as Nancy's (Nothing more lovely could be.)   Thank you so much for your letter, but I'm jealous of this Prof who took you up Bear Mountain "to talk philosophy". My God these Professors, & you in a new hat, too.

Bless you
John.

[Pinbury Park]
[8 Aug 1934]

Dear Florence,

Thank you for your nice letter about the Govr of Bermuda. Would that I had a similar hearty way with decanters & the French.

You ask me "is it bad or not to rhyme *failure* with *pale lure*".

Well, it is a matter of taste, & personal liking, & the squeamishness or robustness of the literary gang one belongs to.

Generally speaking, the best English serious verse makes little use of double rhymes. Our three best poets would have shrunk from such rhymes. I can think of no near parallel in their work.

One might say that certainly the rhymes are not according to the very best English practice. Our greatest men in their greatest moods would not have used them. And that is that.

But Browning when he used them was not in his greatest mood. He was in a mood of high spirits which only once or twice passed into lofty feeling: and he was writing a poem that is, seemingly, being sung, or rather shouted, by young disciples carrying an old scholar's corpse up a mountain.[1]

The double rhymes are of the very stuff of the poem or song, and are so much easier to sing than single rhymes that they are very right where they occur.

Well. What is wrong with them? They *do* rhyme. They gratify the ear's expectancy.

They *are* rhymes, & very clever ones, & no-one but a bad speaker or singer could so pronounce or sing them as to make them sound amiss.

They only jar on the sensitive reader, who reads them & realises that he is not reading our greatest men at their greatest, but reading a robust man, who didn't care much what sensitive readers felt, but still had something worth saying to say; & jolly well meant to say it.

Well: whichever side you were on, take comfort if you can from the subtlety & skill of your dialectic.

Greetings.

John.

---

1. The Browning poem is *A Grammarian's Funeral*. It was published in *Men and Women* (1855).

[n.p.]
Sept 7 1934

Dear Florence,

There is not much to tell you of events here. C. is slowly pulling up out of the illness into health: & is now much stronger & heartier. Then we have had rather a plague of rats, which have not entered the house but have thriven in the hen runs. They are now yielding to treatment (gunshot); but quite recently some clever dog has invented a vitamin that will increase the families of rats three-fold: so that where they now have 10 in a litter, they will have 30 henceforth. It will be the devil, if this man drops any of his stuff near here.

If rabbits can also be multiplied thus, what a chance for the French restaurateur: & the Belgian fur merchant.

Our little festival comes off next week, on Tuesday & Wed. Alas. Willy[1] won't be here to see his play: though I feel sure that it will go well, & be most moving. My *Tale of Troy*[2] is one of the items. It is now 3 times as long as it was when you heard it, but you must not think that I have eaten of this fellow's vitamin.

The *Conway*[3] annual dinner was quite good fun: & I met many old friends there; but it is time that this insane habit, of wasting 3 hours of night in silly long speeches, were altered for the better. No-one wants to speak: no-one wants to listen: yet at dinner after dinner the folly goes on.

John

1. W. B. Yeats was known to his intimates as Willy. J.M. published *Some Memories of W. B. Yeats* in 1940.
2. J.M.'s book, *Victorious Troy: Or The Hurrying Angel*, 1935.
3. H.M.S. Conway was J.M.'s training ship. He published an account of it in *New Chum* in 1933.

Ever the Wanderer, Masefield embarked on an extended business-cum-pleasure tour of the land down under.

[En route to Australia]
[12 Sep 1934]

Dear Florence,

A letter posted today will leave this ship at Port Said tomorrow & should reach you in about 18 days, after which there will be rather a long gap, while we run the 3000 miles to Colombo, the next posting station: & I fear that a letter posted there will be long in reaching the U.S. The *Endeavour* race will have been sailed & all sorts of other things will have happened.

The beautiful bag & rug wh you so kindly sent to me have been most useful: especially the bag. The use of the rug is not now possible: it is very hot already, too hot for much sleep, tho indeed one needs no sleep here: the sun is so exhilarating. I work at my calculations in the mornings, then read Virgil & Homer, then snooze, or study lighter literature, till it is time for a meal, then V & H again, finding V rather more suited to the present Mediterranean mood than H.

We are now crossing the very billows wh gave such a tossing to St. Paul.

There is an excellent library aboard here, for on these long voyages a real supply of books is necessary.

What a pity that you aren't here to enjoy it, most excellent & bewitching Florence, dearest of friends.

John.

Dolphins & flying fish.

[En route to Australia]
Near Colombo.
[n.d.]

Dear Florence,

Did I tell you that when we reacht Port Said, the galla-galla man was busy with his "no chicken, no mongoose" and even cleverer at his job than formerly? He did amazing things for about an hour & a half, & left at last no doubt stuffed, beneath his dirty robe, with chickens (a sort of zoo of these), a rabbit or two, some flags, tin pots, brass pots, stuffs of different colours, & no doubt a lot of our money. I watched him very carefully from a little distance, & I still cannot imagine how the chicken is put into the man's pocket. It is still art-magic to me.

At Aden I found yet another charming letter from you. You say of Aden, that it must be like Eden. It may be, but it would be a bit droughty for Eden. It is a savage sizzling red-hot volcanic rock on the edge of a sunken crater which is the harbour. Cain is buried there; and on the rocks are some water-tanks cut by the order of the Queen of Sheba. But we didn't smell any of the famous Sabaean spice; only a whiff now & then of oil from the oil pumps.

There were sharks in the harbour enough to quiet even Geoffroi; they were all round the ship: I never saw so many except in Brazil.

It was red hot in the Red Sea, but exhilarating. We could not sleep for 5 nights but enjoyed it. Now it is all clammy sick Indian heat, a much more trying thing.

Thank you so much for writing to me. It was dear of you.

Bless you.

John.

[Australia]
19 Oct. [1934]

Dear Florence,

By the time this reaches you, I shall be just starting for home by the Trans-Continental Railway. We hope to be at home just after Christmas.

I know you will be cross, but the Truth must out. We simply love Australia: we love Australia: we love Australia. We are having a glorious time in Australia. We camp by the billibong, we hump our swags thro the mulga, we are regular dingoes about the Mallee. We ride upon our brumbies, listening to the notes of the cookaburra, & sing our hurrays to the Southern Cross. We are having a lovely time, but the first week was very hard going, with interviews & engagements before we were recovered from the voyage.

It is a land & a race unlike anything else. We drove out into the wilds last week & were deeply impressed by the majesty of the forests & the mountains. Pausing in a glen I had a heavenly time watching the foreign birds & hearing their strange song. I am loving this place & people, but you need never fear that you will be ousted, so of that be sure.

New Zealand Cod & Whitebait
and hinemoa.

John.

[Australia]
Octr.26. 1934

Dear Florence,

At the moment, I am out of office as a speaker. I had to speak at a memorial service in the open air last Sunday. It rained as I began, & the audience put up umbrellas, & in the effort to make myself heard the germ got in; & later speeches in the next few day: made the thing worse; & a big speech at the Univ finished it. Nov I have but a sort of a squeak, as when your Doctor in N.Y. deal with me. I am cutting my engagements for a day or two, so as to rest my voice, but hope to be in tune again in a day or two. It ha: been therefore a blessing in disguise.

I have greatly enjoyed the museums & galleries here; & the overwhelming abundance of lovely flowers, which are every-where, at all points, in profusion, in public & private gardens, & roll over the hedges in waves of roses, such as I have never seen elsewhere.

I have no news of you at all, & fear I cannot now have any for a week. I am going out of the city to a sheep station for some days. The shearing is on, wh is one of the sights of Austr, for all the wealth of the land is wool, & the piles of fleece are the harvest. I hope to see the work of shearing in process: but I don't expect to try my hand at it, as it isn't so easy as a master-shearer makes it seem. It is mostly done by clippers now, not the hand-shears, and some men can shear about 350 sheep in one day. You catch your sheep first, then tip him up, grip him with your knees, and run the clippers down his tummy, so that the fleece falls off in a single happy mass. A good shearer never draws blood in a day's shearing: but I'll be able to tell you more about this next week after I have seen.

We just missed the end of the air-race. I had to speak at the Horticultural Exhib[n] just as it finished: otherwise we should have seen it. Only 70 years ago, this place was 70 days from London; usually now it is 38 days by steamer; but the aviator did it in three days, even after some delays of engine trouble.

I send you my thoughts & hopes for a bright & swift & happy recovery. Please give my greetings to Austin & Nancy[1] & to the Judge.

Suppis & Tasmanian Ling Fish.

John.

All sorts of odd Masefields here, the descendants of Ms of Shropshire, of whom I heard years ago.

---

1. Mrs Austin Lamont.

[Australia]
Nov 4 1934.

Dear Florence,

There may be a mail of sorts in tonight & perhaps a letter from you in it, but I must get this off to you this afternoon, as the mail sails on Thurs & this is Tues, so I cannot wait to answer what you say, even if you say it with all your accustomed charm.

We are out here in a great plain of grass, marked only by two little hills & a multitude of dead gum trees, white as old bone & spiky, wh marks where a forest once stood, now killed by the draining of the land. It is now a sheep-pasture, feeding many herds of sheep, wh are now being shorn. It is a thrilling sight to see a shearing. "The shepherds' fleecy care", as poets used to call the sheep, are driven into pens, the shearer darts in, grabs a sheep, puts him out of the pen, stands him on his tail, grips him between his knees, & runs a machine clipper over the beast with a skill wh takes away the fleece as tho it were a glove being pulled off. He peels it off the sheep, even to the ankles & the nose, in two minutes, & then gets on to another. All the time it is being clipped (the wool) it is being gathered & graded, & as soon as it is graded it is baled, & then put aboard a waggon & dragged away into the world.

Sheep are not prone to struggle when caught. If they did, the shearing would be a grim & gory business, but as it is I can only marvel at the ease (apparent ease), with which the thing is done. But I don't feel drawn to the life. I wd like to be able to shear, but would not like to make my living thus, tho it wd be better fun than being a barber & would give you much more sense of the real world. These shearers go about all over Australia & do other things while the fleeces are growing; & are therefore first-rate company.

Bless you.
John.

Back from his shearing experiences in Australia, Masefield was content to settle down in Pinbury for several years.

Pinbury Park.
Oct 4 1935

Dear Florence,

Grateful thanks to you for your nice letter, which came with th un-nice news that Italy has begun another war.[1] This less than 18 years from the defeat of Caporetto, which one would have though enough for any nation for 100 years. Anything may happen now at any time, with results not to be predicted. It is all the doing o two or three people, wielding a tyranny. Italy has been inoculated with a madness, has "taken" madness and is now mad; & will be mad for some time; being mad, she thinks she is holy and wise and glorious; the whole herd thinks it, because these two or three have contrived it. Who would not be a bird, flying in heaven, belonging to no nation at all, unable to hear the noisy scoundrel talking of Destiny & Civilising Missions? Who would not be a herring in the sea, breakfasting off England, lunching off Spain, dining off Italy, & caring not a damn for any of them? Well, wisdom comes, but suffering comes first, & those who suffer worst are usually dead before the wisdom comes, and when the wisdom comes who knows that it is wisdom and either regards or keeps it?

You must call your little dog P.H.M. Lamont; and tell M why I said so.

We are grieved to hear of poor Corliss & of your anxiety. We send him all our best wishes for a quick recovery & a happy convalescence.

We know not quite what to do now. We must watch events for a while; but are rather drawn to a rush to California, if N.Z. & Africa are out of the question. What do you say to that?

Bless you.
John.

1. Italy invaded Ethiopia on 3 October 1935. The Battle of Caporetto, in which the Italian army was routed by the Austrians, took place on 24 October 1917.

Pinbury Park
April 25, 1936

Dear Florence,

I want you to know, that I am at work upon a set of verses for the Harvard Tercentenary.[1] It is not a kind of verse that I (or any other writer) can be good at, but I hope not to disgrace the occasion too utterly.

Tennyson could do the kind of thing better than anybody in the ·ide world.

It was easier to write this kind of thing in the far past, before the ·oets of the eighteenth century had done what they conceived to e translations from Pindar. Now any writer of an ode is like a arodist of an eighteenth century translator from Pindar. Thus ·y ode begins in the good old style:—

> When at Jove's bidding the intemperate East
> Cast forth the Pilgrim Fathers on the strand
> Straight, in contempt of priest,
> (No greater there, nor least,)
> They knelt and worshipped God upon the sand.
> The rude red natives of the forest heard
> The good old hundredth sung, and hearing, feared.

Having made this opening, it is fairly easy to go on, in the good old manner.

> Speak to me Muse, and tell me who they were,
> Who, within Boston bay, or near Cape Cod
> Thus cast their carols on the wandering air.
> A minister of God,
> John Harvard, he was one,
> He and his little flock in unison
> Sang and no other, sang and did not spare.

The rest will follow at a later time. It is very interesting to find that J.H.'s[2] mother[3] came from Stratford, and must quite certainly have seen w.s. that famous bard.

Bless you, dear Florence. You will be on the seas in two weeks from now. HURRAY.

JOHN.

1. J.M. composed and read an ode in September 1936 at the 300th anniversary celebration of the founding of Harvard College. However, he did not include the lines quoted in his letter to F.C.L.
2. John Harvard, 1607–38, first substantial benefactor of Harvard College, which was named in his honour.
3. Katharine Rogers, the mother of John Harvard, had a house at Stratford-on-Avon that is still standing. Acquired by Harvard University in 1909, it is called Harvard House.

Pinbury Park.
May 1 1936.

Dear Florence,

This will be the last letter that I shall be able to send you befor
you sail for these shores, so here it comes to wish you a very happ
and safe voyage to us. May the ship hurry and the mermaids sin
and the sun shine upon you.

The Spring has now come, so has the cuckoo; the fields an
hedges are gay, and the beauty of the Earth almost too great t
bear, it is so clearly the shadow of a real beauty.

So put out the best Spring frock. You won't want it in S Africa
for there it will be the autumn or winter; but here it will be Spring
and besides here there is a poet with an eye for such effects; yo
will search S.A. in vain for such a one. Or can it be that you hav
found one and never let on?

We have been very gay, entertaining a troupe of small boys
who have left us breathless but happy.

Now a most happy voyage to you, and a lovely landing.

John.

Pinbury Park.
[3 Jun 1936]

Dear Florence,

Many thanks for your charming kind letter.

The house seemed very empty after you had gone, and we much
miss you and Tom at the famous game, at which you both shewed
such natural genius. Alas, that the season should have been so
wintry. I hope that the cold has not gone any further. You should
not have refused my rum; nothing like it for sorrow, love or a cold.

I much enjoyed all our talks; but I did hope that you would
have a fine, hot week, to finish up with, so that the may would
have been really good and then we could have gone down the Coln
and seen the sight of the world.

I hope that you are having a lovely time in London. I expect
that the ravishing confections of which we saw some glimpses are
just laying the hearts in ruins wherever you go.

I expect that you had a great collogue with G.M.[2] and settled all
the affairs of the world, and the hash of Benito M the Imperatore.

This typing is a dashing game; but I take to it too late; how unlike you and Tom and croquet.

I have not rolled the lawn since you went, I haven't had the heart, for Florence and Tom are not there to stir one to the fray.

You must come again soon. I loved all the time of your stay and do only wish that it had been longer and the weather a lot better.

Blessings and thanks to you both.

John.

1. Croquet.
2. Gilbert Murray.

Pinbury Park.
[26 Aug 1936]

Dear Florence,

So many thanks for your letter from the ship and for the heavenly handkerchiefs. These are most welcome. As the trade circulars say, they supply a long felt want. The war changed the world in all ways, but in none more deplorably than in the English laundry. Formerly a laundry maid, why the very term is poetry. She was a lavendery maid, smelling of lavender, and smiling and rosy cheeked and wearing an adorable sun bonnet as she hung the things to dry on the flowering apple trees. Poets hung about and made sonnets to her. Bulls, if they saw her, moved to the other end of the pasture and never thought of tossing the gentle soul. She used to do up the handkerchiefs sent to her in neat white squares, fragrant as Araby (of poetry) and they were back on Saturday, if sent on Mon.

How different now.

The last laundry maid married a Brigadier general in 1917.

There is no lavender and no maidenliness in a laundry today. Rough men grab your things as they arrive at the works. They yell Hey, boys, here's some more of thet . . . . Masefield's things. Start up the engines, sons, and feed them into the crusher.

So in the garments go, the hankies sent by Florence, the socks that I bought to go to the Coronation in, in they go; round goes the crusher, down goes the banger; chop comes the hacker; wangle goes the teaser; scratch goes the tearer; zip-crackle-crosh falls the zipper; hurray, they all yell, that got em; that got em; turn on the acid spray, now, to bleach em good. On goes the spray. O says one, thats pure acid, that is. Well we can't stop it now to add the water. Heave em on now to the pounder to powder them down flat. What, some of them fell to pieces, did they, well some stuff is so rotten what can you expect. Well here are the fragments and the bill is 19 and sixpence. What, you don't like our laundry. Some folk got no taste. Do your own wash another time. Yah, capitalist, yah.

And so, after all to open your lovely package and see these exquisite hankies filled me with joy. So many many thanks.

Bless you.
John.

Pinbury Park.
[8 Oct 1936]

Dear Florence,

You ask me about *Queen Mary*. She is a fine powerful ship, steady as a rock in quite big seas (head seas, in our case) and very fast. It would have done your heart good to see her drop the Bremen. The prom deck is bigger and more spacious by far than the prom of the Majestic; and she has besides vast playing fields on the Sun deck.

When these points have been praised, I don't think that much remains to praise. I preferred the Aquitania cabin; and I felt that much of the decoration was deplorable, ugly in itself and shoved in anyhow, without any attempt at a general scheme. The ship contains a vast deal of shiny pannelling, which will be working a bit loose after a storm or two; probably she will creak like fifty thousand rusty hinges; and have to have a joiners gang on board to tighten things up a bit. It is wonderful to have an open window in a ship in a storm in mid Atlantic, and feel confident that no sea will come in. She provides this experience, and it is a deep one.

Then, I did not like her lounges and lesser rooms, such as the library. The Majestic had a majestic library; and the Aquit a good one; this one seemed unworthy. Somehow all this part of her seemed to me to be poky and stingy, instead of ample and easy, as one wd expect from her size. Apart from her prom deck, nothing in her gives an exultation of ease, which her bulk should give. Of all her fittings and decorations, I liked best a landscape by a man called Newton. It looked much out of place, but I liked it; and I also liked a circus frieze in what they call the Verandah Grill; a black panther going through a hoop, etc.

Still, she is steady and she goes like fun; and though she goes like fun she doesn't shake you all to bits. Perhaps the people living aft may have another tale to tell, but to us she was kind.

Bless you. I expect Lew is with you. It is pleasant to think of him with such sweet friends.

Bless you.

John.

[n.p.]

4 Dec 36

Dear Florence,

It seems a long time since I heard from you. I am afraid that your triumphant speech in the cause of peace may have laid you low. I do hope that I am wrong about this. Do please write soon or I shall begin to dread that I am losing my pull.

Lew returned full of your praises (who wouldn't?) after a very very happy time with you all. He enjoyed it all immensely. I am so glad, that he has seen America.

You will know by this time that the crisis is now openly a crisis in this land.[1] Dear Florence, will you please send a few papers to let us know the American view of it. Here I think that the Cabinet are urging that there shall not be a marriage; but I cannot help feeling, that there will be one, and that it behooves us to come to know soon what she is like. I cannot decide from the 2 or 3 little photos I have seen, whether she has character or charm or wisdom or anything. People talk with a good deal of misgiving. The famous eating house in the Strand is now popularly known as The Kings Arms.[2]

Do you remember the marvellous mosaic at Ravenna, of the Empress Theodora? Why should she not rise to her destiny as Theodora did and become our most famous Queen? I've been thinking a lot of divine grace. I do believe that it will come in like a sort of divine wind and blow up even the rottenest and most punctured tires. It so often does. It comes to old men, even, and enables them to do noble works of art. And if destiny has planned to make this lady a queen it may also plan to make her a world-famous great and noble one. I wish it were you in some ways, but if it had been I shouldn't be able to write to you, and you wd never be able to come to Pin.

Why didn't he marry one of your nice young girls when he was in the States the first time?

Roosevelt has made some fine speeches about peace. I do hope that he will try to do something to make peace before it is too late. I came back from Europe feeling things to be imminent and very sinister, more sinister in something the same way of flatulent patriotism, mad nationalism, and hopeless atheism. It is for the U.S to lead; no-one listens to us.

Let me try to thank you once more for all your kindness and thought for Lew.

Bless you.
JOHN.

1. The 'crisis' refers to the great hullabaloo over the intention of King Edward VIII to marry the American divorcée, Mrs Wallis Warfield Simpson.
2. The eating house in question is called Simpson's.

[n.p.]
11 Dec. 1936.

Dear Florence,

I've had an unhappy feeling, that what with your peace speech, Nancy's babe, and the claims of the Clan Lamont,¹ you have just about laid yourself low. I hope the sunny South will have restored the native pep. Good luck to the holiday and may you be just at top form for Xmas Day and the festivities.

We've had a marvellous two days, going to a lot of schools in different parts of London, to see how poetry is taught and encouraged. We were in some mighty poor schools, where the children looked ill in a way that broke my heart to see, but they had a divine courage about them, and a lot of them spoke verse and so plainly loved it, and the mistresses and masters seemed to take such pride and pains, it made my heart ache to think, that in a mean way, I practice a divine art that can link human souls together thus. It is amazing, to know, that our schools and teachers are better than any that we met abroad in almost every way, but in Germany, it is true, there was one man who taught his boys by the method of genius; he was a man apart, who will one day be famous. I fear that boys are everywhere inferior to girls as speakers of verse, but it was refreshing to find so many lads ready to stand up and speak verse to me. I thought the masters and mistresses were just heroic. I've been often unjust in my thoughts of teachers. When I saw what these were doing I was abashed. There was one quite poor girls school, perhaps a quarter of the parents were being relieved by the state. The girls had wanted to make the bare white walls gay, so they had turned to and painted frescoes and pictures for them, full of bright invention and so jolly to see. I was amazed at their work. In a big boys school all the boys are taught to speak verse, and lose THE COCKNEY ACCENT IN SIX WEEKS. LOSE IT FOREVER.

Altogether I was cheered and enchanted, but so much is still to be done and perhaps I may be able to help a very little. Anyhow these humble teachers have done more for this than ever I did for all my being a writer. So let me not be so cocky, but think more humbly and be ready to learn before trying to teach.

I've not read the Housman poems yet but will do so anon. Bless you dear Florence and may you have a happy holiday in the S.

John.

1. Since the Lamonts are descended from Scotland's Clan Lamont, which existed as early as the thirteenth century, J.M. sometimes used the term to refer to the Lamont family. A Clan Lamont Society is still functioning.

Pinbury Park.
Dec 15 1936.

Dear Florence,

I am writing to you today, to wish you a happy Christmas surrounded by a loving and happy family, and a crowd of little beings who love to be near you, and think you very naturally the last word in wisdom and beauty. May it be a happy time to you.

I can never hope to find anything you like or want, but I have sent you a book of mine, and am venturing to send you one or two by others, which I hope you will like.

You ask me about A.E.H.'s[1] posthumous poems. I have only just had them and have not read them all yet, only a few. It seems to me a pity, that they were not left in peace. Two or three of them seem to be neat and witty, coming certainly onto the nail.

Their philosophy seems to me to be mistaken, but I may mistake it. Perhaps universal suicide *is* Europe's only hope. But he did not practise what he preached. He did not buy an eighteen-penny knife and stick it in his heart. He lived to a fair age, and the keen enjoyment of good living. Once when I was a lad, I should have thought the pessimism wonderful; but not now. Ah, my dear, I begin to see now something of the wonder of life, and to mourn that I perceive it with the eyes of age.

But to go on about the poems. They are not good enough. Three might perhaps have been included in his *Last Poems;* the rest are surely inferior utterances of themes which he has done well elsewhere in other poems. His poetical range is very narrow; that gives it its strange perfection. It narrowed with age; that shows its limitation. I think that you must judge him by The Shropshire Lad, not by these. I'm sorry these were ever brought to light. Some like his funeral song, but it is not clinched & convincing, like some of his best terse things.

Put the book away, and be sure that your heart is a lot too noble and too full of love and care and generosity to be improved by an eighteen penny knife. I tremble to think that you are perhaps alone at Palisades with this book of incitement to suicide. Write soon to reassure me.

May this Christmas be a blessed and a happy one to you and all your happy family.

Bless you.
JOHN.

1. A. E. Housman.

[n.p.]
24 Dec. 1936.

Dear Florence,

This is the day before Xmas, and I have by this morning's post rec'd 3 letters from you, one of which I have kept till tomorrow, as bidden on the envelope, but the other 2 I have read with great joy, being the 1st real letters since the crisis began. Thank you so very much for writing and for sending me Mr. W.L.'s article.[1] I cannot tell you how glad your letters have made me; you seemed all gone into the Carolinian wilds leaving as it were no address nor trace.

Well, on a day when I receive 3 letters from Florence, I'm not going to do any work, but write to her instead.

You ask about the crisis. I wish I could write with knowledge about it. I can only give you a rehash, with a few personal impressions. God knows they'll be out of date when you get them.

You know, that London talked a good deal about the pair² all last summer. The press did not. We have a sort of instinctive drill. A suggestion comes, God knows whence, that certain things are not to be in the papers, and lo, they are NOT in the papers; all the rest of the world may scare-head the items and no English paper mention them at all. So this affair was not in the news at all here, until quite suddenly, a few weeks ago.

It began very oddly. A certain northern bishop spoke about the sacramental aspects of the Coronation. There had been some gossip, that the King wished the Coronation service simplified, and this bishop said, that the sacramental part of the service was of paramount importance; and said, in effect, that he wished that the King would pay more regard to these matters of religion. I'm not quoting him literally, but I believe that I do not misinterpret, either the holy sentiment or the devout intention. Now it is very odd, that this apparently chance utterance in the north should have had such results.

At once, the northern papers (and I have not seen them) came out with strong comment on the bishop's speech. At once, the London papers leaped to the conclusion that the bishop was referring to Mrs. S. He, good easy man, was amazed, that anyone should have so misread him, and publicly denied that he referred to anything whatever save religious shortcomings. However, the powder had been lying about loose in great quantity, and any spark sufficed to touch it off. Instantly Mrs. S was in the news, filling many pages of it, and coming into the news reels of the films. At once, the ministers were going and coming, and the question was paramount, was the King to marry her? Was Parliament going to make it possible for a morganatic marriage? Was she to be Queen? What would the Royal Family feel? What would the Nation feel? It was the most interesting thing I have ever known. It is still the most astounding thing of the last 7 centuries or so.

Now it is all over and settled. You must know all the later stages. I cannot fill in the blanks. All sorts of angers, energies and loves were at play. I do not know one least little thing about the part played by the Royal Family in the matter. I'm not very clear about the constitutional side of the question; I did not like the part played by the ministers nor by the Church. I did not like the results. I do not like the hateful way in which the nation has flung the matter aside.

Now what did I like? Well I liked and love the way the King, my master, whom may God preserve, stood up for the woman he loved. He is such a man as has not been promised to our throne for 300 years, when the young Prince Henry died. He had reached the age of 42, without meeting any woman whom he wanted, or finding any friend with whom he could work. In this woman, whom we call Theodora, he found one with whom he could live and work and who could work with him and guard him, too, as she is said to have done, from certain elements in him which were probably due to loneliness. She is a lovely woman; she would have made a royal queen; she would have perfected him, and given to our throne a sense and simplicity well suited to the time. Had the King taken her, there would have been a shock to a good many, who badly need a shock; who do most damnably need to be shown that a real thing is not a sham thing; there would have been this shock, but the Nation who loves the King, would have rallied, and Queen Theodora might have been the greatest Queen to the greatest King we have ever had. Society, such as it is, would have formed a party against her; common sense, wisdom, gaiety and hard simple people would have been for her. As to the King, he was royal throughout, as royal as the King his Father. No nobler thing has ever been done.

Well, he has gone; and we have the ministers and we have the archbishop, and a great soul and the woman he chose are chucked aside. Not 70 miles from me is a waste of a damned derelict Welsh coal field, which the minister ought to have salved and the arch-bish to have saved. Why haven't they got to that, which is their business, instead of to this?

God bless you dear Florence and all your family and all the causes and people dear to you in this New Year so soon to begin.

May God ever bless you.

John

1. Walter Lippmann, 1889–1974, American author, editor and newspaper columnist. His newspaper column was widely read and had considerable influence. A friend of the Lamonts.
2. King Edward VIII and Mrs Simpson, whom he married in 1937 after abdicating the throne in 1936.

Pinbury Park.
Jan 1. 1937.

Dear Florence,

This is New Year's Day, so I must say God bless you.

May it be a blessed year to you in every way.

On the last day of last year, I went through the garden here, and found in blossom:—

Jasmine.
Blue violet.
Primrose.
Pink primrose.
Oxlip.
Arabis.
White roses.
Daisies.
Laurustinus.
And a white flower that I know not the name of.

      Bless you always in all times.
                JOHN.

Pinbury Park.
2 Jan 1937.

Dear Florence,

The mail will go tomorrow, so this must go with it, to bear you my ever grateful thanks for a friendship which means more & more as I grow older, and to wish you a better friend in me as time goes on. God bless you.

Down in the lower garden here, a depression, which we had often noticed, was lately probed by me, with a long stick, which promptly sank well in. So with pickaxe and a spade, a spade, that is a spade and a trowel, I opened him up a bit, and Judith has opened her further, till we see, a biggish hole, with brick and stone work, mortared in, a lot of bits of old pots, probably flower pots of the 1860's; and a tooth, much decayed, which we think may be a pig's. The country folk are of the opinion, that it is the secret passage, so often talked of in English country places, by means of which they old nuns went to visit they old monks (never the other way about, which seems so odd to me) but perhaps they old monks were a lot less coy, and went on the surface.

One old man says, that they do say, that there's a King buried here in golden armour. I see no sign of King nor gold, but think that we are near one or other of the foundations of an outhouse or drainage system. Time will show, perhaps.

The chances of a big war seem rosier every day; the world will be lucky, if it avoids a smash here, during this dread summer, and the year following. The nations seem madder day by day. In fact one feels like that American mother who went to the parade in which her son was marching, and said afterwards, "the whole army was out of step except my Sam".

I have just bought a new oil stove called an Iolanthe, which is a marvel, but a bit of a brute to light.

Your lovely Christmas gift of books are a joy and a warmth to my old heart; I turn from morality to wantonness, and from wantonness to rectitude, with much benefit and delight. Thank you so very much for the lovely gift, and for so much wise and delightful companionship throughout so many more years than most friends can have in life. God bless and keep you dear friend, be sure that your friendship is treasured.

JOHN.

[n.p.]
Jan. 1937.

Dear Florence,

You sent me a pretty card of African beasts at Christmas time, shewing yourself at tea with a tiger and a giraffe, etc. It was never acknowledged, I fear, like so many of your charming thoughts; but I have put it up in my study, on the deck of the Wanderer, so that it faces me as I write; it looks superb here, being of a gay colour. You must see it when you come.

WHEN ARE YOU COMING? THERE WAS A LEGEND ABOUT THE RIVIERA IN FEBRUARY. IS THIS A MYTH OR A POSSIBILITY?

Now listen. What you must do, is to put on your very best raiment and the best hat New York can offer, and then away you must go to Washington, to the great WHITE FATHER. There you must say, that Gitchee Manitu has told you to say this. "IF YOU DON'T GET BUSY AT ONCE THERE WILL BE A BLOODY WAR IN EUROPE BEFORE YOU KNOW IT. YOU MUST TELL THESE POOR EUROPEAN SIMPS THAT THEY ARE A LOT OF MUTTS AND MUST GET AROUND A TABLE AND TALK OVER WHAT THEY WANT. YOU

(OH GREAT WHITE FATHER) MUST OFFER THEM A TABLE TO SIT
ROUND AND JOLLY THEM INTO COMING TO THE TALK. LET
EACH DAMNED LOT OF FOOLS STATE WHAT EACH WANTS TO
FIGHT FOR. WHEN THEY HAVE STATED THEIR WANTS TO THE
FULL, SEE IF YOU CAN'T ARBITRATE AND SUGGEST A WAY OF
GETTING IT WITHOUT GETTING INTO WAR ABOUT IT."

The grammar of the above is not up to the mark, but it is as near
as I can get to the language of Gitchee Manitu. I'm not sure that
Gitchee is not Lake Superior, now that I come to think of it. We
have not yet found any gold in the hole in the garden.

We had Nevill Coghill[1] here for the week end, and more or less
decided to call our Oxford show

THE OXFORD SUMMER DIVERSIONS.

First night:— Perhaps a ballet by me, and a Music programme by
a symphony orchestra. In Rhodes House.

Second night:— A dramatization of part of PIERS PLOWMAN[2] in
the garden of New College, if fine, (BIGGISH IF).

Third night:—DEVIL'S DYKE by Christopher Hassall[3] and a
short farce to follow; in the garden of New College; if fine.

Fourth night:— A mixed grill of spoken poetry, mostly modern, in
Rhodes House

MEMBERS OF THE LAMONT FAMILY WILL BE EXPECTED IN THE
FRONT ROW.

Bless you. A charming letter reached me from you yesterday for
which I thank you. I have the uneasy feeling, that you are very
tired from Christmas and the other racketty times you have had. I
wish you'd come and rest a bit here. WE DO REST YOU HERE AT
PIN.

JOHN.

Will you ask Austin if he wants a rather rare French book with
plates of rigging etc. L'Encyclopedie Methodique 3 vols £25;–;–.
It seems a thumping sum for a book; and I daresay he already has
it.

---

1. Nevill Coghill was born in 1899. He became Professor of English Literature at
Oxford and Warden of Exeter College.
2. *Piers Plowman* by William Langland, c1311–99. The most ambitious poem in
Middle English to be extant.
3. Christopher Hassall, 1912–63. Biographer of Edward Marsh and Rupert
Brooke, and librettist for a number of the musical plays of Ivor Novello.

[n.p.]
Jan 1937.

Dear Florence,

Thank you so much for your letter of the 9th, which came here on this 18th, only nine days. The Queen Mary is laid up for winter overhaul, and I expect my Christmas letter went by some old dug up replacement ship; we ought to do better than a fortnight; we did before the war. However, the Xmas mail was in such a mess this year, that the poor postman had to deliver on the Sunday after Xmas Day, to get the Xmas mail clear. I hope that future letters will take less time to get to you.

Thank you ever so much for your fine stand beside the old firm for Prinny[1] and Theodora.[2]

No-one now has a good word for either of them. It is very odd. The English are often rather a kindly people, but in this case, they have neither charity nor sense of proportion. The wildest stories are being told. I have the feeling, that they are being put about by people who wish to divert attention from ministerial action. As it chances, we have been seeing a lot of people from LITTLE LONDON. They see only the LL point of view. They are often fantastic, but this is the kind of thing. "Of course, he gave T's husband £40,000 to be divorced. He gave her all the Crown Jewels, and all Queen Alexandra's jewels. He is said to have mortgaged all the income of the Duchy for years, and to owe fabulous sums, which have all gone to her. He was an insufferable little man, nervy and without any character, or poor character, and always associated from choice with a rotten set. He would not do as his ministers wanted; he is said to have refused to be King at the time of his father's death, until begged to it by his mother." etc, etc, etc, never a barrel of better herring, it is all after the above dirty sample. I feel sure, that it was rotten bad silly policy to get rid of him. Already, there is a widely spread contempt for him; all his virtues and splendid past are forgotten; and it is not so much the man who is despised, it is the institution of royalty. People feel that if baldhead[3] and cantuar[4] can flout royalty, they too can. A man was here who said that his garage man was saying, "The dirty little tyke (Tyke means dog) he jolly well deserved the kick". I am so savage, that the lousy ministers let the thing pass in such a way, that remarks of that sort can be passed. The press is now after younger brother, in a way that makes me wonder how long it will be before the institution of royalty is again respected. If baldhead and the priest had said "We regret your choice, but you are our King and we will see to it that the lady you have chosen shall be our Queen," they could have done it. It would have divided society, into the real and the sham, but.

Men ask, but how could he have married her? It would have split the realm from top to foot. B would have resigned and who would have taken office? I do not know. I think that Lloydie[5] would, or Winston.[6] I do not doubt, that either would have formed a cabinet, quite as good as the usual bunch. The word would have gone to the press, that Theodora was to be accepted, and by this time next year, she would have been the most popular Queen for centuries. But she would have been a Queen forced to great deeds, as Theodora and Aspasia; no folly would have been tolerated, she would have had to be a paragon, and I believe she is so clever that she would have been one. No-one at present says a good word for her. No doubt there will be some more muck-flinging when her decree is made absolute in the Spring.

A man was here a day or two ago, a very good fellow, of high position, but not very clever, still, with good means of knowing facts. He said, that ministers met in the early autumn, talked it all over, with the American papers before them, agreed, that Prinny was too independent, and that Theodora would not do, and then decided to get rid of him. One of the complaints was, that he liked to do things for himself, instead of through ministers, another, that he would not go to church. I suppose not half of one per cent of the adult male population of this island does go to church. Church is a dull routine from which the spirit has gone, and Prinny shewed a wise instinct in keeping away. If he had made cantuar turn to and brighten up the lives of men a bit, religion would have brightened too. Whatever harm he did to the church by not going to it is as nothing to what cantuar has done by speaking and acting as he did. He is loathed for that by every person I've met except one.

Religion is his business. Well, this Xmas, the little boys all over England have been singing to the well known tune of Hark, the herald angels,

> Hark, the herald angels shout
> Stanley B has kicked him out.

"Him" in this instance is the one King we have had who felt for the poor and spent hours of every day down with the downs and outs. One of his last official acts was to go to the depressed areas in South Wales. Lew has just been there and you may take it that they are depressed. His remark was, SOMETHING MUST BE DONE. Well, the minister and the arch bish did not want anything done. They wanted, the one to say, that every avenue would be explored, and the other to call for a week of prayer about it. Damn their guts, my dear, I'M so savage about it. Somebody who was here said that Theo was (as an American always would be) very very eager to get these depressed areas brightened into life spots. It is just the one thing that an American queen could have got done. She and he together were just what this old land needs. And now there are these damned little tykes singing the above carol. How is Royalty to be respected again?

Well, the present man is very like his father, and like his father never expected to be King, and like his father will buckle to and be a wonder. God save and bless him.

And you, too, dear Florence.

JOHN

1. The Duke of Windsor, formerly King Edward VIII.
2. The Duchess of Windsor, formerly Mrs Wallis Warfield Simpson.
3. Stanley Baldwin, Prime Minister of England, who engineered the abdication of King Edward VIII.
4. Archbishop of Canterbury.
5. David Lloyd-George, 1863–1945. He was Prime Minister between 1916 and 1922.
6. Sir Winston Churchill (1874–1965) was a known supporter of King Edward VIII.

Pinbury Park.
Feb 15 1937.

Dear Florence,

I was much afraid, that you were ill, or were going to be ill; so your letter, that told me, that you had been ill, and were now living the normal New York life again, was a great relief. I'm so glad that you took such a short way with these Dissenters, the microbes in your throat. Confound their politics, frustrate their knavish tricks, addle their mangy chicks, and God save Florence. I do hope, that now you are over the winter infections, and will have clear health and fair days.

I wrote you a most mangy letter last week. I suppose the news ran out or something. There isn't much to tell, this week. Did I tell you of the wolves? You may have seen it reported, for it roused some emotion here.

There is at Oxford a small zoo, which I have never visited, but often passed. It is some few miles out of Oxford, on the Banbury road (I think). As you go by, you see camels and humped cows, buffaloes and yaks and things grazing in the meadows, and think, O pastoral scene; this is the sort of thing Job used to survey, before he was tempted, (or whatever it was he was). Well, those are only the decoy. In cages, further in are beasts of prey. Among these were some wolves. One night, a fortnight back, these wolves found a little hole 7 inches across in the wire netting, and out they got through that hole, three of them, and killed a sheep and went off into Wytham wood after eating some. Next morning there was a pretty stir in Oxford. The wolves were loose, and Red Ridinghood might be re-enacted at any moment. Out came all the University guns and dogs, out came the farmers, and their men, the air force was warned, the local artillery manned their cannon. Any dog bigger than a Pekinese went in peril of his life. A day of horror passed. One bicyclist saw one of the wolves, who shewed his teeth at him for one shocking second. Somebody shot one of the wolves just in Oxford that night.

After a night of horror, a second wolf and an Alsatian dog, in mistake for a wolf, were shot, but the third was still free. The third had a run for his money. He got into a field of sheep the next night and killed fourteen; but was himself shot next morning. So now all three are dead. I did so hope, that they would get into that vast old Shabbington wood, miles from anywhere, and almost deserted, and settle there in peace and raise cubs, and then go for the South Oxfordshire Hounds and hunt them round the county. However, it was not to be. Dis aliter visum.

The last wolf was shot well within Oxford town, on the outer Banbury Road. The fame of the MacDonald, who killed the last British wolf, in (I believe) 1712, in some Scotch fastness, will now be somewhat dimmed.

At odd times for some time, we have been busy, clearing the moss off walls here. Lately, I have taken to clearing ivy also; it is a ruin to walls and to trees, too. So I go around with an axe, a very sharp and nice one, newly bought. When my financial American friends give up their calculations and come to relax at Pin, they will say, What has come to all the ivy which used to be here? Then,

I, so as to make them feel at home, and to know that their national legends are not neglected here, shall answer, like the Father of their Country, "I will not, on this occasion, with all the evidence so plumb against me, tell a lie. I did it with my little hatchet."

By the way. In reading over about the wolves. My meaning is not too clear, I fear. I wanted the wolves to get away and establish themselves in Shabbington. So that when the S.Ox hounds came to hunt the fox there, they should rouse not the fox, but the wolf pack, which far from being hunted would hunt *them* and pull them limb from limb, munch scrunch, and jolly well teach them a little humanity to foxes.

Bless you.
JOHN.

Pinbury Park.
Feb 17 [1937]

Dear Florence,

It occurs to me, that in all our years of friendship, I have never told you a tale of which it might be said that it brought a blush upon the cheek. This record ought now to be disturbed, and shall be, I trust, in this letter.

Though you may read no further than the above, and I daresay won't, I do want you to know the following true tale.

You may remember a few days ago asking me about a poet who died not long ago, whose posthumous work was (I think Mistakenly) made public.[1]

On his death-bed, he began to thank the doctor for all his care and attention to him, during his illness. He spoke with much feeling and emotion, which was of course something that he never did when well. The doctor was moved and made uncomfortable by this display of feeling, and also felt, that it was bad for his patient, so to bring it to an end, and to introduce a more genial mood, he said, I do want to tell you something I heard yesterday. I was talking to an actor, who has just returned from Hollywood, and asked him "what did you do at Hollywood?"

He replied, "Well, I did what all men do at Hollywood, one of two things. I either lay on the earth and looked at the stars, or I lay with the stars and looked at the earth."

At this the patient shook with laughter and continued to shake for some minutes. At last he spoke and said, "I'll tell that story as soon as I reach THE GOLDEN FLOOR."

These were almost his last intelligible words. By this time, I hope the angels are chuckling over its success with the Trinity.

You are now off to the Bermudas, I expect, and seeing the flying fish all day long. Good luck and good cheer.

JOHN.

1. The poet in question was A. E. Housman.

Pinbury Park.
11 March 1937.

Dear Florence,

You write from the sunny south. I write from the wintry north. England nearly always has a winter, but you never can tell when it will come. Sometimes it is June, sometimes May; but this year it is now. We have been under snow all this month so far. Great drifts of it, lie on all the high ground, and last night the drifts got doubled. We went over to Oxford, to see & hear 2 operas, which Nevill Coghill was producing. We had an uneventful passage there; with clear roads; but I felt, that the night was going to be bad, so after the plays, I wd not go to N's party, but started for home. It was all clear till past Burford, but then the snow began; and grew worse all the way home; it was a foul drive; with the stuff clogging the windscreen & tending to stop the wipers. However we got home at about 1 in the morning; and now the filthy stuff is all melting, and Pin is in such a mess as never was. It is fun to see the tracks in the snow round Pin; rabbits all round the house, also foxes, and the marks of the foxes' brushes, where they just touch the snow.

I am furious with our ruling classes, as ever. They make the world a filthy mess with their stupidity (by OUR here I mean MAN'S not only the English variety) and then say that they must arm for security. Here we are committed to an enormous silly unthought-out madly wasteful scheme for re-arming, and on this we are to spend some colossal sum of which we know before hand at least one third will be wasted and chucked into gunmakers' profits without scrutiny, without appeal and without protest. This from the very men who refuse to spend shall we say half a million or any less sum, on opera houses, national theatres, and ballet houses in the Empire's capital; and the same men who have waited year by year doing nothing about the depressed areas, saying that they had no money. It makes man sick at heart.

I don't doubt, that we need the arms, and may have to use them this year or next; but that inhumanity should have these billions and humanity nothing but the dole and the amateur is hard to bear.

You may not think there is a danger of war here. I think there is great danger.

I am to speak to America about the Coronation some time before the Coronation week, through your National system. Mind you listen from the Riviera or wherever you may be.

Bless you
JOHN.

Pinbury Park.
July 7, 1937.

Dear Florence,

Thank you for ringing us up and for your letter. I hope that the Clan Lamont is now settled in and enjoying the pibroch and the haggis, on their native heather. Hoo's a wi ye the noo?

Deil wumman ye no maun gae callin a wee bit clockie a clock the noo. In bonnie Scotlan they ca siccan a clishmacliver a wag at the wa.

I'm sad to think of the poor letters I've written you lately. I have never been so busy, I do believe.

Bless you and yours, and may the rain and the midges alike hold off.

Love to the Clan from us all.

John.

Pinbury Park.
22 July 1937.

Dear Florence,

Thank you so much for the happy three days with you on the Loch,[1] and for all your care and kindness. It was sweet of you to have us, and to give us so happy a time. Thank you, too, for having Judith. It would be hard to say which of us enjoyed it most, or which of the many delights we enjoyed most.

On the whole, I liked best the evening in the car in Glen

Douglas and the sight of the sea current rushing up the loch at Ballachulish. I shall always have happy memories of our walks along the loch side in the forenoons.

Thank you all so much for these and the other most happy times.

We were safe at home at five minutes to nine last night 12 hours to a tick from your door. We will draw a veil over some of the journey, for the train was crammed, with, I suppose nearly 1000 people; however, we slept and ate and read our books, and thought how kind our fellow travellers were to the women and children. We had a cheering tea at Padd & at Kemble were met by Lew.

You will have many beautiful memories to take home from the loch; thank you so much for letting us share them. I do hope that we weren't a great addition to your house keeping problems. Please give our loves to all the family.

I hope that the sheep dogs really played up and did their piece.

Bless you and thank you,

John.

I think my old grandfather passed Rossdhu in the lake steamer, which was running even in 1824.

1. During the summer of 1937 the Lamonts rented a spacious house known as Rossdhu on Loch Lomond near the town of Luss, and filled it with various children and grandchildren. J.M. and daughter Judith also paid a visit.

Pinbury Park
[n.d.]

Dear Florence,

There is just a chance of the Queen Mary, if this goes today, so here goes.

I hope that the enemy has now been so far chastened at the polls as to be afraid of any further malice. I hope so, damn his wicked eyes. Good luck to you, I say, and may the truth be thrust down his false throat, and stick in his lying gizzard.

We had a gale here yesterday; pretty bad. I had to go to Kemble to meet a train in the worst of it; and found the road to the station blocked by a big tree across it, so I had to go a long way round, by the Roman road from Ciren. Here, I came in for the very worst weather I have ever driven in. The car was as nearly as possible blown over in one gust, and the hail was so blinding that I had to stop. I could not see the road five yards ahead. Of course this vehemence was only a few minutes long. After the bad gust, it became not quite so bad, and no more trees came down, nor did I get blown over. I felt the wind lift the car in the big gust. I would be prepared to say that all four wheels were off the road for an instant. What would you have said, if you had read English poet blown out to sea? There you would have said, I always said he wanted ballast.

The gusts were 105 miles per hour at 3 recorded times. Nothing to you New Yorkers, but tough going to us.

I told you of the new house. We havent quite got it yet but I rather think we shall have it. It is a plain solid rectangular quiet Victorian house on the river, in full view of Witnam Clumps, which would be distant about 2 or 3 miles I think. You can fish and swim from the lawn, and it will be easy to have a boat or two, and go a rowing. It is about 7 or 8 miles from Ox, and 4 from Abingdon. About 1 from Dorchester. The pub is the famous Barley-Mow, where you used to get swindgeing good teas after rowing. I suppose we may move there about May, if we get it. If there is to be a war, I would rather be near Ox than here.

The house is called Burcote or Burcot Brook, because Burcote or Burcot Brook flows through the garden.

> Dear Friend, come soon and look
> At burcote or burcot brook.
> Put on your coat and surcoat
> And take the ship for burcote
> And beg the good Herr Gott
> to land you at Burcot.

Bless you.
John.

P.S. If you were to sail to London from N.Y. you could come right to our garden all the way by water.

The Masefields were settled into their last home, Burcote Brook, at Abingdon near Oxford, by the beginning of the New Year in 1940.

[n.p.]
[20 Jan 1940]

Dear Florence,

This is to thank you for your 9th letter, dated New Years Day, safely received this morning. I judge that it was posted on the 5th. I have had all your letters now, except 3 and 4. Someone has seized those, or sunk them or lost them, for which they will suffer in the future, however they may exult now.

There is no remedy against the loss of death. It is a cruel pain; and there is no comfort for it. The friend is gone and the voice is silent, and the sympathy and knowledge removed from near-by. It is all loss and anguish.

The very greatest have tried to give comfort; and have for long times together given much; and though all their systems are out of favour, men come back to them, from very suffering. And though they be out of favour, why should they not be true? It does not need much experience, to know that we are parts of a mystical being, that those near us are parts of our parts of it, and that it being eternal, they too are eternal, and not the less there for being discarnate. The rose flowers in June, and lingers on in blossom till Xmas and then is as a dead tree, but the rhythm of which June is a part is undying and the idea of the rose is eternal and the withered blossom and the dead tree are as dust.

Buddha did find Enlightenment. Christ did find that he had conquered death, and began to sing upon the cross. Mahomet did talk with something divine till he shouted with the fire of it about mercy and compassion, to people who knew nothing whatever about either.

I doubt that this will ever reach you; still, let me hope it may.

God bless you in your sorrow.

John.

Burcote Brook
[6 Mar, 1940]

Dear Florence,

Many many thanks for Letter 14, safely and gladly received this 6th March.

It was not visibly Censored, but perhaps the Censors can do their sleuthing without leaving any marks; they are probably subtle dogs at their jobs now. Only one of your letters, I think, has been visibly opened by a Censor. I cannot understand why he did not pant to open others when once he had seen what a phoenix of a writer you are.

You have won our grateful thoughts by what you do and say for the Allied Cause.

Colonel Kermit Roosevelt has been doing great things over here. He was in our Army, and obtained leave to command a force of volunteers for Finland. Just before he left, he made a speech, which was broadcast, and very likely made public in the U.S. It was the finest speech of the war, so far; the sort of speech Leonidas might have made. The only modern parallel to it is Garibaldi's letter, before "going out from Rome". It is astounding how G's letter, and this simple speech make the utterances of the dictators like the ravings of a sick hyena and a mad gorilla, not like the utterances of men at all. So, if you feel sad about the U.S. you just look up Col Kermit Roosevelt's broadcast, and be proud you belong to the nation that produced such a man. It is a superb thing.

You blame me for not working by a fire; well, I have done without a fire for 30 winters, and can last without one for a few more, I hope. My ink was frozen solid for weeks together, but I am independent of ink now. It still freezes hard, and I have never seen so few flowers out by the 6th March. However, the birds are singing and nesting. Spring is on its way.

Peace, too, must be nearer than it was; but still remote, I judge.

I suppose the Germans will have a crack at us pretty soon; and then we shall know more about it.

Cheer up, and don't you be depressed; if nations get into messes, they also sometimes get out of them, and cut fine figures in doing so.

Bless you.
John.

Burcote Brook
24th. June. [1940]
Dear Florence,

I am sorry to have your letter of June 3rd, with the news of Dean Woodbridge's[1] death.

He was (to me) one of the Pilgrim Father kind of American, not often seen now and hard to replace, and certain to be much missed.

I am sad to think what a gap in your life his death will make. Few people can have many mental friends; one makes them only at certain times; for the mind is a lonely thing; and when one of them goes a part of life ends; and there's no comfort, I'm afraid; it is one of the conditions of this living.

Still, you had thirty years of his friendship and advice; not many friends get so much as that.

I only met him once, on the memorable day when he ended his book on Plato. You will have his books with you.

"His spirit is thine, the better part of him"

but that is no comfort; one wants the friend back, to speak to.

Alas, I can give no comfort. Death is the end of association and of ways of life. Only Buddha, so far as I know, gives any help at these times. Even so, in real grief, what help can Buddha give?

One can only HOPE. HOPE is a pretty good deal.

The more one thinks of it, the more it seems.

So hope on, and Hope shal delivre, hit is no drede.

John.

1. Frederick J. E. Woodbridge, Professor of Philosophy at Columbia University and Dean of the Faculties of philosophy, political science, pure science and fine arts. He died 1 June 1940. Under his guidance, F.C.L. took an M.A. Degree in philosophy at Columbia in 1898 and later became a close friend.

Burcote Brook
July 1, 1940

Dear Florence,

This is your birthday, for which I wish you many happier returns than this one. I cannot send you any gift, save pleasant thoughts of you and wishes for your happiness.

I am sorry that your hopes of a quiet party in the South of France have had to be postponed for this while. Never mind,"There'll come a time";¹ and we shall enjoy it all the more by and by, perhaps.

I've been reading a great many books about Russia. You would much enjoy the older books. It is a land of endless theory interspersed with occasional frightful violence, and therefore throwing up extraordinary figures, and many remarkable brains. There was plenty of savagery going around. Ivan the Terrible is said to have nailed the French Ambassador's hat to his head, because he did not take it off on coming into the imperial presence. I wonder would things become easier if this were always done to ambassadors. We are perhaps too old to try, but a young Nation might make the experiment; it cant lead to a much worse hash than exists.

I do wish I could say something to cheer you up; you seem as doleful as though your rum had been stopped for the voyage. Do think of that poem of Hardy's about the young female baggage, who had been warned against being ruined, but went the primrose path and found it by no means so bad.

"O its awfully nice to be ruined, said she."

Ted was along here one day last week; a hell of a military swell. Cheer up and bless you

John.

1. Thomas Hardy, 'The Ruined Maid', from *Poems of the Past and Present* (1902).

[n.p.]
Nov 16. [1942]

Dear Florence,

I am writing at once to say, that yesterday, Sunday the 15th, we had the very great pleasure of a visit, (tho a brief one) from Tom, Jr.[1] and three friends. They turned up in a car on their way from some service journey to somewhere near here, and could not stay long, because they had to get to town before the black-out, and it was certain to be foggy on the way. He was very well and cheery, we thought; and it was such fun to see one of the clan, whose face now reminded us of you, now of Tom, now of Corliss-Austin-Eleanor-and little Tommy. (Corliss, perhaps, most of all.) We could not exactly stay them with flagons, but we comforted them, I hope, with apples, and shall hope to see them again soon.

Today, your two letters of late October reached me together. My best thanks for these, and for so kindly getting me the particulars of the State Papers. I judge that the things I want to see will be in Virginia somewhere, if they are anywhere. They are not important to the soul of man, I fear, but have some interest to students of colonial history, and out of the way events. They interest me; but then I am fascinated by these pioneers, living on the creeks and clearings, shooting now a grizzly bear, now a dusky savage, and anon celebrating Thanksgiving with rum from a Jamaican pirate.

Thank you, too, for the packages you so graciously send us. All are welcome and fill us with glad thoughts of you.

I am sad to think that everybody is anti-British, that is, anti-English, for I do not accept the word Briton. It is evidence of the great cleverness of the enemy, that after five years of re-iterated atrocity the world is preferring the doers of the atrocities to those who stood against them. This cleverness will continue of course; it will be directed to wrecking collaboration among the nations after the war; and if it be succeeding now, during the war, it will succeed when the link of alliance is removed. Granted, that we are imperfect, very imperfect, consider a little what the alternatives to us will be. The german the japanese the modern Italian the vichy Frenchman, and the plausible indian babu, who knows jolly well that if once we lose control in India the north-western Moslems will come down from the hills and cut his yapping throat in three. Well, if the world prefers that kind of man and that kind of world, securus judicat, perhaps, but let me be dead.

Russia yaps with the rest, that she alone is saving liberty. Only 3 years ago, she was cutting her own silly throat by helping to ruin Poland. $3\frac{1}{2}$ years ago she refused without common civility to join any common cause in Europe. However, dear Florence, you know very well, that with all our faults (wh are appalling no doubt) we are the bird that hatched the American Eagle. So cheer up about us, and sock our detractors good & plenty in the solar plexus.

Bless you.　　　　　　　John.　　　(of course, we'll pay duty, gladly.)

So glad the Bish was nice, and that the Walrus wrote a nice letter.

1. Thomas S. Lamont, stationed in London during the Second World War as Lieutenant Colonel and Procurement Officer in the United States 8th Air Force.

[n.p.]

June 27. [1943]

Dear Florence,

Your letter of June 13th came yesterday, much more quickly than usual, by some chance. I am grieved indeed to think of you still in bed, being treated by doctors with a drug of which I have never heard for an illness which has not yet been diagnosed, and this in NYC in a clammy heat-wave. May the weather soon mend, and the patient soon be free of bed and doctors. Good luck to you and a speedy recovery.

Thank you for writing to me in your misery. I wish that there were some way of getting this to you quickly, but alas, war holds us.

You ask me no small question, when you ask me what a poet means by a rose or the rose. Generally, he means something; I would go so far as to say that. What he means, you have to decide from what he is trying to say at the moment and that in modern times is not always so clear, but sometimes a clue is provided, and sometimes clever young men provide theories in their reviews, etc.

Dante had a sort of suggestion of a rose in Paradise. There is a wonderful winter-blossoming rose in AXEL.[1] You can generally safely bet that when a poet makes a rose his symbol he is feeling intensely, and doing his best to suggest the thoughts welling up upon the feeling. If you will relax a little and not worry your brain too much about the thought, the feeling of the poet's mood may suggest the thought. If it doesn't, put the thing down for a while and try again in another mood. Remember, that a rose and fire are both extreme things, of passive and active beauty, and are used often by poets when no other images are extreme emough. Pascal[2] used fire to express a mood which plainly burnt him up and through.

Ada is at Bronshill Court, Torquay, South Devon, still, but I have not heard from her since early in the year. I have not heard from R and V for a long time; poor souls; god alone knows how they must be suffering. Where they are living now I cannot tell. I must write to Ada, to ask.

YOU DID TELL ME ABOUT THE UNCONSCIOUS MAN STILL TREADING WATER. But when your letter takes 9 weeks, and my reply 8 weeks, and each of the 17 weeks has been full of battle murder and horror, little quiet romantic incidents like that get shoved aside.

Get well, dear Florence. May the doctors soon have you up and about, merry as your usual self.

Bless you.

John.

1. *Axel* (1890) a symbolist play by the French poet Villiers de l'Isle Adam, 1838–89.
2. Blaise Pascal, 1623–62, French theologian. Author of *Lettres Provinciales* (1656–7) and of *Les Pensées* (1670).

Burcote Brook
14th Sept. [1943]

Dear Florence,

I wait a word from you, and hope that it may be soon, and reassuring. Dear, I do hope that things are better, and that you are off your island, back in N.Y. "better dwell in the midst of alarms, than have Tom ill¹ in a horrible wilderness", for in illness all is wilderness that has not skill at a close call.

May all be well with you, and may I soon hear that it is all well. God damn these Pin-gangs who cause these upheavals in life and friendships, and keep man from his real enemy, disease.

I have come to see that memory is frequently abnormal. I was reading only 2 days ago of a family who always talked Sanskrit at meals. I need hardly say that these bastards were german & are now mercifully dead. Then only last week a sporting journalist died; cricket was his specialty; he knew the details of every important match for fifty years, but he had also a religious streak and knew by heart the HYMNAL, Ancient & Modern, about 500 hymns, mostly tosh, and all the book of Psalms, with their numbers. Well, if I had a memory like that, I would get a friend like you and try to keep in mind all her good points.

Bless you.

John.

1. T.W.L. had a serious heart attack during the summer of 1943 at his summer home in North Haven, Maine.

Burcote Brook
Oct. 29 [1943]

Dear Florence,

Your letter of Sept 28th came today. Many many thanks.

I hope that by this time you have both visited Franconia[1] & had a happy stay, and got back to NYC; doubtless a frightful railway journey, but worth it twice over. I hope it has been restful.

The reason your letters are so long in coming, MAY be, that some come by sea, don't you think, and so have to wait convoy or clearance of some sort? This last took only a month.

I wonder, have you read Alexander Blok,[2] a Russian poet, now dead? If you can get any good translation of him you ought to read him.

Going to London, the other day, a thick fog supervened; the train was 2 and a half hours late. Coming back in blackness, we stopped at a halt, a little sort of platform, where trains never stop save by special request. As the train was long and the platform only a few yards, the descending passengers had to be lifted down and stood on their feet, and then guided off the premises. I have never been out in thicker fog. I could hardly find my way on a straight road. The poem you ask about, is of two ladies, who directed Cheltenham Ladies College. It was written by the girls:

Miss Buss and Miss Beale
Cupid's darts do not feale.
How different from us
Miss Beale and Miss Buss.

Bless you.
John.

I seem to remember having seen Miss Beale, many years ago; but I may be wrong about this.

I was writing about certain feats of seamen, standing on their heads aloft and so forth. I believe that in our sailing Navy, about 1870, men always stood, with folded arms for a minute or two on the summits of each mast when the ships paid off. Later, I suppose it was stopped, but I was brought up by men who had done this or seen it done. In a 3 decker, this meant 220 feet from the water-line. I have seen some mad pranks played aloft with my own eyes, but never saw a man stand on the truck. I have seen a man lie flat on the truck and do the compass needle trick, spin himself round horizontally, with arms and legs flying. A man was doing this close to my ship, in a ship not 300 yards from me; when he fell; and was, of course, killed. I did not see him fall; but his example darkened my goings aloft for a time; and checked any wish I may have had to do that particular stunt. It is an easier stunt, than standing with folded arms, which I could never have dared; never. Probably you in your girlhood thought nothing of it; how different from us, in fact.

Most tender thoughts and greetings, dear Florence.

J.

1. An attractive town in northern New Hampshire.
2. Alexander Blok, 1880–1921. Symbolist poet.

[n.p.]
Feb. 9th. [1944]

Dearest Florence,

Your first letter about Tom's illness¹ came 2 days ago, but I was not able to write sooner. Alas, I feel for you, and roughly guess at the nature of the trouble, and know the strain upon you. I am hoping, that you are now out of N.Y. and perhaps down in the sunshine, where Tom can lie out in the open, and get the great healing of the light. There was nothing like sunlight for healing; I always felt, when I was in the business. May we soon have a letter, to say, that Tom and you have both found it so, at somewhere or other in S.C.

The world seems to have had a mild winter this time, so perhaps NY has not been so hard to bear as usual. I hope that you could get South without much trouble.

Since your political letter came, of course, the papers here have been a good deal discussing the fourth term.

To the philosopher, it seems a good thing that a nation should be able to turn out its governments before they have had time to do much evil, but, then, it is never a good thing that a nation should be completely upset at brief intervals. The thing to aim for, is a Civil Service of the very best and most carefully trained people in the nation; with this in being politicians, even of the usual kind, can do comparatively little harm.

Mr. Dooley² used to be very wise on these points; it is just possible, that the above is a paraphrase of the wisdom of Dooley.

Dear, may Tom swiftly mend, and your anxiety give way to rejoicing, and the sun shine gladly upon you both.

John.

1. T.W.L. continued to be seriously ill with heart trouble.
2. Mr Dooley was the pen name for Finley Peter Dunne, 1867–1936, American humourist and journalist.

[n.p.]
March 1st & 2nd.
[1944]

Dearest Florence,

After long silence, I have had in these 2 mornings, your letters of Jan 14th, & 28th, and of Feb 4th, the last having come with the speed almost of light, only 27 days. So many thanks.

Alas, I fear that you have had a weary and an anxious time. I can only hope that the next day or two will bring word that you have been able to take Tom into the warmth of the South.

In your letter of the 4th Feb you ask me a question, about which I expect you will have forgotten. The answer is Yes. Gladly, Certainly. So that if you have forgotten what the question was, you will know that any way it was a cheerful question with a gay reply.

About the Alaskan who broke his knee. No, he did not marry the Red Indian girl who mended it; he did not even try to seduce her; he thought she was a heavy handed slut who enjoyed inflicting pain.

A young American was here not long ago, who had seen Indians operating and bone-setting; he said that until you saw them at it you could not understand how skilled they are. He had lived in the wilds as an Indian, with Indians, and said that no other life afterwards had any taste. Various travellers have said the same; even white women captured by the braves have regretted being brought back to their Xtian homes. Well, after a little at sea, shore life is kind of dead; I daresay to get away from a pilgrim Father or pilgrim husband was like a real breath of Paris.

I am glad that I did not tell Mr. W any more tales of bed-time. I have not told you many, have I? When you meet me again, I will tell you some, if still able to speak from rapture at seeing you again.

It seems to me, dear, that you kind of believe the god damd ;erman gang to be on the way to smash fairly soon. I do not know what you are going by, and I am loath to question the conclusion, but it is not my reading of the signs. Some day, I would like to write about old T.H. and his "consciousness the Will informing". I read him a lot; more than anybody, except perhaps Dickens, and think him the best of the men in whose time I've lived. I am so god damd glad that I was able to shew him that I admired him; and I will never forget him. His reading of the signs is not mine, but his wisdom is very great, and seems to come out of the earth and the climate, as a breathing from the soil & the spirits of it.

It is no good my trying to write of European questions. They change over night and by the time this reaches you may be profoundly changed. But one thing is very clear to me at present, or perhaps two... These we must talk of when you are here.

It is cold, a little snow is falling, but the sun is really hot upon my face as I write; we have daffodils out & many other flowers.

Now dearest Florence, may your anxieties be speedily over and your patient able to go fishing with you in the Laughing Waters of Southern Carolina; or golf, if you prefer it.

Blessings and thanks to you.

John.

[n.p.]
April 8. [1944]

Dearest Florence,

It is good news, that you have got the patient & yourself away to the South. I hope that the sun and the quiet may soon restore you both.

Now as to your questions. The tradition is, that the poem beginning "My mind to me a kingdom is" is by Sir Edward Dyer, who was born 1540 or so, and died 1607. The chances are that he was the author. He was one of the great friends of Sir Philip Sidney, and like Sir P, a chief ornament of Elizabeth's court. She liked having very clever, good-looking young men about her, and I fancy liked to make them think that she loved them. Being very clever, they saw her little game, and apart from the fact that she was a bit too blue in the leg for a young man's bride, the love of any such lady was much too risky a matter. She played off 4 or 5 of them against each other; and their lives were lived in danger. Dyer was employed on missions abroad. His work is not much known, except for that one utterance, but some think he wrote the Health song with the chorus, Down among the dead men, which is still well known here. Anyhow he was Philip Sidney's great friend, that is a good deal of glory.

The phrase IN MY END IS MY BEGINNING is the device of Mary Queen of Scots. She was a Catholic, who for 19 years of prison expected to be murdered by Elizabeth or E's orders. She made this device a comfort to her, thinking that Death would set her free to a more real life. It is said, that the Pope blesst some bread & wine, and enclosed both elements in a tiny jewel, which someone brought to her in prison, so that she might have the sacraments unless actually suddenly cut off. Now bless you, and may you both recover wholly in the sunny south.

But of course, there are still lots of questions to answer, so here goes, at the second lot.

The Old Lady. Well, the name may have lapsed, but years ago, in sunny Boston, I was told, that that was what the paper was always called, and in my innocence, I always believe what I am told. Perhaps the name only goes in Boston, but as to this Eleanor would be able to tell you with more certainty.

The heart-shook tree. It was 3 feet thick for a full forty feet, and I have cut it all up into small chunks, and burned most of it. It was like me, it needed to be psycho analyzed, but as this wasn't done in time, lo, a sheer hulk lies poor tom bowline.

The Holist scheme. Dear, I missed the speech, and do not know what was proposed, but dear, do consider this:— For years before this war, the damd bastards of germany were forming pro german gangs in every land in the world. They had small, powerful gangs in each of the lands which they have now plundered and enslaved, and you may be sure, that the gangs are now big and much more powerful. The problem before us, at present, is to get the german bastards out of the lands they have enslaved. We are some way from that I judge. But, when it is done, the task of getting unity into the freed lands will be not small; and getting rid of these great pro german cliques may be the very devil. The task is made all the worse by the differences of tongue. To myself, who love France devotedly, France is the main question; but before it becomes that, there looms the fact of enemy power. From Dover, you look at Germany, remember. Let us end that fact first.

John.

[n.p.]
May 7th. [1944?]

Dearest Florence,

You may boast of your cold April in N.Y. Last night, we had the hardest frost of the winter; and the thermometer in my study as I write this at mid-day is just above freezing-point.

I wrote to you last week about a famous old NY song, such as we used to sing in little old NY in our happy childhoods. It now occurs to me to ask, do you remember two other songs of those glad days:— "Jimmy on the chute, boys, won't we have a day"; and "Pretty Jenny Slattery", who used to be at Macy's? There was a third, more solemn, "The bells had just done ringing", which I am sure you sang; it was everywhere; with a pathetic death at the end "a soul had passed away". Have you the words of these masterpieces, by any chance? The tunes I cannot forget, possibly.

I came upon a nice American poem the other day.

"Observe the happy moron,
He doesn't give a damn.
I wish I were a moron.
    By God, perhaps I am."

The nightingale has returned, but I know not whether they will nest here this year.

I hope that you can get to Palisades a good deal, and that the patient mends with the weather. May you yourself be getting a little rest and quiet, too, for you have had not much of a year of it, so far, I fear. May you get to Maine, later on, for the happy summer. Bless you, dear.

John.

[n.p.]
May 23. [1944]

Dearest Florence,

After long, long silence, suddenly 3 delightful letters by one post from you, dated April 25. May 2. and May 11th, almost yesterday's bulletin, in fact. So many many thanks.

I was so touched at your saying you pray for me. Dear, keep right on at it, for there's need, but dear, you did ought to take on one of your own size in sins, not an outsize.

Now, you ask, why I love France. Because the best in France is the best there is. Or WAS the best there was. Anybody practising arts when I was a beginner knew that France was the world's teacher in the arts there was no doubt of it; our masters were French. France was bled white in the great war; broken by it; the natural checks on the scoundrels in her politics were killed; and the unity the war gave her was quickly lost after the peace; she needed a queen then; you ought to have stood up in your famous brown dress at Versailles, and called out "Francais. Avec Moi. La Gloire nous attend." Try it next time; don't forget.

No man likes ALL in another nation. But think of Geoffroy & Genevieve & beautiful Yvonne and her grand husband; and wonderful chaps like Giraud;[1] and the virtue and honesty of the work done under your eyes wherever you go in France, and the rightness of the French mind, whenever you seek its judgment. In the early days of the last war, I saw the purity of French devotion, too. It is appalling to me to think of France under these god damd bastards.

You remember a little hair-cut-shop where you went chasing a Luny for Austin? Alas, it has copped a packet and gone off the map. I was there the other day, and like the chap in the bible "it was not".

Good luck to your sweepstake. I hope you will rake in all the 82 plunks.

Bless you.
John

1. General Henri Honoré Giraud, 1879–1949. A leader of French resistance to Germany after the establishment of the Vichy government.

[n.p.]
May 24. [1944]

Dearest Florence,

I sent off a note yesterday, roughly acknowledging 3 lets, but reserving my thanks for the clippings, till I had read them.

You ask, why I was not interested in the English Moslem. I was. I am not much drawn to the Moslems I meet, as a rule, but I AM drawn by Mahomet; he was an inspired Prophet. I do not understand how a man once persuaded of that could ever cease to believe it; what took your guy, that he ratted on it?

You ask me what I think of Heard.[1] I met him only once, long ago, and liked him personally. I have not read his work, I fear.

It has been the bleakest May I ever saw, and the driest year in memory. The well is nearly dry; all the wells here are; but I have got a nice broken flower-pot, and if there be no water I shall give up washing, and just scrape myself in the manner of Job, but not if I develop boils.

You mock an english drought; we know better. Our plants and things are used to a lot of rain, and soon wilt without it.

It has frozen like irish hell five nights this month.

Well, cheer up and bless you dearest girl.

John.

1. Gerald Heard, 1889–1971, English author and editor.

[n.p.]
26 May. [1944]

Dearest Florence,

To my horror, I find that I have let a week pass without keeping a promise.

Do you remember Stripling?

Well, a week ago, I was in a place; I daresay the censor will not mind if I go so far as to say that it was in sunlight, when I saw a smile which seemed somehow familiar; and then I saw that it was attached to S. He seemed hardly changed in all these years, and had heard somehow that Tom had been ill, and asked eagerly for news of you both. When I said that Tom was much better, he asked me twice to be very sure to let you both know how glad he is to think of the recovery. I promised to do this, but a week has gone. However, I do it now.

I hope that you will urge on all you meet the VITAL importance of France to civilization. All nations owe much to her. Western Europe in a way depends on her. No nation has more real virtue; and if misery has given her skunks great temporary chances, you must never think that the skunks are the nation, as they may be in germany.

Cry, Vive la France, wear a tricolour in your hat. En avant, chérie, vive la France et les god-dams.

John.

[n.p.]
15 June. [1944]

Dearest Florence,

Your letter of May 29th reached me yesterday. Many thanks for it.

While it was on its way the invasion began; so now you will know how much of the sweepstake will be yours.

You ask, why I do not comment more upon affairs? Well, for many reasons. Affairs in war change with great suddenness and completeness; & you must reflect, that my comments are sometimes eight weeks and always more than two in reaching you. Often, as it is, when they DO reach you, you wonder what the angel I'm talking about; things have moved on so, since I wrote. Then, too, there is the Censor; and I have beside the certainty, that the enemy has many many agents very shrewdly on the pounce.

I long to talk with you, as we talked about the pin-gang, years ago. If & when we meet again, we will talk so, once more, I hope. For brother & sister, we are a very devoted couple, and I think there are no topics in the world that we have not discussed, except, perhaps circumcision and Virginity. As to the former topic, I vote we leave to the Moslems, who understand it better; but as to the second, I would ask, About how much of it can exist in Europe at present? And how much will be left when the war ends?

I missed the speech you ask about. But when we meet, we must talk over the Spanish business, for it was of great importance, and in all ways fatal. You might be interested in the Spanish poet LORCA,[1] by the way.

I loved your tale about Wallace[2] for second choice. Alas, the moron poem is by another, not me. Dear thoughts to you.

John.

---

1. Federico Garcia Lorca, 1898–1936. Spanish poet and playwright.
2. Henry A. Wallace, 1888–1965, Vice-President of the United States, 1941–5.

Decr. [Dec 17, 1944]

Dearest Florence,

Thank you so very much for your charming nice letter, with the glad tidings of Eleanor's recovery, and the extra-ordinarily clear and compelling article by Tom. This, we read with much approval, and have imparted to others. Do, please, urge Tom to print it, and to have it printed over here.

The german theory of war is, that it shall be made profitable. Before 1914, in high peace, they sent expert critics and valuers to our best collections; what might be left to the generals or junior officers, and what might be left to the troops. In Poland, before this war the same course was taken. All the best things were noted, and, later, removed. In Belgium, women were sometimes compelled to pack up their fine table-linen, sheets etc, and actually to address the parcels to the wives of the damd thieves. In France, at this time, as a result of this kind of thing, woollen and linen things hardly exist. The god-damd bastards have skinned Europe; and I can only hope that if the allies get into germany they will examine every house, and burn every house found to contain any article not made in germany. The god-damd bastards are the god damdest bastards going and, do, dear child, be sure, that they are at their skunks tricks all the time; and that some of their most dangerous agents are those who claimed to "have escaped from the Nazis"; escaped be damd; they are agents; and I judge that you'd have learned it by this time, if things had worked out otherwise than they have. Well, dear, bless you, and preserve you from their dirty games. Thank you so much for admirable letter & article.

John.

In Italy, so far, almost all the museums have been robbed to some extent by the swine; and all the coin collections have gone.

[n.p.]
Jan 3rd. [1945]

Dearest Florence,

Many many thanks for your letter of the 13th Dec, here today. I am sorry that I mis-read what you said about the Ballet.

You were talking about Rilke.[1] I think you will find a good study of him in Bowra's[2] book on Symbolism; a very fine book on various recent poetry, which is largely the experience of strange individuals remote from the filthy age they have dwelt in, which has no religion, no speech, binding its societies.

As a result, you have them talking of their own souls under symbols difficult to understand. What they say may seem very important. It is worth trying to understand what they mean.

But you must have preferences in art; you must have standards.

Look upon possible poetry as the WORK of Beethoven, all his work. Well, you can, if you wish, say that the Grosse Fuge is the last supreme thing in art. It gives a sort of image of a turbulent, rude, dead, angry savage, who has been batted on the head by a mule, and gagged by burglars, trying to say something of much importance concerning human life. You realise that it is that. Very well. But do not tell me that it is as precious as the 9th symphony or the big concertos or the best of the divine sonatas.

Half a dozen great poets have shewn what great poetry IS. Usually, it is readily communicable, like love and tenderness and inspiration generally.

Bless you; may your New Year be full of all these three.

John.

1. Rainer Maria Rilke, 1875–1926. The greatest German poet of his generation.
2. Sir Maurice Bowra, 1898–1971. Classical scholar, critic and wit. Warden of Wadham College, Oxford. *The Heritage of Symbolism* was published in 1943.

[n.p.]
25th Feb. [1945]

Dearest Florence,

Just as I posted a letter, grieving that you had gone to the South, whence letters take 3 months on the road, a lovely letter came from you from NY. Many thanks for this, and also for a happy package, which came yesterday.

I am so glad, that you are not in the South; that is, for my own selfish sake; I daresay, it would be a good thing for you & Tom to be away in the land of cotton, eating water-melon, and the amazing dishes the old negro cooks contrive. Sometimes, I could wish that I were there myself, going down the Mississippi on a raft, and tying up at night.

I am glad, that you have heard some recent facts about enemy occupation. If you will turn up Lord Bryce's Report,[1] published about 1915, during the last war, you will see, that they have only repeated themselves on a much more lavish scale. They were not brought to book for their crimes in 1918; and no doubt think themselves immune now.

You may be able to find a report now published here, on some of their recent doings in Poland. But recently I have been seeing

German Official photographs of their occupation in Russia and the Ukraine; the sort of thing the bastards print in germany to cheer their bastardly swineries to greater efforts. Do not think of them as civilised beings; they are a vast conspiracy to wreck humanity; and to spread evil in every land; their touch is death. Do read Exupéry's little book LE PETIT PRINCE;[2] that is a book of light & sweetness, the real France again.

John.

1. The Bryce Report was published by a Committee chaired by Lord Bryce. It was appointed to consider and advise on outrages alleged to have been committed by German troops in Belgium and France.
2. Saint Antoine de Exupéry, 1900–44. French aviator and author killed in action in Second World War. *Le Petit Prince* appeared in 1943.

[n.p.]
20 March. [1945]

Dearest Florence,

Perhaps at this moment, you have received the startling news, that you & Tom have been unanimously elected members of the NATIONAL BOOK LEAGUE,[1] and are still breathing hard and wondering What the hell? Well, it was my doing; I am the President of the concern, and could not bear not to have you in the body. It will bring you no immediate benefits, but, then it will give you no duties, nor any obligations, till after the war.

But, even before the war ends, you, as Members, may receive free of charge the League's publications; and after the war, the League will have very jolly rooms near Piccadilly, in which you will be able to meet the sages whose company you so often delight in; and it is then that your duties may begin. They are simple, but as President, I do beg you to perform them.

Our aim, as League, is, to foster the right use of books, and the habits of study & serious reading.

But my side aim, as President, is to have a place in London where Americans and lovers of books can BE SURE OF HAVING DELIGHTFUL COFFEE; tea, if you must, but COFFEE, the drink of Arabian sages certainly.

Your duties, as Members, will be to raise Hell whenever the coffee is the usual London muck described as such. The yoke is easy & the burden is light as someone says somewhere; and I do hope that two such discriminating souls as you & Tom will not shrink from bearing a hand at this task.

The ROOMS are very beautiful; I think, myself, that some of the woodwork must be of the time of Charles the First; and I do hope to see them a centre of HUMANISM: so do not be vexed at my cheek, "beloved snail"; but come & join the dance. (Carroll).

Blessings to you.
John.

1. British literary society founded in 1925 with headquarters in London. J.M. was the first President of the organisation.

[n.p.]
June 9. [1945?]

Dearest Florence,

Your letter of the 28th arrived today; rather more quickly than usual; so many thanks.

I am so glad that C.C.¹ has done so well; and can only hope that he is now in less danger somewhere. I will not ask where he is, for no doubt whereabouts are best kept secret; enemy spies are everywhere still.

I think you may not know that ANTOINE is SAFE & SOUND; after being mourned as dead in that damd den at Buchenwald.

About the said den; it is only a large scale systemization of what the enemy did in the last war; they were not punished at all for what they did then; and unless the guilty are hung this time, they will repeat the war and its horrors just as soon as they can; their minds are like that; they are just what Caesar found them 2000 years ago.

A young Dutchman was here a few days ago; perhaps I told you of him? He was under their thumb for 4 years, and said, that they were not too bad, in his out of the way town until the Normandy landings, and that then they became appalling, and took EVERYTHING. He had 4 gestapo sergeants with their lady friends in his house. The lady friends were of the sort who were so much amused when Don Quixote hailed them as "Fair virgins". They had a rule, of not robbing the houses they lived in, but of sending out, for old silver, china, linen, lacquer, etc to the neighbouring houses, and so all houses got picked, and my Dutchman was reduced to making tulip bulbs into coffee; he said they make not bad coffee; English coffee; the sort you'll have to kick at at the N.B.L.

> Bless you.
> John.

1. Charles C. Cunningham, son-in-law of the Lamonts. He served as Lieutenant Commander in the U.S. Naval Reserve in the Second World War and was assigned to several aircraft carriers in the Pacific Far East.

> Burcote Brook
> June 11th. [1945]

Dearest Florence,

This is in answer to your letter of June 4th. That is, I am replying to something you wrote only one week ago. Dammee, girl, as the wicked Bucks used to say in the novels, this is almost like old times.

I am so very glad for all your sakes that Teddy[1] is under respite. Perhaps the war may end sooner than we think; for in my view the japanese are people with breaking-points; and I don't expect their people to stand what the god damd bastards the jermans couldnt.

Bombing is the hell of a strain, dear, and the bastards are getting the hell of a bombing; but nothing I hope to what is on its way.

You ask me to tell you true, when we are to have a good talk again. Well, when we parted, I thought we should never meet again; now, I am not so sure; perhaps we shall. Any how we HAVE met in the past, and the majority of people can't make that proud claim. So cheer up; and have a romping good time in Maine, with many a jovial picnic, with Judge and family.

> Blessings attend you all.
> John.

1. Edward Miner Lamont, second son of Mr and Mrs Thomas S. Lamont, grandson of F.C.L. and T.W.L. At the age of 18 he had just entered U.S. Naval Officers Training at Princeton, N.J.

[n.p.]
July 26. [1945?]

Dearest Florence,

I was so glad to have your letter of July 15th, only 10 days from Maine.

What fun, to think that you may be in England next summer. Well, the winter will be a fatal time in Europe, I fear; and it is ill guessing what sort of a holiday any European country will be able to offer after it.

Do not dread the floating mines too much; not very many will be out in the Atlantic; after the last war, which was pretty mine-y, no Atlantic line suffered loss that way, after 1918.

I do not know whether the censorship is abolished or not; I have not heard. Anyhow, I am not going to talk about the war.

But I must say that I am glad to think that C.C.[1] will be back in the U.S. and may even be with you now.

Did you come upon the poems of Harry Brown,[2] a young American? If not you'd better hop it to the book store and lay in a supply.

The election results are being declared today, most of them; and so far my hopes have failed, my main enemies are routed, and all my prophecies are completely wrong; however, only a third are yet declared; and the best may come later.

However, no party can make a worse mess of things than the other parties have made in the past; so let us be of good cheer, and cultivate literature upon a little oatmeal, as somebody translated Virgil's opening line once.

Bless you.
John.

1. Charles C. Cunningham.
2. Harry Peter M'Nab Brown, 1917–, American poet, novelist and playwright. Author of 'The Poem of Bunker Hill' (1941).

[n.p.]
February 4th. [1948]

Dearest Florence,

One goes over this in the mind, so often, and foresees all the horror, and then the blow falls, and the horror is something that cannot be foreseen, nor lightened.[1]

I telephoned to Murray first; he was out, walking; but I left the message; then telephoned to Lindsay,[2] who was in London; so I left the message there; and telephoned to Mrs. Binyon,[3] who heard it with audible grief. It is in the papers. Murray & Lindsay must both know.

It is so sad to think of all your hope and all your struggle ending thus. I had hoped for Tom to benefit from the sunshine, and to be with you in Maine for another summer or two; and able to be his old, vital self and enjoy, as only he could.

That is one of the great things, perhaps the greatest thing, that he saw the magnificence of enjoyment, saw that the world can be made to bring forth great fruits, by any-one who cares enough for fruits, cares enough, that is, to make sure that those who care shall have, not only now, but through the long ages, for which his beneficence has prepared and sown. You who bore a hand with him in all those years of laying great bases for futurity must know how his power is in the world like a great glory that will burst forth long hence, in many a fair mind, in many a noble quickening, in the America that you both foresaw and strove for. May all this be a little star in the darkness, that is dark dark, god knows, my dear.

John.

1. After several years of ill health, Thomas W. Lamont died of heart failure on 2 February 1948 at Boca Grande, Florida, where he and F.C.L. had gone to escape the winter's cold.
2. A. D. Lindsay, 1879–1952, Baron Lindsay of Birker, English classicist and Master of Balliol College, Oxford, for twenty-five years. Translator of Plato's *Republic* into English.
3. Mrs Laurence Binyon, wife of the English poet.

[n.p.]
Feb 9. [1948]

Dearest Florence,

I cannot help thinking that you may now be at the Palisades, so I send this to New York.

I am grieved not to have written a better and fuller & more ample notice of Tom. What should have been made clearer was his extra-ordinary clearness of mind (an American trait, by the way, never an English one), combined with a gay good humour. The combination is even rarer than the qualities by themselves, and together they could persuade into wisdom, that precious food that men avoid if they can like poison.

Then another point of rarity was his habit of looking at things in the biggest and most generous way. This bigness of aim, greatness of conception, is very very rare, & it is one of the foundations of all genius. Only America shows it at present; and how wonderful it is.

"Great things are done when men and mountains meet".

I felt at Harvard that time, that Tom and America were on the top of the world, doing and preparing things such as man has not yet known, of splendour and glory. He has laid great bases which will shoot with all sorts of wonder for centuries to come, through all the States.

We send our constant thoughts to you.

John.

March, 1948

Dearest Florence,

I am grieved to know that my letters have been so blank for so long. It is old age that does it, not deadness of heart; just the dull stupid pressure of time on a brain never very good, and now done for.

This is an Easter in March, always an unusual thing; but this March is like our Summer at its best; and I hope that you at the Palisades have something of the sort, with cloudless sky and many birds in song.

You may perhaps have noticed here, on a clear day, a white patch of road on the downland? I always wondered where it went; so I went to find out. It runs up into the downs as a road, from a farm, & after a mile or so splits into tracks that go on across the downs, as these tracks do. It is the loneliest part of the downland, & not so lovely as most, except for sky larks that are everywhere. Who made it a road, and left it where he did, is preserved on old maps I think. It isn't a place to take you to, but we know others that are. So come along.

John.

July 2nd. [1948]

Dearest Florence,

You ask about G. M. Hopkins.[1]

I had better begin about the conversions to Roman Catholicism. For several centuries, men have been going over to Rome from the reformed churches. They go for many reasons, but chiefly for three, or mixtures of the 3. One, from the feeling that the Roman Church IS the church, and has the real tradition of the early Xtians. Two, from a delight in ritual and a feeling that worship should be accompanied by intense and splendid ritual. Three, from the sense, very strong in some souls, that religion is a mystical thing. Many churches make it a practical thing, and are too narrow to provide anything for those who want something else. The Roman Church is not narrow. It has a special place for those who want mysticism, for those who want to preach, or teach, or proselytise; and its directors are very cleverly picked, and are always on the look-out for young men perplexed, as youth often is.

I do not know why Hopkins became a Cath. I suppose the Eng Church did not satisfy him, and the R church got him in his perplexity. I know nothing about his religious life, but was told that he was very unhappy as a Jesuit, (if that be what he became). Someone described him as "the squarest possible peg in the roundest possible hole". He was, I judge, somewhat too in-dividual to be easy to squelch into utter obedience, or whatever virtue his order needed.

Well, that was his affair; and it is over. His poetry is our affair, and may now be considered.

When he wrote, when I was a child, or shortly going to be a child, for I think he was as remote as that, the world of literature was under the school of perfection. Tennyson, a limited but flawless master, was the god, and smooth, perfect verse was everywhere. Men were longing for something rougher.

I was never a monk, but I judge that after 50 years of flawless Offices, the temptation to say the lords prayer backwards may be strong in many monks. After 50 years of sweet verse, Browning seemed like the only possible escape. Well, he wasn't the only escape. Hopkins had another way, and it is rather fresh and queer; and has a new kind of cock to it, and it is as cheerful as a red-herring after a year of ship's provisions.

Of course, he was not published till long after the end of the whole Victorian time.

I feel that he did three or four fine things, and about a dozen other odd and queer things. He was very devout, and the depth of his feeling makes the odd manner glow now and then; but I cannot feel that even his 3 or 4 fine things are perfect things; they have startling instants and bad instants and that is not how the masters are.

I am no great shakes as a writer, god knows, but I can certainly say this, that if Hopkins' way be right, then the masters are wrong, and I know that the masters are NOT wrong; they have uttered the truth in the final way, in the words truth chooses.

When Hopkins is well spoken, by really choice speakers, as by the reciters we had of old, then some of his queerness and repetition can be made very delightful.

I am so very very glad that you have all reached Maine well and cheery. May you have a most lovely summer.

Bless you.

John.

1. Gerard Manley Hopkins, 1844–89. English poet and a member of the Society of Jesus. His poems were published posthumously in 1918, with an introduction by his friend Robert Bridges. A second edition, edited by the poet and theologian Charles Williams (1886–1945) came out in 1930.

[n.p.]
July 28. [1948]

Dear Florence,

My grateful thanks for your kind letter about Lew's book.[1]

The story-tellers are coming along nicely. They took for one day the romantic theme of poor Amy Robsart. But you will say, who is this Amy Robsart? What is she to me?

I fear you may not know of her. This, my dear, is one of the heavy prices you unwittingly paid for your boasted independence. I suppose you will say she was nothing at all compared with Tecumseh anyway, nor with J. Paul Jones, nor with Billy the Kid.

She seems to have been a brunette.

We have today paid a sad visit to the cherry orchards, to see the last of an amazing cherry-crop, amazing beyond memory of man. The last cherries were either little and black, or big and of exquisite ruby red; I never saw such things; these last were not so much for eating as for preserving.

Thank you for your most thoughtful & understanding letter. You do not say how you are, nor how Eleanor is. Do obey the Bible wh says, "Take a pen & write quickly".

John.

1. A posthumous novel, *The Passion Left Behind* (1947) by Lewis Masefield.

[n.p.]
Augt. 5. [1948]

Dear Florence,

You have often spoken of the Clumps as a landmark you look out for, when plunging down from Nettlebed. Yesterday, I thought I would send you a view of them, so I did one, & now enclose it, such as it it. Perhaps you did not know that they are only about a mile from this as the crow flies.

Did you know about the nitrate ship that blew up at Brest, the other day? She was not quite so fatal as the ship which blew up at one of your Gulf ports last year, but she made a pretty general average in Brest.

I was (as Homer wd say) "delighting in the bath" at the moment, when suddenly the house, windows, pictures, etc. rattled and shook for half a minute together, as in the war, when an attack was on. There was a thunderstorm at a little distance, & I thought that some building had fallen, being stricken by lighting, but it was this ship at Brest a good 230 miles away. It is strange that it should have had such an effect, but I suppose all Nature here is jumpy since the war, and leaps when a fire-cracker goes off.

I hope soon to hear that you are well & Eleanor better. Bless you.

John.

Burcote Brook
Oct 1. [1948]

Dearest Florence,

The Book League people have asked me for the addresses of your children;[1] and, alas, I am not quite sure of the present address of any one of them.

Please, if it would not be too great a bother, would you most kindly jot down the addresses on the leaflet enclosed, and presently let me have it? This would be warmly appreciated by all hands.

The N.B.L. are giving an overwhelming show of precious French books and mss. It is a superb thing, and I do wish that you could see it. You would come out of it, wearing a tri-color skirt, with seven fleur-de-lys in your bonnet, and singing a Ronsard Hymn.

Bless you.
John.

1. J.M. wanted the addresses of F.C.L.'s four children so that they could be informed that they had been made life members of the National Book League.

Burcote Brook
Sept the 7th [1952]
Dearest Florence,

I am hoping that this will be at your home in N.Y.C. when you arrive there, to wish you a safe return, and a happy stay in the golden fall at Happy Laurel Hollow.¹ What fun to see the Indian Summer a few weeks from now.

Did you ever know of a case in which a woman disguised herself successfully as a man? There have been a good many cases here in the past; one, very famous, of an army doctor who was found to be a woman.

I have seen several successful disguises made by men; & was reading last night of a tale told by Mrs. Garrick, the wife of our famous actor. She was in a little country town, & going out with her little dog, she came upon an inn, with a little balcony over the street. On this balcony, a farmer was telling all hands of his adventures in London, & convulsing everyone with delight; Mrs. G was also (discreetly & becomingly) convulsed.

Soon, she noticed that her little dog was trying to get to the balcony; & it was only *then* that she discovered that the farmer was her husband, David Garrick; the dog knew him sooner than the wife.

It makes a nice story.

As a rule, writers avoid disguising their characters, knowing the limitations of disguise; but in the days of beards & longish hair, disguise was much easier and authors used this device a lot.

Bless you & let us not disguise our friendship.
John.

1. The country house of F.C.L., after the death of T.W.L. in 1948, was at Laurel Hollow, Long Island, N.Y.

[n.p.]
Sept 30. [1952]
Dearest Florence,

I am hoping soon to hear of your being well recovered; & perhaps out at The Laurels again, enjoying the sun.

I had a charming dream of you last night in which I had the honour of taking you to see an amazing team of 14 Italian & Spanish riders, doing what used to be called "a musical ride" or horse-dance, upon a stage of great splendour. You were in great splendour wearing blue, with what used to be called smasher hat, on which a diamond the size of a hen's egg shone. You were looking, my golly, superb; & the riders were all on great horses, & each rider was 6 feet 4 inches tall; and all were poets, & I knew them all, & told you about each one; & I had a great book by one, in ms., all sonnets, in English, which I read to you.

One of the sonnets began with a quite good line. Then the poet wrote,
"O that I could remember what I wrote for the 2nd & 3rd lines".
At that I turned to you and said "How well I know that feeling about the wonderful lines that shine, & then fade out of memory".

But you will want to know about smasher hats. They used to be something like this:

[water colour sketches]

but they smashed so many hearts that they were suppressed by an Order in Council many years ago; though you may see them now & then in portraits of saints, etc.

It is horribly cold here; and one of the earliest winters on record.

I am trying to paint, still, but it is too long a task, & I have no time for it really. Please write soon & tell me of your being away in the sun on Long Island.

Bless you.
John.

[n.p.]
7 Oct. [1952]

Dearest Florence,

Thank you for your letter, and note, & for two gracious gift parcels, most precious, and for the news that you are out at Long Island in quiet & sunlight. With my thanks go my wishes that this may find you out of pain, and able to live your life again, free from doctors & Miss M. I will not address you as Doc, if you prefer, but for a few times I had to do it, because it is an honour, well-earned, & much appreciated by your friends.

Over here, with all sorts of feudalisms everywhere, many are particular about the mention of such distinctions. If, at a Levee, a Sir should ask an Admiral, "Please what is the time?" The Admiral might say, "By my watch, its just noon", but a recently made Lord who has kind-of-bought his title, might say "By my gold watch and chain, its ten to."

You were asking about J.[1] She is at the moment living here altogether while her Oxford landlady remains unable to take her during the mid-week, as usual.

We have had a wonderful crop of apples; & it has been fun doing up boxes of them for friends who have not any. Soon, I shall go over to Bosley's Farm to see his barn when the Annie-Elizabeths are there. These are glorious red & gold apples, averaging a pound in weight each. The barn full of these is a wonderful sight; I do wish you could see it.

Please do not regard Trollope's short stories; but *do* read his *Hunting Sketches* book; that is very good; & read *The American Senator*, too, for the hunting scenes in it. He was a leisurely novelist, very good, indeed, with an enormous range of character, & wholly English in his manner; he was not a short story-writer.[2]

Blessings & thanks & thoughts to you.

John.

1. Judith Masefield.
2. Anthony Trollope, 1815–82. Prolific Victorian novelist. The *American Senator* was published in 1877 and *Hunting Sketches* in 1865. He produced five volumes of short stories between 1861 and 1882.

[n.p.]
Oct. 24. [1952]

Dearest Florence,

I grieve, if I never acknowledged your kind thought in sending me the clipping about your geological survey of the sea-floor. This safely reached me and interested me very much. I hope that by the time the new continent emerges and becomes habitable man may have learned some rudiments of humanity; & make a wiser use of his very brief allowance.

Gilberto was here yesterday (with RB) and seemed in very good trim; full of anecdote as ever, and going off tomorrow to address a public meeting. He is a wonder, I must say. He had a story of young Swinburne as an undergraduate at Oxford. ACS hurt his ankle, while out for a walk, & could hardly put his foot to the ground. A friend who was helping him home got him to talk of poetry; soon ACS was a fiery fountain spouting poetry; & as the god took possession, the ankle was forgotten & he resumed his usual sort of trot, & was back in College on time.

I have decided to read all Shakespeare again, from the beginning, & have now begun upon him. I shall play certain scenes with chess-men on a board, & wish all the time that he had been a story-teller and not a dramatist. Be comforted; I will not inflict my views on you.

I hope so much that you have found a perfect cook; and have also found a complete release from the plasters. All blessings & grateful thanks & all glad & happy memories to you.

John.

[n.p.]
25 Oct. [1952]

Dearest Florence,

This morning I have had another wonderful parcel from you, and send you my all unavailing & imperfect thanks for it. When was there such a friend as you, in all the long lists of such?

I wrote yesterday to tell you of Gilberto. I heard from him today, that a Frenchman named BALDENSPERGER[1] (a rather odd name for a Frenchman) has translated Shakespeare's sonnets into French (very odd game for a Frenchman to try to play). I hope to get the book, & to read how he does it. How would you begin to do it? "Des choses les plus belles on desire profiter", etc. It would be a happy exercise to put a boy's French class to do.

I hope that your poor tormented back does not take from you all zest and interest in these things. But no doubt at the moment the election is the main issue and shuts out most of life from every American.

Like you, we are rather stumped for lack of a cook, as our good Mrs. G wishes to leave, & at the moment this land is hostile to the idea of service of the sort, and I suppose too busy with other schemes.

John.

1. Fernand Baldensperger, 1871–1958, author.

[n.p.]
Nov. 4. [1952] 12 noon
(7 a.m. with you)

Dear Florence,

My grateful thanks for a lovely letter from you, dated 8 days ago; your air mail marks it as 5 days ago; but thank you for it, whichever day it was.

I think of you as probably now at Laurel Hollow, voting, and then planning to march in a parade on 5th, and to sing with 50 massed bands, to the tune of *Home, sweet home*

> "Through East Side and West Side although you may hike
> You may take it for gospel there's no man like Ike.
> Ike. Ike. Sweet sweet Ike
> O vote, boys, for Ike", etc.

Well, I would love you to have the pleasure of seeing Ike roll in as President with a grand majority; & then to have him come in to tea, to say "Mrs. Lamont, I owe my position to your belief in my cause & all your work of it. I want you right now to be my Secretary for Foreign Affairs & English Ambassador..."

I was a lad at Yonkers when the D of M¹ came there with his affianced Consuelo² for some reason. Perhaps they came to see the Palisades or the Indian Summer Woods. Anyway, they *did* come & went to the big hotel for something.

The courier or dragoman made the arrangements as a rule; but this time something miscarried; he didn't; so the hotel clerk asked the D—

"What accommodation does youse party require?"

The D said, "I haven't the least idea."

"Land", the clerk said. "You must be a green one, sport. When did you come over?"

This was reported to me by one who was there, so you may add it to your history book. It was just before the marriage.

The D wrote a good life of the great general Marlborough, the first Duke, to whom Blenheim was given by a grateful country. Late in life, he was much interested in religion; and became (so I was told) a Roman Catholic.

I hope that the excitements of this day will not be too exhausting to you. I bless you daily.

John.

1. The Ninth Duke of Marlborough, 1871–1934.
2. Consuelo Vanderbilt, 1877–1964, daughter of Cornelius Vanderbilt.

[n.p.]
[9 Nov. 1952]

Dearest Florence,

Many thanks to you for a lovely packet of delights received here this morning.

Thank you, too, for the glad news that you are off to the polls to vote for Ike.

I am able now to send you my glad congratulations on the success of your party; and I know with what joy Ike will be received by almost all the Americans I know; but by none so gladly as by you, and by none whose good opinion is worth so much. I only hope that it (the success) has not led you into any wild excess, such as window-smashing on Fifth or along Broadway; or firing off rockets from the solarium.

Here, we go along in cheer. We have a friend to help our household along; and a new housekeeper will be coming later.

All best wishes & thanks & thoughts to you.

John.

[n.p.]
[27 Nov. 1952]

Dearest Florence,

This is your Thanksgiving Day.

May I use the Day to utter my Thanksgiving for you, & for your letter, & for all the countless & precious acts & thoughts of friendship that have blessed me from you, all beyond all price, beyond all thank, beyond all thought.

I hope that as I write, Miss M will be waking & resolving to show that she, too, gives thanks to you in a tenderer recognition of your wonder.

I hope that all the Clan may be there to show their thanksgiving for you, & that the day may be in all ways a blessed & glad one to you.

John.

[n.p.]

[28 Nov. 1952]

Dearest Florence,

My thanks again to you for your welcome letter, telling of the results of the transfusion.[1] May all your treatments help you & give you pep.

I do not at all agree, that men of genius should run away from universities. They go to such places in youth to learn certain things & to be with many young men of their ages, to discuss all things, hope all things, and try all good things. If any talent is weak enough to be quenched by a don, in God's name let it be quenched, but as a rule genius is a protecting oil from which don-doctrine runs off without making any impression whatever. In some cases don-doctrine rouses rebellion in the genius. In Shelley's case, Shelley was expelled; in Swinburne's case, Jowett was wise & talked A.C.S. into friendly moods. Youthful genius is not often defiant & rebellious; it is more often modest, & too acutely conscious of its own point of view to argue with the settled opinion of one whom genius must perceive to be deficient.

Some defiant young men leave or are sent away from universities every year. I have seen a good many of these, and they have not been geniuses, but freaks, nuisances & misfits, who have done no good and are no good. A University is rightly admired. It is an earthly paradise created by the learned & the thoughtful for the maintenance of Knowledge, thought & the love of God & good things. It is said that there was once a heavenly paradise, in which a conceited spirit rebelled. He was not a creator, but a miscreator, and the world feels that on the whole his rival Kingdom has not been a success.

However, let me not go on like this, lest I seem to talk through my hat instead of asking what sort of hat you have for Christmas parties? No doubt a smasher hat, as in my lively dream of you.

All blessings to you now & always.

John.

1. F.C.L. had had a blood transfusion to strengthen her heart, but she steadily grew weaker.

[n.p.]
[18 Dec. 1952]

Dearest Florence,

I hope that this may come to you at about the right day, to wish you all the gladness that Christmas can bring.

You have brought life & gladness to many many people; & so much of both to undeserving me, that your pillow must ever be bright with little fairies of blessing. May it be brighter than usual this time, & may you feel that some of the brightness comes from my grateful heart.

John.

On 29 December 1952 Florence Lamont died quietly at her home in New York City, at the age of eighty.

In a comment the next day in The Times *of London, John and Constance Masefield said:*

'The news, though for some days dreaded, will bring great grief. Few spirits more brave, daring, gay and delightful have ever gladdened friends.

'To this country she was ever the staunchest of allies. Few English visitors to New York during the last forty years have failed to find in her a welcoming clever hostess, thoughtful, helpful and fore-seeing, whose friendship, later, endured and grew.

'There was in her look and bearing such a spirit of gaiety, life and wisdom that none who knew her will ever think of her as dead. This living gaiety was of her very nature. It gives a matchless charm to those Letters from China and Japan published by her early this year.[1]

'England has had no finer friend. Those who knew her will ever remember her as a most rare spirit, active, even to the last, in all great human causes.'

Fifteen years later, on 15 May 1967, John Masefield died at his home in England two weeks short of the age of eighty-nine.

1. *Far Eastern Diary, 1920*, by Florence Corliss Lamont, published privately, 1951.

Index